BOOKS, BABIES
AND SCHOOL-AGE PARENTS

Also by Sharon Githens Enright

Development of the Boundary Structuring Questionnaire:
Teen Mother Version (Dissertation)

Also by Jeanne Warren Lindsay

(Partial listing)
Do I Have a Daddy? A Story About a Single Parent Child
Teenage Couples — Expectations and Reality
Teenage Couples — Caring, Commitment and Change
Teenage Couples — Coping with Reality
Pregnant? Adoption Is an Option
Your Baby's First Year: A Guide for Teenage Parents
The Challenge of Toddlers: For Teen Parents —
Parenting Your Child from One to Three
Teen Dads: Rights, Responsibilities and Joys

By Jeanne Lindsay and Jean Brunelli:

Your Pregnancy and Newborn Journey:
A Guide for Pregnant Teens

Nurturing Your Newborn: Young Parents' Guide
to Baby's First Month

By Jeanne Lindsay and Sally McCullough:

Discipline from Birth to Three: How Teen Parents
Can Prevent and Deal with Discipline Problems
with Babies and Toddlers

Books, Babies and School-Age Parents

How to Teach Pregnant and Parenting Teens to Succeed

Jeanne Warren Lindsay, MA, CFCS
Sharon Githens Enright, Ph.D., CFCS

Morning Glory Press

Buena Park, California

Library of Congress Cataloging-in-Publication Data

Lindsay, Jeanne Warren.
    Books, babies, and school-age parents : how to teach pregnant and
parenting teens to succeed / Jeanne Warren Lindsay and Sharon
Githens Enright.
        p.   cm.
    Includes bibliographical references (p.) and index.
    ISBN 1-885356-21-8 (hardcover). -- ISBN 1-885356-22-6 (pbk.)
        1. Pregnant schoolgirls--Education--United States. 2. Teenage
mothers--Education--United States. 3. Teenage parents--Education
--United States. I. Enright, Sharon.   II. Title.
LC4091.L55 1997
371.93'086'5--dc21   97-5793
                                                                            CIP

MORNING GLORY PRESS, INC.
6595 San Haroldo Way   Buena Park, CA 90620-3748
714.828.1998; 1.888.712.8254   FAX 714.828.2049
Printed and bound in the United States of America

CONTENTS

12 Building School   206
and Community Support

- Help from school network • Is school a friendly place?
- Advocating for students • Becoming a resource expert
- Frequent guests enrich offerings
- Promoting school/health/social service partnerships
- Working with community advisory council
- Support from advisory councils
- Service organization support • Tips for success

13 Finding the Dollars   226

- State funding • Additional sources of funds
- Collaboration within school district
- Tips from grants director • Community funding
- Common mistakes in proposal writing
- Grant-writing works • Sharing services
- Fundraising — a necessary step

14 Outreach, Marketing,   242
and Public Relations

- Drop out because of pregnancy?
- Recruiting eligible students • Teen parent panels can help
- In-school publicity • Reaching out to community groups
- Value of service projects • Handling media publicity

We both became enamored with teen parents when we started teaching in teen parent programs in the early 70s, Sharon in Ohio and Jeanne in California. We found our students eager to learn. For many, learning became more important *because* of their parenthood status.

At that time, our jobs were unique. Services for teen mothers were just beginning, and teen fathers were almost always ignored. We knew, however, that the young moms in our classes needed more than reading, writing, and arithmetic. They needed to learn the art and skills of parenting. They needed to graduate from high school and prepare themselves for the world of work.

Most of us who were teaching teen parents didn't get much support from our schools or our communities in those early years. If we were lucky enough to know other teen parent teachers, we helped each other. Most important, as we worked with these young parents, we learned from *them* . . . and we saw their accomplishments. Our teaching made a difference.

In this twenty-first century, the world has changed for all of us, and perhaps especially for teen parents. Leaving school at 14, even 18, today almost ensures a lifetime of poverty for oneself and one's family. Teen parents continue to have enormous needs, needs that teachers play a primary role in meeting. In conjunction with families, health and social services, churches, youth organizations, and others, we struggle to provide services that help young parents cope with their current realities, to empower them to take charge of their lives, and to go on to productive and satisfying futures.

Our working lives still revolve around the world of teen parents. Sharon directed GRADS (**G**raduation, **R**eality, **A**nd **D**ual-role **S**kills), school programs for adolescent parents in Ohio and 16 other states. Jeanne is the author of 18 books, almost all of them for and about teen parents, and she edits the *PPT Express,* a quarterly newsletter for people working with school-age parents.

As we work with teachers, we encounter many already doing a great job working with teen parents, but who welcome assistance in honing their helping skills. We meet individuals just entering the field of teaching young parents. "I have this new assignment . . . and I need help," they say. We talk with teachers concerned about the pregnant and parenting students in their day-to-day classes. Often these teens are offered no support services to help them continue their education, learn the art and skills of parenting, and become job-ready. "How can I help them when I already have a full teaching load?" these teachers ask.

Books, Babies and School-Age Parents is designed to help both the beginning and veteran teacher or program coordinator in teen parent programs, and also those other teachers and administrators who see a need and would like to develop such a program. Our intention is to supply the nuts and bolts of developing, coordinating, and teaching in an effective program for this special population.

Above all, we hope to convey our deep respect and love for teenage mothers and fathers, and acknowledge the role a special teacher can play in the development of these young parents' dreams for themselves and their children.

Jeanne Warren Lindsay
Sharon Githens Enright, Ph.D.
August, 2003

Why Serve
Teenage Parents?

This simple question evokes many different responses. A
teacher, social worker or nurse who works directly with teenage
parents would answer much differently than a principal, school
board member, or legislator. Since access to a teenage parent
program in Florida became a state entitlement fourteen years
ago, a full range of reactions by this state's school districts has
been noted. Some districts serve teenage parents vigorously,
some do so hesitantly, and a few begrudgingly.

These reactions, no doubt, reflect the varied opinions of the
taxpayers, voters, editorial boards, and policymakers of our state.
And the debate over welfare reform, including the prominent
position that young unwed mothers hold in that maelstrom, is
about to begin again. The Florida Legislature, in a remarkable
parallel to Congress, attempted to "fine tune" the welfare reform
package that Congress passed in 1996.

Though a full-time observer and a part-time participant for
some time in "the debate," I was both flattered and daunted when

Jeanne and Sharon approached me to write the foreword for this wonderful resource. Knowing them and their outstanding work for years, the notion that I could add to their manuscript was an intimidating one. I eventually agreed in the spirit of Florida's finest educators, those who teach teen parents and who never shrink from a challenge. I thought I might try to explain why it is that they, like their counterparts in so many schools in other states, are driven to do what they do.

The simple truth is that teenage parents and their children are getting our attention, our time, and our resources like never before. Four historical facts lend perspective to this truth and help us understand why it is the case.

The first of these is that teenage girls, as a group, are no more fertile today than they were four decades ago. While there have been some increases and decreases in this span of time, the number of births per 1,000 teenagers in most geographic areas has not significantly changed.

The second fact is that the sequence of events that follow teenagers' conceptions has changed dramatically. In the past, the most common remedy to an unplanned and unintended teenage pregnancy was simple — marriage. In contrast, 83 percent of Florida's teenagers age 18 and younger who gave birth in 1995 were single.

The third important consideration is the change in the relationship between educational attainment and wage earning from only two generations ago. In the postwar American economy, many individuals and couples were able to maintain a modest middle-class standard of living and raise a family without the completion of post-secondary or even high school education. Clearly those days are long gone. Far from any guarantee of success, a high school diploma in today's labor market is an absolute minimum in order to earn even subsistence wages.

Finally, the economic costs of early childbearing and its attendant results have soared in recent times. Even conservative estimates are staggering. Understandably, taxpayers are less and less willing to shoulder that burden.

As primary prevention efforts yield only the most modest success, it becomes clear that no simple solutions can address this complex problem. Yet, there are reasonable approaches to reducing the burden of dependence on public assistance associated with teenage childbearing. At the core of these efforts is education.

Nearly all of us agree that too many of our youngsters become sexually active at an early age. Many of us are beginning to recognize how frequently these initial experiences are unwanted. We can also lament the obvious — that many teenagers who are sexually active do not take steps to prevent conception. The most extreme extension of this is the increasing incidence of intentional pregnancies among adolescent girls. There is little at this point in time to indicate that our teenagers are likely to reduce their sexual behavior in the near future, or that those who are sexually active will suddenly become more responsible contraceptors.

We have heard, and will continue to hear, the polarized interpretations of this information. Some will say that society should not be economically straddled with the huge cost of the "mistakes" or the "poor judgment" or the "immoral behavior" of young unwed mothers. This group believes that a diminished stigma associated with teenage childbearing has resulted in a proliferation of the problem. Personal responsibility, combined with the proper "disincentives," would result in less of it.

The opposing camp points to a "victimization" and a genesis of interrelated factors that separate girls who bear children in their teenage years from those who don't. This group maintains that the event of girls growing up in fatherless homes, combined with experiences of child sexual abuse, combined with the hopelessness associated with grinding poverty and the vulnerability to the advances of adult men, are to blame.

The debate between these two sides continues, while the costs of early childbearing continue to mount. Teenage pregnancies and the babies that result continue to get our attention, our time, and our resources. On the surface, there would seem to be no common ground between those holding such different opinions. A closer look, however, indicates that there should be considerable agreement.

Who among us can believe that an uneducated teen mother is

preferable to an educated one? Can any of us think that an
unemployable teen parent is preferable to an employable one?
Could anyone support the idea that a teen parent dependent on
welfare is preferable to a self-sufficient one?

Aside from the direct costs of babies born to very young
mothers, we are just now drawing the connection between early
childbearing and juvenile crime. A study cited in *Kids Having
Kids* (1996) shows that the teen sons of adolescent mothers are
nearly three times more likely to land in prison than the sons of
mothers who gave birth in their twenties. Should we be surprised
at the figures that indicate many incarcerated youth were born to
teenage mothers, were disciplined harshly or randomly or not at
all, were victims of abuse or neglect, or were raised in fatherless
homes?

Assaults, rapes and murders committed by teenagers scream
for our attention, our time, our resources. Teenagers bearing
babies quietly get them.

What further complicates our search for solutions is that this
group of young parents is such a mixed bag. Last year's graduating "class" of pregnant and parenting students in Florida includes a valedictorian, a homecoming queen, several who received athletic and academic scholarships, and dozens of gifted,
talented, and honors students. Many pregnant and parenting
students have specific learning disabilities, emotional disturb-
ances, or limited English proficiency. Teenage parents come in
all races and ethnic groups. Though the birth rate is higher for
African-American and Hispanic teens, 61 of Florida's 67 coun-
ties had more births to white teens than minority teens in 1996.

Truly, the group of teen parents is a heterogeneous one.
Nevertheless, empirical research and anecdotal evidence tell us
that more than three-fourths of Florida's young mothers share
three characteristics: they grew up in poverty, they were victims
of some form of maltreatment (most notably sexual abuse), and
they were impregnated by an adult man, not a school-age boy.

When we remove the passion and the rhetoric, when we lay
aside the emotion that this topic so quickly evokes and reduce
the discussion to the most cold, selfish, economic terms, another
simple truth emerges: All of us, as individuals, as a community,

and as a society, benefit from educating young mothers
and fathers.

For each teenage mother . . .

- who receives prenatal and postnatal care,
- who recognizes her worth and value other than her sexuality,

and for every teenage *parent,* mother or father . . .

- who bonds with their newborn infant,
- who learns to properly raise their child,
- who maintains contact at school with caring, responsible
  adults who model appropriate behavior and good values,
- who succeeds in small incremental steps,
- who is imbued with goals and ambition,
- who continues or resumes their education,
- who experiences opportunity and hope,
- who graduates from high school and looks beyond,
- who comes to understand the assumed but usually unspoken
  connection between education, gainful employment, and a
  better life,
- who is empowered to strive for independence and self-
  sufficiency,
- who aspires to improve their lot and that of their child,
- who succeeds in a role in addition to that of parent,

. . . **for each of these we, the taxpaying public, benefit.** All
altruism and humanism aside, for each of these teen parents, we
save tax dollars!

The more our policymakers grasp this concept (which has
been obvious for a couple of decades to those who teach teen
parents), the more valuable *Books, Babies and School-Age
Parents* becomes. Newcomers to teaching this special group of
students will think of this volume as indispensable. And even the
most veteran teacher of young parents will find strategies and
techniques worth adopting in these pages.

Indeed, one of the most frustrating aspects of working with
teenage parents is a sense of isolation. So often, the teachers of
young parents, particularly those in rural and small school

districts, say that none of their fellow teachers have work days quite like theirs. Consequently, even the most empathic co-workers cannot quite appreciate the special challenges that are inherent in working with pregnant and parenting students.

This book will go so very far to reduce that sense of isolation. *Books, Babies and School-Age Parents* gives the satisfaction that comes from the exchange of ideas, the enthusiasm that comes from comradery, and the relief that comes from knowing, "I'm not the only one with this crazy job I love!" How special it is that these things (usually experienced only briefly at a conference attended by like-thinking people from distant places who have similar jobs) are now bound in a book that can be referred to over and over.

"The debate" will continue. Taxpayers, voters, editors, and elected officials will express diverging opinions in every forum from the cocktail party and the panel discussion to the school board meeting and the floor of the Senate. More pregnant and parenting adolescents will stay in or return to school. More programs will be created, and existing ones will be expanded.

The young parents are thought of quite differently by different adults, some who know them and many who do not. They may be seen through eyes of sympathy or eyes of disgust. They may be treated with compassion or with scorn. By a growing number, they are considered an opportunity, young people who need our help.

We can be certain that teenage parents and their babies *will* get our attention, they *will* get our time, and they *will* get our resources. We can invest these now, in their education and that of their children, or pay a much higher price later. The fund of information contained in this book makes the investment much easier.

Max Schilling
Former Teenage Parent Program Specialist
Department of Education
Tallahassee, Florida

ACKNOWLEDGMENTS

Many, many caring teachers have shared with us their expertise in working with pregnant and parenting teens. I (Sharon) have learned so much from the caring and wonderful GRADS teachers with whom I have worked, and I thank them for sharing their stories with me during the past six years. Teachers whose comments I pass along in this book include Bonnie Thompson, Mary Jo Guidi, Mary Potter, Pat Tucker, Barbara Cain, Bonnie Beckman, Joan Durgin, Kathie DeMuesy, Ann Durusky, Jeanette Abell, Pat Clark, Pam Frazier, Linda James, and Susan Scott. I also thank Margaret Carels for her help.

Throughout my years of teaching and working with teen parents, I (Jeanne) learned a great deal from other teachers working with this special population. Because of my current work, I continue to interact with teachers, and I interviewed some of them in order to utilize their expertise here. Teachers and others who were interviewed included Sue Kaulfus, Jan

Figart, Patricia Miles, Ray Larsen, Ann Terry, Gloria Parmerlee-Greiner, Meri-lin MacGibbon, Brenda Egan, Joan Koch, Ruth Frankey, Linda Miller, Irene Dardashti, Sheila Maggard, LoLita Pfeiffer Dawson, Susan Todd, Patrice Hall, Barbara Edenfield, Win Van Cleve, Ginger Masingill, Susan Siepel, Rosann Pollock, Chantal Phillips, Pat Alviso, Lee Powers, Nancy Buzzell, Becky Roth, Leslie Dragoo, Jackie Silver, Gretchen Almstead, Pat Guerra, Liz Irwin, Dot Rhodes, Karen Hoelker, Mike Trover, Emily Runion, and Connie Graff.

They represent twelve states and a tremendous variety of school programs for pregnant and parenting teens. They all contributed to this book, and most of them are quoted.

We are especially grateful to Max Schilling, former Teenage Parent Program Specialist, Florida Department of Education, for his careful editing, for his fine Foreword, and his Afterword. (Yes, we let Max have the first *and* the last word here.)

The quotes from pregnant and parenting teens and their parents are mostly from interviews conducted for earlier books. Names have been changed to protect their privacy.

Others who critiqued the manuscript include Sharon Rodine, Fern Marx, Susan Batten, Sally McCullough, Judy Peterson, Evelyn Lerman, Connie Blair, Genie Wheeler, Sue Kaulfus, Irene Dardashti, Linda Miller, Dorothy Wallace, and Kathi Lindsay. Our book is better because of their help.

Tim Rinker designed the cover, and David Crawford contributed the wonderful photos of students in his Teen Parent Program at Daylor High School, Sacramento, California. Steve Lindsay helped with the interior design of the book, and Ellen Beck contributed the clear explanation of Internet use on page 58. Carole Blum and Karen Blake spent many productive hours proof-reading, and we appreciate their careful work.

We especially thank our husbands, Steve Enright and Bob Lindsay, for their understanding and support during our months of intense work and late nights. We appreciate and love them.

Jeanne Warren Lindsay
Sharon Githens Enright

To those caring and tireless teachers
who find joy in helping teenage mothers and fathers
work toward satisfying and productive lives

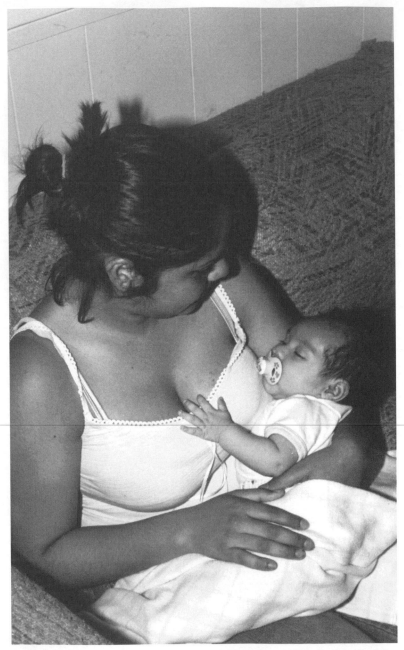

"When I realized I was pregnant I thought my life had ended."

When I realized I was pregnant I thought my life had ended. My dreams of college, of even finishing high school, were over. I was ready to drop out when I read of the Teen Parent Program. I decided to enroll, and the support I got there made all the difference.

I only missed three weeks of school when my baby was born. My mother works, and I had no one at home to care for Travis. But my school has a child care center, so he went to school with me. I'll graduate in June, and then I'm going to college to learn accounting.

Elisa, 17, mother of Travis, 16 months

Do parents need an education?

Strange question? Think back a generation. If you were young and pregnant, you were not *allowed* to continue your education. Our culture valued education highly — *unless* the individual became a parent before her high school graduation. When that happened, school usually was not even an option.

Schools are the social institution with the greatest opportunity
and capacity to educate and intervene in the lives of school-age
parents, fathers as well as mothers. Schools are also important
places for socialization with peers and, among some groups, for
acculturation. The best interests of schools are also served when
they work aggressively with teen parents to help them remain in
school and be successful while there. When students who
become parents experience success during their school years,
their children are more likely to be successful in school, too.
Simply put, when we teach the parent, we teach the child.

It would seem that schools would welcome teen parents with
open arms, but this is often not the case. Today, however, few
schools would dare admit to pushing students out because of
pregnancy or parenthood. First of all, it violates federal statute.
Second, it doesn't make sense, at least to many of us.

Some young parents have the strength and the family support
to continue life as it was before baby. They go to class and grandma cares for the baby. They come home, play with the baby,
and do their homework. They participate in extra-curricular
activities. They don't appear to have added problems or burdens.

How many young parents do you know who have this happy
reality? Many do not, but your school may assume that because a
few students have babies and are attending class regularly, there
is no big struggle for other adolescent parents. Or are there
people in your district who assume pregnancy and childbearing
doesn't happen among your community's teenagers?

Half a million teens deliver babies each year in the United
States. One-third to one-half of those babies are fathered by teenagers. That's a lot of young people coping with adolescence *and*
the adult world of parenthood. Juggling the responsibilities of
these two worlds often requires help. The "regular" school
program is not enough. For proof, witness the number of teen
parents no longer enrolled in school. Teen parents need support
services on campus. They need to access social and health
services as easily as possible. They should be able to continue in
their regular academic work including remedial help, advanced
college prep classes, and workforce preparation as needed.

Those who have been turned off by school and have dropped out also need services. Enhanced educational and support services in a regular school setting may be adequate to retrieve some school dropouts, but not all. Many who have already dropped out may not be willing to return to the school where, for whatever reason, they previously experienced little success. A more flexible alternative school may be their answer.

Reducing Adolescent Pregnancy and Childbearing

The best way to solve the problems of early childbearing is to do all we can to help teens delay pregnancy until they're physically, emotionally, socially, and financially ready to parent. The fact that teens are far more likely to give birth in the United States than in any other developed country is our national disgrace. As a society, and more practically, in each community we must take targeted steps to reduce the number of births to our adolescents. The responsibility of adolescent childbearing does not fall on the shoulders of teens alone — it also rests upon our societal and economic institutions and families.

Adolescent childbearing is a very complex issue. Many risk factors are associated with early childbearing, such as

- economic poverty
- low academic achievement, poor school attendance, and school failure
- victimization, notably child sexual abuse, but also other forms of maltreatment
- mothers who are distant, uninvolved or underinvolved, in unstable partner relationships, are survivors of sexual abuse, or were teen mothers themselves
- fathers who are absent, distant, uninvolved, or abusive
- experiences of loss or grief, particularly the loss of a close, caring, guiding adult family member
- relationships between older men (age 20 and over) and younger teen women (age 17 and younger)
- communities that are unsafe, violent, or lack safe gathering places such as recreational areas or community centers
- communities that lack health care systems that are accessible, affordable, respectful and inviting

• communities that lack organized youth activities with trusted
  and caring adult leaders

Teens with several of these risk factors in their lives are likely
to have little hope for a bright and healthy future. Teens with
even one risk factor may have diminished hope. Effective
strategies for preventing teen pregnancy and childbearing need to
focus on instilling protective factors in the lives of children and
youth. When youth have hope for a positive future, they are
more likely to abstain from sex, or if they are sexually active, to
use contraceptives wisely and effectively.

As communities strive to develop and refine promising
strategies to reduce their rates of teen births, we believe it is
critical for the program coordinators, nurses, social workers, and
especially teachers, to assert themselves in this dialogue. Because teachers spend more hours each week with students than
any other adults (other than parents or close family members),
they have a better grasp of, or can more effectively express
young people's struggles, either before they conceive or after.
Who better to enlighten their communities as to which efforts are
most and least likely to effect a reduction?

Until teen childbearing disappears from our culture, however, we cannot afford to ignore those young people who get
pregnant each year, the half-million who deliver babies, and
the teen men who father at least a third of these children. (The
other fathers, adult men, represent a separate problem that will
not be solved through school programs for pregnant and
parenting teens.)

Our common goal of education for all has come to mean
special help should be available for those who need it — the
physically challenged, the slow learners, and, theoretically at
least, the economically disadvantaged. Perhaps the true measure
of our public education system is how well it is applied to those
who need it the most.

Does this special help also apply to teen parents? Does the
fact that a 15-year-old has a child have anything to do with her/
his educational needs? Of course it does! In fact, targeted
programs and services for teen parents and their children can

contribute to teens delaying subsequent pregnancies and to reducing the risk factors in the lives of their children.

Preventing School Dropout

The early months of pregnancy are extremely important from an educational standpoint. The young woman may not feel physically well during this time, and she is likely to be in emotional turmoil. Her grades may drop dramatically or she may simply quit attending school. School may not seem relevant or important when compared with the other events in her life. She may view pregnancy or parenting as her ticket out of school, a place which has been the source of many problems and much failure.

This can also be a time of confusion and upheaval for young expectant fathers.

Sometimes school personnel fail to understand the importance of school attendance for young parents. A few years ago in southern California, the mother of a pregnant tenth grader received the following letter from her daughter's principal:

> *. . . Denae really is going to have some problems achieving a high school diploma. Right now, though, her biggest and most important concern has to be the coming baby, and its and her care. I know that both you and she will be fully involved and enjoy the new one.*

The letter was written on school stationery and signed by the principal. Apparently he had already decided that, because Denae was pregnant and had failed two classes in the ninth grade, he should invite her to be a school dropout. One wonders if this principal often programmed students for failure early in their high school careers. Or did he feel that if a girl has a baby she "should" be home, with her education no longer important?

Denae did not allow her principal's prophecy of failure to prevail. She moved to a neighboring district which provided child care for students' children, and through much hard work, · managed to graduate on schedule. Soon after graduation she was working and supporting her son.

One wonders how many young parents in Denae's home

district never graduated from high school, never were able to
hold promising jobs, because of this principal's short-sighted
attitude.

Title IX Guidelines Apply

Title IX Guidelines of the Education Amendment Act of 1972
state that no school receiving any federal funds may discriminate
against any student based on sex (being male or female). Marital
and parental status is specifically addressed in §106.40. It states
that a school shall not apply any rule concerning a student's
actual or potential parental, family, or marital status which treats
students differently on the basis of sex.

Pregnancy and related conditions are also addressed. Public
schools shall not discriminate against any student because of
pregnancy, childbirth, false pregnancy, termination of pregnancy, or recovery therefrom. This student cannot be excluded
from any educational program or activity unless the student
requests voluntarily to participate in a separate portion of the
program or activity. The school cannot ask a pregnant or
parenting student to obtain a physician's certificate stating that
the student is physically and emotionally able to participate in a
regular school program unless the same certification is required
of all students requiring the attention of a physician.

If a school operates a special voluntary program for pregnant
students, the program must be academically comparable to that
which is offered to students who are not pregnant. Attending a
special program is strictly voluntary, and no student is to be
required or even "counseled" into such a program.

The school shall provide a leave of absence for the period of
time deemed medically necessary by the student's physician.
The student is to return to school at the status she held when the
leave began.

It is imperative that all school staff members understand Title
IX. A clearly understandable summary of the law and its ramifications for school policies should be included in student handbooks and in informational materials sent to students' parents.

Since a school's primary responsibility is to educate children,
"letting" pregnant or parenting students drop out is not the

answer. Consistently following up on students who are repeatedly absent or who simply quit coming to classes should be standard procedure. Each time a school helps someone stay in school, whether a pregnant teenager, prospective father, or teen parent, it increases that young person's chances for a self-sufficient, productive life. Conversely, each time a young parent drops out, the likelihood of both the teen and the child being economically dependent on public assistance is increased.

As you work with your district, avoid being pulled into a "moral debate" — although what could be more moral than helping school-age parents become educated? Or more immoral than discouraging/excluding them from continuing their education? Focus instead on the problems of teen mothers and fathers in terms of sex equity, dropout prevention, new parenting responsibilities, and economic self-sufficiency. Stress the needs of the innocent children of the teen parents who are the next generation of students and citizens. Few school administrators are able to ignore the fact that the infants of today's teen parents will be entering their school system in a few short years.

Enhanced School Services Needed

Meeting the educational needs of students is the first and foremost mission of all schools. However, standard school services simply are not enough for pregnant and parenting teens. They need enhanced services.

During pregnancy, healthy mothers are vital to healthy outcomes for both mothers and babies. Pregnant teens need early and regular prenatal care which is accessible, low-cost, and available in an inviting, caring environment. Schools need to be partners with health care providers, by linking the teens with health care services or by offering on-site health care.

Health and wellness education are also important to healthy outcomes for mothers and babies. School programs for pregnant teens need to have a strong curricular emphasis on health, wellness, nutrition, and prenatal self-care. Following delivery, the post-partum check-up and continuing health care for parent and child are essential.

Many students have no trusted family members or friends

who can provide child care. Safe, high-quality developmental child care and transportation are necessities for these young parents if they are to continue attending school, *and necessary for the children.*

Social support services may also be needed by pregnant or parenting teens. For example, some teens are not able to live at home, and some live in unsafe homes. They may need assistance in obtaining safe, nurturing, structured living environments.

Teen parents often need help in avoiding another pregnancy in their teenage years. They may need counseling to help them address the problems which might have led to the initial pregnancy or which may impede their ability to parent their children effectively.

They need help as they move rapidly from adolescence into adult responsibilities, including preparing for the world of work. Generally, teen mothers who continue to attend school or return to school are more likely to postpone a subsequent pregnancy for at least two years than are school-age mothers who do not attend school.

Making a Difference

I dropped out after tenth grade. I never liked school and saw no reason to go. But after I got pregnant I knew I'd have to support my baby so I enrolled in the Teen Parent Program.

I'm taking auto mechanics along with my required classes. By the time I graduate I think I'll be ready for a job – and I know I won't have to settle for minimum wage!

Susan, 18, mother of Jessica, 1

A lot of times I feel like I can't make it any more. I need support. I don't get it at home much, but I do get support in the teen fathers group. It helps knowing I'm not the only teen dad. It makes me feel a lot better.

Daric, 16, father of Kianna, 1

Susan and Daric are ahead because their school districts understand the need for special services for pregnant and

parenting students. They didn't have to settle for the impover-
ished, uncertain, often grim future faced by many teenage
parents, a future that has become even more uncertain due to
changes in the welfare system.

In the majority of school districts in the United States, however, Daric and Susan would have had no teen parent program,
no support group for teen dads, no opportunity to prepare for
employment, and no on-campus child care. Susan would never
have returned to school. Daric, too, would have been less likely
to stay in school and do his best to handle his responsibilities as
a father.

You and your school district, through your concern for this
vulnerable segment of our population, can make a profound
difference in the lives of young parents and their children. The
potential for influencing young lives cannot be overstated.

A variety of teen parent program models are described. No
one model has demonstrated that it works better than all the
others. Your community can determine which model or
combination of models best fits your needs.

The following chapters contain many suggestions for developing strong, supportive school programs for teen parents. Staff
qualifications, program organization, curriculum development,
workforce preparation, teaching the art and skills of parenting,
working with teen fathers as well as mothers, helping pregnant
and parenting teens deal with losses, all are important. So are
measuring your program's effectiveness, collaborating with
families, school staff, and community, funding programs, and
outreach. These chapters provide guidance for looking at the
many needs of pregnant and parenting teens. Obviously, most
programs cannot do it all, at least not immediately, and some
chapters you may choose to ignore at this time. You, of course,
decide what teen parents in *your* community most need, and
what you and your community can do to meet those needs.

Know that you are needed.

School-age parents need enhanced services to stay in school.

CHAPTER 1

Designing Services for Teen Parents

Without special services, schools often are unfriendly places for pregnant and parenting teens. School-age parents need advocates, people who will help them negotiate through the difficulties of staying in or returning to school. For teens who are still enrolled in school, this can be done by providing supportive staff and services in regular school settings as well as alternative schools.

Some young people are not able to learn in a school of 2,000 students, and may need more individualized attention and instruction. The one-to-one relationship between the caring adult/ teacher and the student makes the difference. Young parents need the caring, understanding, and respectful relationship that says, "I value you as an individual; you're going to be a good parent and citizen."

This kind of environment cannot be overstated. It is here that many young parents respond to the first caring adults with whom they've had contact in years (if ever).

Twenty-five percent of teens who become pregnant drop out of school before conceiving. You need to have a strong outreach to these disenfranchised teens. Sometimes, having a special teacher who advocates for them, or a special program that addresses their many challenges, is enough to attract them back into school. One pregnant teen expressed it exactly this way:

Sometimes I want to forget about my worries, but I can't. What I did is I started going to school. That gets the worried out of my mind.

For those adolescents who do not re-engage with a secondary school, an additional option of an enhanced GED (General Education Diploma) program might meet their needs.

Extremely important for these young people is a strong "search and serve" mind-set in the schools, an understanding of the importance of finding teens who have dropped out of school, and of getting them back into the system. We have to find them before we can help them. See chapter 14 for more on this topic.

Importance of Comprehensive Services

Throughout these chapters, a wide variety of school services for teen parents are simply referred to as teen parent programs. TAPP is a frequently used acronym for TeenAge Parent Program. Many teen parent programs in Texas are called PEP (Pregnancy, Education and Parenting). GRADS (Graduation, Reality And Dual-Role Skills) refers to the network of teen parent programs throughout Ohio and in some areas in other states.

This book advocates educating pregnant and parenting teens whenever possible through a well organized and, preferably, daily class focusing on their special needs. Many of the teachers quoted are working in such programs. Ideally, all pregnant and parenting teens would have access to this kind of program. In addition, for teen parents unable or unwilling to attend a full-time school program, possible alternatives, such as independent study, will be discussed.

Comprehensive services designed to meet your students' health, social, and educational needs are preferred. Some school districts provide comprehensive services for teen parents and their children at a single site, including on-site child care, a health clinic, counseling services, workforce preparation, and transportation.

Separate or Alternative School for Some

In many school districts, large and small, pregnant and parenting students may choose to attend their own separate school. This model is most common in large city school districts such as Albuquerque, New Mexico (New Futures); Miami, Florida (COPE); and Louisville, Kentucky (TAPP). In some districts, a self-contained classroom is located on a school campus. In the past, many districts offered these programs at churches, YWCAs, and other off-campus locations. This is still the practice in some areas.

The separate school provides most courses required by students, including academics needed for graduation and some elective courses. Parenting courses are traditionally offered, and sometimes workforce preparation is available. Often, small separate schools do not provide adequate college preparatory courses such as advanced math, science, and language. Equity and quality of program offerings must be continually monitored. Students who enroll in the separate or alternative school program must have an education experience equitable with that which is available at their home schools.

Often, especially in the larger teen parent programs, other professionals such as counselors, social workers, and health-care providers are located on-site to offer social support and health services. A child care center is often on-site. Teachers usually have a full teaching schedule, with a teacher preparation period, although sometimes part-time teachers or aides are utilized.

The teen parent program in some districts starts out with one teacher and the "little red school house" approach. The one teacher does her/his best to teach math, English, science, social studies, and other academic subjects along with the prenatal health and parenting classes — and at the same time helps students link up with the various community resources designed to meet their needs. If the teacher has a wide academic background along with family and consumer sciences training, s/he may be able to intervene effectively. An integral part of the program may be generous use of community resource people as guest speakers.

Early programs tended to be at sites away from "regular" school. In fact, in California during the early 70s, pregnant minor programs were funded under special education, and were specifically excluded from comprehensive schools. Apparently, the California Legislature considered pregnancy contagious.

As a result, many California teen parent programs were and still are located on continuation (alternative) school campuses. Teachers with good outreach techniques soon discovered this was an excellent approach to the dropout retrieval challenge. The smaller continuation schools, with a more individualized approach to teaching combined with prenatal health and parenting classes, and in some districts, child care, drew dropouts back into an environment of learning.

Special Services in Comprehensive Schools

School districts across the United States illustrate an amazing variety of programs and services for pregnant and parenting teens. More and more, teen parent programs are being developed on comprehensive high school campuses.

The California School Age Families Education (Cal-SAFE) Program was established in 2000 to increase support services for pregnant and parenting teens in California. Cal-SAFE programs demonstrate the effectiveness of teen parents continuing their education at their home school, but with additional services provided to help them in their new role of parenthood. In addition to their academic and workforce preparation classes, Cal-SAFE students generally spend one period a day in a parenting class and one period earning credit in the child care center on campus. The Cal-SAFE goal is to access sufficient resources to support a seamless, cost-effective service delivery system from point of entry into the program until graduation.

GRADS is a model in-school family and consumer sciences instructional and intervention program for pregnant and parenting teens, male and female. GRADS, developed in Ohio, operates in 75 percent of Ohio's school districts and in sixteen other states. The mission is to promote personal growth, educational competence, and economic self-sufficiency. Objectives, similar to those in many other comprehensive programs, are to:

- increase school retention, retrieval, and graduation rates
- have healthier mothers and babies
- increase knowledge and skills in positive parenting practices
- prepare participants for the world of work
- increase knowledge and skills of balancing work and family
- delay subsequent pregnancies

The GRADS model consists of five basic program elements plus a sixth optional component:

- A trained family and consumer sciences teacher to direct the program
- Curriculum and instruction based on the *GRADS Competency Analysis Profile* along with the *Adolescent Parent Resource Guide*
- Home and community outreach to strengthen involvement of family and community agencies and organizations
- A local advisory council to build a strong base of school and community support for the program
- Evaluation and research to demonstrate program effectiveness
- Optional component: On-site child care based on local policy and resources

Schools are free to enhance the basic model to fit the needs of students and resources of the local community. For example, programs may include transportation, health care or health professional involvement, counseling services, WIC (Special Supplemental Feeding Program for Women, Infants and Children), University Extension, TANF (Temporary Aid for Needy Families), child support enforcement case workers, legal counsel, grandparent support groups, mentor parents, and more. There are as many adaptations as there are programs.

GRADS teachers usually teach three classes during the school day, and have a teacher preparation period and two conference

periods. These conference periods provide time daily for teachers
to have individual student conferences, make home and hospital
visits and other parental and family contacts, work with social
service agencies and health care providers, and with other school
staff. This schedule allows the teachers to provide support for the
wide variety of needs of teen parents.

In schools with high concentrations of pregnant and parenting
teens, GRADS is offered as a daily elective class. In schools
with few pregnant and parenting teens, the teacher may travel
among several schools during the week, meeting with students in
each building two or three class periods a week.

Outside of Ohio, some schools which have small numbers of
pregnant and parenting students offer one elective class daily for
GRADS students. The teacher teaches other classes, but has one
additional conference period to meet the many needs of the
GRADS students.

Program for Pregnancy and Postpartum

Another approach is utilized for the TeenAge Parent Program
(TAPP) in the school district of Okaloosa County, Ft. Walton
Beach and Crestview, Florida. Two off-campus programs are
designed primarily for pregnant students who usually remain for
a minimum of one semester, then return to their home schools.
Located on vocational education campuses, the programs offer a
full academic program, vocational training, a required course in
parenting, and a physical education class designed for pregnant
and parenting teens.

Students normally have a three-week maternity leave and
have learning packets with assignments from school on which
they work as their postpartum schedule allows. When the baby is
three weeks old, both mom and infant return to the TAPP classroom. "This extends the bonding period and enables the social
worker and the teacher to reinforce appropriate parenting skills,"
Barbara Edenfield, TAPP coordinator, explained.

The baby comes to school with mom until s/he is about two
months old. At that time the school, working through a local
non-profit agency, helps the student find appropriate child care.
Some students prefer home day care which must be licensed.

Others choose a licensed child care center.

At the end of the semester in which she delivers, the student returns to her home school, whether a comprehensive high school or a vocational program. The district provides transportation for mothers and babies to and from their homes, the child care facilities, and school, using buses with car seats.

Each week Edenfield contacts each child care site to check on the baby's attendance and to see if there have been any difficulties. If the baby has been out more than three days, she calls the parent to ask if there is a problem.

Follow-Up Support Provided

Some schools report that when teen parents leave a special program to return to their home high school, the success rate is not good. Without supportive services, many young parents, unable to cope with the demands of school coupled with the demands of early parenthood, drop out. Edenfield, however, reports that about 95 percent of their TAPP students return to their base school. She helps that success rate by calling each young mother at least once each semester. This is in addition to checking with the child care centers and following up when babies have been out more than three school days. "Teen moms always have my phone number. If they have trouble with transportation or child care, they call me and I help them solve it," she said.

In addition, periodic counseling groups are scheduled at the high school. "It gives the young moms a chance to get together and provides a support or mentoring situation among them. It also helps us identify other students on the campus who are parents," she said. This has been offered at six-week intervals during the regular school day. The group, led by a social worker, is scheduled at different times throughout the day so that students will not be pulled from the same class again and again.

"Here in Florida, girls who are receiving TANF (Temporary Aid to Needy Families) must now either be working or, if of school age, in school. We are seeing more and more parenting teens who had dropped out of school now coming back and asking for help. We're trying to develop ways to meet their needs," Edenfield concluded.

The requirement that school-age parents receiving welfare be enrolled in school is going into effect across the country. The difference in Florida is that child care for teen parent students who enroll in or complete a teenage parent program is mandated. In many states, the school attendance requirement is difficult to enforce — if there is no one else to care for the child, the school-age parent cannot be forced to attend school.

Serving Middle School Students

As more younger teens become pregnant, more younger students will need enhanced educational services. School districts across the country are struggling to find ways to meet the needs of pregnant middle school students, which may be quite different from those of older school-age parents.

School districts that provide separate schools for pregnant and parenting teens may be able to serve these students easily during pregnancy. They attend the same separate school as the older pregnant teens. However, many districts do not have the resources to serve these younger parents for the duration of their schooling, nor do most of them want to remain in these school settings for several years. Besides, these programs are rarely equipped to provide the long-term career-focused education teen parents need.

Some districts with in-school programs have a high school teacher who travels to the middle school two or three times a week, or even daily, to meet with and teach pregnant students. Clearly, this type of service is better than no service, and may be the best that some small, rural districts can offer. However, since pregnant students in middle schools are rarely the norm, these adolescents may feel very different than their peers and unwanted by their schools. A program that relies on a high school teacher traveling to a middle school may find this approach is inadequate for these very young parents.

In some districts, middle school parents are simply ignored. Others promote these young people to high school, simply because they don't know what else to do with them. Neither of these are acceptable educational practices, as they are not in the best interest of the students. We need to explore ways and try new models for serving young parents not yet in high school.

In Cincinnati, Ohio, two middle schools have high concentrations of teen parents. One school has one full-time GRADS teacher, and the other, two full-time GRADS teachers. Having teachers on-site all the time has made a big difference, and these teachers help the students transition to the high schools by connecting them with the high school GRADS teachers.

In Carlsbad, New Mexico, the GRADS program is on the high school campus. Pregnant middle school students are encouraged to enroll in GRADS. When a middle school student enrolls, the bus picks her up in the morning, and she attends the GRADS class the first period at the high school. She is scheduled into the child care center for her second period. Then the bus takes her back to her school where she continues in her regular academic classes. After her child is born, she may enroll him/her in the high school's child care center.

Toledo, Ohio, has pioneered a new model for very young parents. Joan Durgin, family life education specialist for Toledo City Schools, spearheaded a collaboration among the school system, Toledo Hospital, the Medical College of Ohio, the Toledo Museum of Art, and other agencies and organizations. Two teachers provide the educational component for participating students. One covers the academics and the other is a GRADS teacher. Most of Toledo's young pregnant students choose to attend this separate program during pregnancy, but usually opt to return to their home schools after delivery.

Barbara Cain, the GRADS teacher, travels to each home school several times weekly to provide young parents with needed educational and support services. As students transition to the high schools, Cain also helps link them with the high school GRADS teachers. This model is working well in this urban area.

If we are going to retain our youngest, most vulnerable young parents in school, we need to explore and develop models that work best for them.

Critical Transition Points for Teen Parents

There are certain critical transition points for teen parents, times when they are at highest risk of dropping out of school.

One critical transition point is when students transfer back to their home schools after attending a separate school for pregnant and parenting teens. There is abundant anecdotal information about the high dropout rate of teen parents at this time. The second critical transition point is when teen parents return to school after being a prior school dropout. Teens who have previously met with little school success are quite likely to continue to be sensitive to any school difficulties or failures.

The third critical transition point is when teen parents move from middle school (usually after completing eighth grade) to high school. As I (Sharon) reviewed the Ohio GRADS data on school dropouts, I found that the ninth grade students have a higher dropout rate than students in any other grade (including grades seven and eight), even though compulsory school age in Ohio is through the eighteenth birthday.

Special attention needs to be paid to teen parents who return to their home school or who attend a new school for the first time. This can be accomplished with transition plans that are carefully crafted and implemented by students and teachers together. Visits to the new school prior to the transfer can help, as can maintaining contact with current or former favorite teachers. Most of all, though, students need to form attachments to a few key people, or even one person, in the new school. A staff member at the new school who befriends teen parents, is attuned to their special needs, and helps address their needs can make a huge difference to teen parents attending a new school.

Offering Choices to Teen Parents

Ideally your district won't stop with one kind of teen parent program. Even in a small district, the school-age parent list is likely to include a wide variety of young people from the high-achieving college prep students to our most reluctant scholars.

You may develop a superior program in a comprehensive high school, but in the process, not attract dropouts back to school. You may offer excellent services at an alternative school, but not satisfy students needing advanced placement classes. You may also miss the students who simply don't choose to transfer to the alternative school, or who enroll in a vocational school.

Services should be designed to meet the developmental age range of participating students. A 14-year-old parent may need services that are different than those for a 17-year-old.

For three years, Charlotte County Public Schools, Port Charlotte, Florida, provided one school-age parent program at the alternative school. "We realized there were kids we weren't reaching," Chantal Phillips, supervisor of alternative programs, explained. Phillips reported some young people didn't want to come to the alternative school. Others found it logistically difficult to get there. "In addition," she added, "our numbers were growing, and we couldn't expand much more at that location."

Of the three comprehensive high schools in the district, one appeared to have the greatest need. It was the furthest away from the alternative school, and the area it covered included a number of housing projects.

"We have found that most kids prefer the alternative school when they become pregnant or have a child. A few, however, want to remain at their home school, and we decided to suggest to the others that they consider staying there. Sometimes they don't make the best choice for themselves when they choose the alternative school without much thought. It's a long bus ride, and it's still a school. We want them to understand how both programs work, then make an informed choice. Ideally, we would have a program in every high school," she concluded.

No Special Program?

If there is no special program or class for pregnant and parenting teens at your school, you may want to organize one. If you're in a very small school, with only a couple of teen parents attending at one time, a daily class may not be feasible. But you can still offer support. If there are two or more students, form a support group.

A pregnant teen may experience a sense of isolation. Suddenly she is outside the mainstream of teen life. She's having new feelings and experiencing physical changes. Talking with other teens undergoing similar experiences can help. A support group gives her a chance to talk about her feelings, get information about her health and her baby's health, and learn about

needed resources available to her in the community. After the
baby is born, the young parent(s) will probably need positive
peer support and enhanced educational services more than ever.

According to Sue Kaulfus, former PEP (Pregnancy, Education
and Parenting) Program Specialist, state of Texas, a few small
schools in her state have only one or two pregnant or parenting
students. The person in charge meets with these stu-dents on a
regular basis. "We prefer that they meet at least every week,
every day if possible. Being with the student regularly is the only
way the teacher can keep up with their needs. They can't get
credit for the parenting education for school-age parents course if
they don't attend a regular class on a daily basis."

Kaulfus reports that independent instruction can be provided,
perhaps on a weekly basis, at lunch or after school, either with a
group or an individual. If the school chooses to use the parenting
education for school-age parents course, it must be taught by a
certified home economics teacher with approval by the state.

"Our mission is graduation — keeping pregnant and parenting teens in school until they graduate," Kaulfus explained. "Our
dropout recovery rate is about 38 percent. When PEP first gets
started in a district, it's usually quite small. By the third or fourth
year, there is tremendous growth because of dropout recovery."

Kaulfus described one area in which 17 small school districts
make up one program. One of the districts serves as the fiscal
agent. Each school has a teacher mentor, but everything is
planned and coordinated from one place. If a school has only two
students, for example, PEP offers transportation, parenting
classes, and academic counseling to make sure the student is
taking the courses s/he needs and receives career/job counseling,
self-help counseling if needed, and child care as necessary.

Independent Study Plus Peer Support

Many of us firmly believe teen parents provide valuable support for each other as they work in groups, but we know many
pregnant and parenting teens are not in school. What can we do?

First, we can do everything possible to recruit these students
into our school programs.

If we're unsuccessful in our recruiting, independent study

may be adapted to meet some of the needs of students who do not attend regular classes. In California, independent study usually means the student spends one hour per week with the teacher. The student is expected to work 20 hours on the assignments supplied by the teacher. These assignments are designed to cover the academic classes the student would be taking if attending school full time. Graduation is the goal.

Some independent study teachers working with pregnant and parenting teens design assignments which include material relevant to the special needs the teen parent has in addition to pursuing math, English, and other academic subjects.

Occasionally the teacher schedules group appointments with several pregnant and parenting students. Meeting at least once each week, and preferably more often, the group can learn together about prenatal care, prepared childbirth, parenting, community resources, and other relevant topics. Class discussions, speakers, field trips, and other activities are planned for these meetings. In some states, home tutoring can be organized in a similar manner for pregnant and parenting teens who qualify.

The GRADS *Adolescent Parent Resource Guide* (1997) with its independent and group activities for each competency provides a model for preparing assignments for independent study students and activities for group meetings. All of the *Teens Parenting* and other textbooks from Morning Glory Press include workbooks and curriculum guides which also provide many individual and group activities. A Comprehensive Curriculum Notebook is available for each of the *Teens Parenting* texts, as well as videos and board games.

Similar individualized planning is needed for teachers who work with individual students within a school, students who attend full-time, but who are not scheduled into a teenage parent class. For some teachers, this means a group meeting two or three times a week with students who are pulled out of their regular classes for these sessions. Teachers often schedule these meetings at different times from one week to the next, so the student will not be called out of the same class each time.

If the student is scheduled into a study hall, the pull-out plan can work well. Calling a student out of someone else's class, however, can be frustrating to that teacher, and can shortchange the student's learning in that class. Yet the student needs the teen parent teacher's assistance. What is the best approach?

Perhaps you and your students could brainstorm some ways to achieve your goal of helping teen parents meet their special needs without calling them out of other teachers' classes. Would it be possible to meet during lunch? Perhaps your own lunch period could be scheduled after your students go to their next class. Or would you and your students be able and willing to meet before or after school? One approach might work for awhile, perhaps for a semester. Then you might decide on a different solution the next semester.

In some schools, the teen parent teacher meets individually with students with no credit attached. In Florida and Texas, for example, students are usually expected to take a one-semester teen parenting course. After completing that course, they are eligible for ancillary or continuous counseling services from the teen parent teacher. Some teachers report, however, that with no credit attached, they don't feel they can ask students to do anything beyond keeping their individual appointments and attending occasional group meetings.

If this is your situation, we have two suggestions. First, some of your students probably *want* to learn more about parenting. Try planning exciting assignments on topics that truly interest them. A reader-friendly book about discipline coupled with suggestions for applying new ideas might appeal to them.

Secondly, what can you do about developing a credit plan for the student who is enrolled full-time in other classes? In some schools, an in-school independent study plan is acceptable. A teacher can design a course, complete with goals and objectives, that will meet the student's needs. The student earns a specified amount of credit if s/he meets periodically with the teacher and completes the requirements for the course. Students are more likely to be able to earn credit if you meet with them periodically during study hall, lunch, or before/after school.

Check with your school administrator or curriculum director. If no such plan is currently offered at your school, suggest that this be done. If you go this route with students, you will also want to figure some way of having those group meetings.

A daily class with other teen parents will, for most students, result in more learning than working alone. In the absence of such a class, however, independent study, whether for a full-time in-school student or for the non-attending teen, can also result in valuable learning. Adding peer interaction through periodic group meetings will increase that learning.

Challenge of Continuous Counseling

The programs described provide only a sampling of the wide variety of enhanced educational services developed for teenage parents in school districts across the United States. An integral part of most projects is the goal of helping teen parents find and use the personal and community resources they need to meet the challenges and crises in their lives.

Some programs serve students only during pregnancy and for a short time after childbirth. Others are designed as follow-along programs. If the mother and/or father are 14, or even younger, when their child is born, they may need significant support for several years in order to graduate from high school and become ready to join the workforce. If the program is organized as a one- or two-semester class with little or no services provided after the course is completed, the young parent may not have access to continuous counseling or case management assistance. This can limit their successes rather than sustain them.

These issues become a problem if the school program is the only way in which teen parents receive case management. Some school districts contract with community-based case management agencies that come into schools and/or meet students at home, and provide long-term support.

In California, young parents may enroll in a Cal-SAFE program as many semesters as needed to graduate. Teen parents may continue in GRADS programs until they graduate. In Texas, students may enroll in the PEP parenting education for school-age parents course for up to four semesters.

In Florida, if a student is still in school after completing the required child development course, s/he continues to be eligible for all ancillary services until graduation from high school.

These include child care, social services, health services, and transportation for pregnant and parenting students who are currently enrolled in or have completed a teenage parent program, and for their child.

Even if teen parent students are eligible for continuous enrollment in a teen parent program, they often encounter scheduling difficulties. There are not enough periods in the day to take civics, English, workforce preparation, math, science, art, music, and a teen parent class. Your role is to advocate for your students according to their individual and most immediate needs and preferences. Some will need a daily teen parent class for several semesters. Others will benefit from a semester or two of participation in the special program with less formal interaction with a caring teacher along with the option of utilizing ancillary services during his/her remaining semesters in the school.

In your role as advocate for teen parents, you need to be involved in overall scheduling decisions at your school. Is block scheduling being considered? This may mean double periods for most classes resulting in a year's credit within a semester for one course, then progression to a different course the next semester. Some GRADS teachers have commented on the difficulties sometimes caused with this system because teen parents may have a double period for GRADS one semester, but no time for the program the following semester. Teen parent needs can't be scheduled that neatly.

Continuing instruction and intervention are critical and needed by many students. Ideally, your students will have the flexibility to schedule into your class for the equivalent of one daily class period each semester.

Be aware of any reform efforts being considered in your school. If you anticipate that the changes might be detrimental to students in your program, you need to be at the discussion and planning sessions with all the other stakeholders.

Teen Parent Programs Evolve

No teenage parent program ever began as a "model" program. Even today's finest had very modest, humble beginnings. Expect your program to evolve. The best programs have an appreciation of where they started and an eye to the future as to how they can improve. Let your strategies, interventions, choice of model, and plans for expansion or improvement be driven by questions such as:

- How can we keep more young parents in school?
- What can we do to serve students and their children better?
- Is there something we can do to encourage those who have dropped out to return?
- How can we improve attendance?

Ask these of the students. The most insightful answers may come from those who had dropped out, and your approach may change depending on your current students' needs.

Understand that no single program model can possibly be a perfect match for all young parents. Know that you are doing the best you can, for the most you can, given the current circumstances.

Take steps to avoid burning out. Your students are likely to be some of the neediest, emotionally and economically, in your school or district. Your effectiveness is diminished if you are consumed by those needs. Build a support network for yourself and others working with the program even as you are building support networks for the teen parents.

Expect that program changes (expansion, improvement, adding a new model) are apt to happen gradually. That having been said, look for every opportunity to influence the "gate keepers" and key decision makers so that you can serve teen parents better, and serve more of them.

Advocate for your students and for program changes based on their needs. Recruit others to be advocates, too. It's easier and safer just to do what's allowed, but it's far more rewarding to do what's best for the students.

If you are involved in designing teen parent programs for your district, you must have a clear understanding of the needs of the students in *your* area. The more you know about the range of possibilities, the more effective your planning will be — and the more likely that your district's teen parent program will make a positive difference in your students' lives.

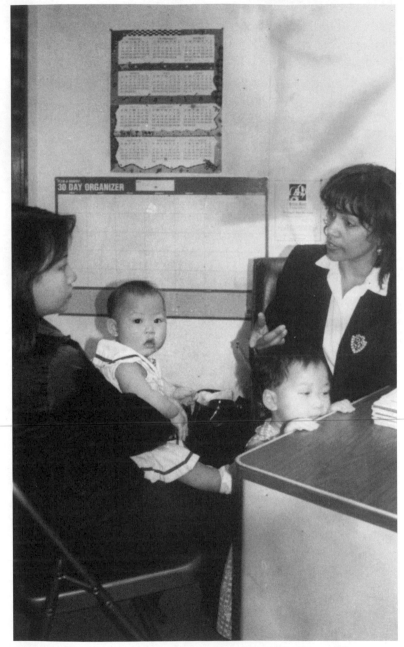

The heart of the teen parent program is the staff.

CHAPTER 2

Special Staff
for Special Students

It takes special people to work with pregnant and parenting teens, and the heart of the teen parent program is the staff. During this intense period of students' lives, everyone with whom they come in contact, professional and support staff, is important. Generally, however, it is the teacher who has the most contact with the students, and it's the teacher who has the greatest opportunity to help them become competent, self-sufficient individuals, parents and citizens.

When you work with pregnant and parenting teens in a school setting, you have a challenging and very special opportunity. Not only do you need to be well qualified for your role as teacher, child care worker, administrator, counselor, nurse, or whatever your position may be, you also need extra doses of *understanding, enthusiasm, compassion, and patience.*

Most important is *wanting* to work with young parents in a positive way.

Teachers Change Lives

At times, your students will act like children, and at times they will seem very grown-up. It is imperative that you take a non-judgmental approach, that you accept each student for who s/he is today, with faith in the person s/he will become.

When you work with teen parents, you are working with adolescents who are taking on the adult role of parent, often before they are fully prepared to do so. You can have a greater impact on their lives if you are friendly, empathize with their situations, and refrain from giving unsolicited advice. One of your important roles is to help them make reasoned decisions. You can't make decisions for them. To meet these standards, you need to have a good self-image, and to recognize your own values. Honesty is important, and so is a sense of humor.

For students, having teachers with these qualities is important. Teen mothers and fathers need a safe and supportive environment where they can learn about balancing their role of adolescent with the role of parent. Teachers need to be personally concerned and professionally involved, but not become a surrogate parent or overwhelmed with the issues and problems young parents bring into the classroom. A teacher who regularly takes students' issues and problems home at the end of the school day is a likely candidate for burn-out.

Every teacher in every classroom should *care* for the students being taught. In a teen parent program, this translates to accepting pregnant and parenting students as human beings who need to feel loved and challenged. They should have limits set for them, and know they can trust the staff to be there when they need help. Rachel, a young mother living in Florida who is now in nurse's training, responded well to her teacher's help. She wrote:

> *Towards the end of my junior year in high school I found out that I was pregnant. I felt very uncomfortable about attending the high school during my pregnancy, so I decided to finish my senior year at a school called Teen Parents West. It was a great decision. Many of the girls there were potential dropouts so the teachers worked very*

hard to keep us interested and motivated.

I had always hated high school, and received poor grades, but my senior year was a great experience. I enjoyed learning and becoming more responsible. The teachers kept me motivated every day, and that is an important part of being a good teacher.

Flexibility Is Crucial

The ability to be flexible is especially important in a teen parent program. Attendance may be a problem. A guest speaker is planned, and half the students are absent. The teacher needs to take advantage of teachable moments. Daily plans are important; so is the ability to adjust those plans as the needs of students indicate. A student's baby cried all night? Today may be the best time to brainstorm and investigate effective ways of dealing with a crying baby. A teacher with a rigid personality or inflexible lesson plans may struggle with this kind of teaching.

Max Schilling, former Teenage Parent Program Specialist, Florida Department of Education, explains this concept by saying, "Cognitive learning cannot take place in a state of affective disorder." When the student is upset, learning may not happen.

Sue Kaulfus, former PEP Program Specialist, state of Texas, thinks flexibility is one of the most important characteristics needed by a teen parent teacher. She said, "Schools want lesson plans and objectives, and that's fine. But when you deal with student crises, those lesson plans may blow up in your face. Susie may come in saying she was kicked out of her house last night, and she will upset the whole class. Your lesson plans go out the window because you must deal with this emergency.

"The needs of the students must be met before they can learn anything that was on those lesson plans. A typical math teacher may not care what happened at home last night, and that's one reason so many of our kids drop out. Our teachers *must* care, care enough so the student can begin to learn the math and the English. If your administrator walks in, and you're not at quite the right place in your plans, that's okay. You have to meet the teachable moments. That's the way it has to be."

As human beings we are all different. Because we are

different, we are each unique and special. A teacher must respect individual students and the decisions they make. Students can sense a teacher's non-acceptance because of early pregnancy or what the teacher perceives as a poor choice of partner or other evidence of irresponsibility. There are also teachers who have difficulty with students of different ethnic groups and religions.

Some teachers are not completely accepting of lesbian and gay students. Yet, according to the May/June, 1999, issue of *Family Planning Perspectives,* lesbian teens are significantly *more* likely to become pregnant than are heterosexual teens. The study cited came from the 1987 Minnesota Adolescent Health Survey Behaviors which involved 36,840 public school students aged 12-19. Several other state studies have reported similar results.

A teacher who is hostile, judgmental, rigid, humorless, critical, condescending, or punitive doesn't belong in a teenage parent program. The teacher who is too permissive or overly sympathetic will also cause difficulties among students.

Pat Alviso, former director of the Teen Parent Program, ABC Unified School District, Cerritos, California, spoke of a teacher who has been in the program for several years. "Her staying power is her non-judgmental ways. She is very flexible. Things don't have to be a certain way. She doesn't prejudge, and she has problem-solving abilities. She sees the big picture and tries to work it. She knows her students are still adolescents, and when things get tough, she knows it won't be this way forever."

A teacher of pregnant and parenting teens has key roles to play with students and on their behalf. Four of these roles are trust builder, facilitator, probing questioner, and networker. Filling these roles well is critical to the success of the student, the success of the teacher, and the overall success of the program.

Building Trust

Several years ago I (Jeanne) asked 23 pregnant and parenting high school students who among the school staff they had talked with concerning their pregnancies. Three had not been in school. Of the others, only eight had talked with a school counselor about this issue. Two had talked with the principal, two with teachers, and three with the "narc" (security officer). Five told *no one* at the school.

When I expressed surprise that almost none of them had spoken with a teacher, one responded vehemently, "Ms. Lindsay, haven't you ever been in the teacher's lounge? Teachers report *everything* they hear from students!"

Building trust with any student is important. Building and maintaining trust with pregnant and parenting teens is crucial.

Gaining the trust of your students is one key to the success of your program. Trust may or may not come easily, as some young people have learned to trust only themselves and their families. For some, even family members have neglected, abused or abandoned them, and trusting adults is very difficult.

Strategies for building trust include:

- Use discretion in contacting and meeting with students in regular school settings. You quickly become known as the teacher who works with pregnant and parenting students. If you personally call a female student out of class, other students may assume she is pregnant. Use an alternative method to contact students, such as a note from the guidance counselor, or a message delivered by a student courier.
- Use a private conference area, preferably one with a telephone. Students will be more relaxed and willing to communicate in a private space. When a phone is available, you can coach your students to make their own contacts.
- Inform students that the conversation will be held in confidence. Also inform students about the exceptions to confidentiality, particularly the legal requirement for you to report suspected child abuse.
- Request a student's permission to discuss or "partner" with another professional, such as the school guidance counselor, if the student reveals information about a situation you believe needs additional professional intervention.
- If a student is reluctant to talk with you at a particular time, ask if s/he would like to come back to talk at another time.
- Make commitments to your students only if you fully intend to follow through.

Trust-building strategies help you work more effectively with your students. Pat Clark, a former GRADS teacher at Eastland Career Center, Groveport, Ohio, believes extensive note-taking during a first conference with a potential student can be detrimental to trust-building. She said, "During my initial individual conference with students, I don't take notes. I want it to seem more like a conversation. When the conference is finished, I write like crazy. Otherwise, I forget important details."

Facilitating Students' Problem Solving

A teacher needs to facilitate the development of student self-responsibility, problem solving, and self-sufficiency. There will be situations in which student problems are heartbreaking and appear overwhelming. Your role is to guide students through these crisis situations. If you *solve* problems for your students, they don't gain the skills to solve their own problems.

Susie's search for housing illustrates this point. Susie has a two-year-old child and has been living with a foster family. On her eighteenth birthday the foster family informs her that she has to move out. This is April of her senior year. She goes to her teacher for help.

Teacher: *What do you see as your alternatives?*
Susie: *My mom kicked me out when I got pregnant, and Dad said I can't live with him.*
Teacher: *Do you have any other relatives in town?*
Susie: *Yes, my grandma, but she said she doesn't have room for me.*
Teacher: *Have you contacted any agencies for help?*
Susie: *I left a message for my social worker.*

The teacher's goal was to empower Susie to find her own solution. She showed her how to use the area resource agency directory, and allowed her to use the phone. The teacher recommended she try the Family Service Agency first. Before Susie made the actual phone calls, Susie and her teacher role played how to make the calls. Working with her social worker, Metropolitan Housing, and the Family Service Agency, she was able to find housing beginning in July. Her grandmother agreed to allow

Susie and her child to live with her until that time.

The student used resources provided by her teacher and solved her own problem. Had the teacher found the housing for her, Susie would not have learned the skills to take steps toward adult independence.

Most important here was Susie's growing ability to cope. Also important is the teacher's state of mind. A teacher in a teen parent program in California reported that she was transferring back to the high school where she had previously worked as a counselor. "I'm tired of solving students' problems," she said. Her mistake was in thinking *she* should solve other people's problems. We can work hard, however, to help our students improve *their* problem-solving abilities.

Your role as facilitator is extremely important. When your students are exploring their alternatives, suggest options they haven't mentioned, or point out consequences of options they may not have considered. You can also coach them in identifying situational factors, and recognizing their values and goals related to the problem.

As you coach your students, you can expand their thinking and their horizons. You can do this in the context of real student problems or use case studies as part of their learning activities. Case studies give students an opportunity to develop their problem-solving skills using hypothetical situations.

Probing Question Approach

Leading students toward adult independence requires questioning techniques which focus on the continual development of reasoning and problem-solving skills. Examples of probing questions that can help students develop these skills include:

- What do you see as your alternatives?
- What are the consequences of this plan for you? Your child? Your family? Your community?
- How do you think your child will someday feel about your decision and action?
- What would happen if everyone set similar goals and achieved them?

- What happens daily to make it difficult to . . .? Monthly? Yearly?
- Which of these barriers do you think would be most difficult to overcome? Easiest to overcome? Why?
- Which of these barriers do you presently face?
- Is there anything you could do to eliminate or lessen these barriers? Why or why not?

Appropriately phrased questions can lead students to higher levels of reasoning, and can show that you are really listening. You can display empathy through your tone of voice and your questions.

Avoid judgmental statements and absolutes such as "I see your only alternative as . . . ," or "If I were you, I would . . . ," or "The best choice for you is . . ." *Remember — your role is not and cannot be that of solving someone else's problems.*

Both the GRADS *Adolescent Parent Resource Guide* and the *Teens Parenting* Curriculum are written with a problem-based approach. Case studies of typical teen parent experiences are central to this approach. Many learning activities are accompanied by processing (probing) questions.

As you encourage your students to make good decisions and to solve problems themselves, you will find some who have a particularly hard time. Their problems may be bigger, or they may have had little experience in problem solving. Perhaps up to this point, their parents have been in control, but now expect them to "be responsible."

In contrast, some teen parents have been making the majority of the decisions in their families for years. Unfortunately, they probably have not had the maturity and skills to make reasoned decisions.

Still other teen parents, particularly those who are survivors of trauma or abuse, have "learned" they are not allowed to make decisions for themselves. These teens have a difficult time identifying alternatives. They learned there is only one option, and that option is whatever someone else has chosen.

Talking with a trusted adult is important for many of us. If you are approachable, and if your students know that no matter how busy you appear to be, you have time to discuss their concerns with them, you probably will make a positive difference in their lives.

Support Staff Attitudes Matter, Too

Transportation in many school districts is an important part of the teen parent services. For many schools, this means pick-up at the students' homes, transportation to school and to child care. Standing at a bus stop with a baby or a long bus ride with a toddler are not likely to inspire good attendance for student parents.

Remember to include the bus driver in your team approach with students. The bus driver may spend as much time with some students as their teacher does. Students have a hard time dealing with a bus driver with an "attitude."

Susan Siepel, executive director, Carlsbad AWARE, Inc., Carlsbad, New Mexico, spoke of the bus driver's important role. "We got a bus driver one time who didn't believe in our program, and it was horrible. She would make negative comments as the teen parents got on the bus, and we lost students who wouldn't put up with that treatment.

"Luckily, the driver resigned at the end of the year. As soon as we learned who our new driver would be, the GRADS teacher and the child care center supervisor made an appointment with her. They explained that our kids are unique, and how much we would appreciate her understanding of their needs.

"We explained that they can't run to their locker, then run to the bus. Instead, they have to run to the locker, then all the way across the campus to the child care center. They need extra time, and the driver's day might be a little longer than it would be on another route. We assumed she would be positive, and she was."

Staff Development Possibilities

Most educators who are hired to work with pregnant and parenting teens have had little or no prior training or experience in working with this special population. Very few universities offer classes in teacher education programs on this issue. Therefore, teachers' expertise is learned on the job. If you would like help in addition to on-the-job training, there are numerous opportunities for professional development.

If you're trying to start a program for teen parents, or if you're a teacher newly assigned to a teen parent program, one of the most worthwhile things you can do is visit as many other effective teen parent programs as possible.

Ask another teacher to mentor you. A mentor teacher would be willing to answer questions throughout the school year and share learning activities, resources, and professional development opportunities with you. Having other teachers and programs as professional resources are valuable because you will learn different ways of handling various situations. The more you know, the better equipped you will be to decide on the best strategies for your students.

In some states, the State Department of Education houses an educational consultant who focuses on educational programming for pregnant and parenting teens. These offices may produce materials for use in teen parent programs. Materials that may be available include annual reports of programs in the state, directory of teachers in the state, competency list, instructional resource guide or curriculum, and program implementation materials. These state offices may also sponsor professional development opportunities, such as new teacher workshops, state conferences, and regional professional development meetings. Other technical assistance may also be available. Check with your State Department of Education for information.

A strength of the GRADS program is the leadership provided by the Ohio Department of Education. The state leadership helps coordinate program funding, new teacher training, professional development activities, curriculum development, program evaluation, yearly newsletters and updates, and program marketing. As an example, see page 262 for a description of professional development opportunities sponsored by the Ohio Department of Education for GRADS teachers.

Look for other opportunities for networking and in-service training. Some national and state organizations focus on adolescent pregnancy and parenting. National organizations and many state affiliates sponsor yearly conferences and the opportunity for networking. See the organization listing on page 256.

If you would like information on your state's adolescent pregnancy, parenting, and prevention network or organization, if any, contact the National Organization on Adolescent Pregnancy, Parenting, and Prevention (NOAPPP), 2401 Pennsylvania Avenue NW, Suite 350, Washington, DC 20037. 202/293-8370.

Help from the Internet

An excellent source for both professional development and other information that definitely should not be overlooked is the Internet. It is not only a fast way to find out the latest facts, figures, and statistics available, but also offers a way to expand your networking opportunities. Think of it as a virtual community of others like yourself sharing ideas, problems, and solutions.

The most familiar component of the Internet is the World Wide Web. As more and more federal and state agencies are providing information on the web, it is worth your effort to learn how to search it. The quickest way to find specific references is to use a search engine such as www.Yahoo.com> The search engine you choose should be easy to use, have the ability to fine-tune searches with extra commands, and return the most relevant information first. Once you begin using the web, look for those sites that are not only informative in and of themselves, but contain links to other sites of interest. Two examples are:

- **CYFERNet** <www.cyfernet.mes.umn.edu/> — The cooperative extension system, in conjunction with land grant universities, county governments and the USDA, provides educational outreach programs in all 50 states. The web site contains practical, research-based, children, youth, and family information in six major areas: health, child care, building organizational collaborations, promoting family strength, science and technology programs, and strengthening community-based programs.

- **Campaign For Our Children** <www.cfoc.org/> — This web site contains access to a variety of information links, including a "Teacher Connection" for the exchange of ideas, questions, and solutions.

Bear in mind that the Internet and the World Wide Web are still evolving. Take advantage of a source that can provide up-to-date information at your fingertips.

Professional Development Among Teachers

Seek out other educators near your location who also work with pregnant and parenting teens. And don't ignore teachers of other at-risk populations (disinterested, unmotivated, discipline or substance abuse programs, adjudicated youth, migrant or homeless services). There is often significant overlap in effective strategies and techniques used by good teachers.

An experienced teacher might be willing to mentor you in your new educational role. Join or form a "community of learners" with other teachers in your district or community. Hold regular monthly meetings. Some of the best professional development takes place when clusters of teachers meet regularly to discuss teaching and learning theories and strategies, and delve into teen parent issues. "Teachers helping teachers" might be the most successful approach to professional development.

The thirteen GRADS teachers in Stark County, Ohio, for example, hold monthly meetings. Sometimes they share tips among themselves, and other times they invite guests for a focused presentation or discussion. Kathie DeMuesy, GRADS teacher, Hoover High School, North Canton, quipped, "These meetings help me keep my sanity!"

If no one else is providing professional development for teen parent teachers, perhaps you could take the lead. Sharing ideas and techniques with other teachers can be terrific. All you'd have to do is contact teen parent teachers in your area, set a day and a time, and invite them to your school for an hour or two. Ask them to bring their favorite teaching techniques and suggestions for helping teens deal with the special needs of early pregnancy and parenthood.

You might like to organize a full day meeting, perhaps on a school holiday or Saturday if you don't have a professional development day available. Develop a mailing list of teachers in your area. Invite three or four experts to present workshops — and remember that an "expert" may be the teacher down the hall, or it may be you. The simplest lunch plan is for each participant to handle lunch independently. Or you could order box lunches or ask attendees to brown-bag it. At the end of the session, identify key issues to discuss/share at the next session. If there is enough interest, set the date for the next get-together before adjourning.

You might find you have organized a more helpful meeting than some of the better funded professional development meetings offered to teachers. The secret to success is to focus on the special needs of your very special population — pregnant and parenting teens.

Of all components of a teen parent program, you, the teacher, are the most important. You are the grease, the guts, and the glue of the program. You are the person who has the most contact with the students, and you become their advocate, their mentor, their confidant, their trusted teacher. You have many important roles in addition to educator — trust builder, facilitator, probing questioner, and networker. Seek out professional development opportunities to help you grow in this very important profession of a teacher of teen parents.

Teaching pregnant and parenting teens provides opportunities to instigate positive change in students' lives. Your teaching *will* make a difference.

With appropriate support, school can be a positive experience.

CHAPTER

Getting
Organized

Few kindergartners experience more trepidation about starting school than some teachers new to the world of teen parents. We've talked with teachers who have been handed the teen parent teaching assignment not long before school is to start, or in the middle of a semester. They tend to express dismay as they say, "I'm going into this class and I have no idea what I'm doing!"

Their district's professional development didn't do enough for them, or they were assigned too late to have it at all. Or, and this is most likely, little was available in the training that applied directly to their specialized role in the teenage parent program.

Chapter 4 focuses on curriculum development with an emphasis on the competencies your students need to master, and on the strategies to help them accomplish these tasks. This chapter deals with your role as program facilitator. Each teacher in a teen parent program plays an important part in facilitating optimal development among the students — from the time you first hear of a potential student to the student's actual class enrollment, and throughout the on-going instruction and support needed until the student graduates.

"Organization" to some people means setting rules, having a routine, and minimizing surprises. Being organized is important for a teen parent teacher, but it's a different kind of organization. Teen parents' lives are constantly changing, sometimes in dramatic ways. True, they need stability, and school may be the most stable part of their lives. But their needs will change. There will be many crises. Parenting, workforce preparation, relationship problems, academic study, simple survival — which is more important? No matter how good you are at organizing, you'll not be able to "solve their problems." You will be able to provide some structure *with flexibility.*

Careful record keeping is important because it will help you help students. When they enroll is a good time to collect basic information. You need to develop a plan of study with each student and track their competency attainment in all areas of study in your class. See *Organizing TAPP: Useful Forms for Teenage Parent Program Teachers* (1997), prepared to accompany this book.

Creating an Inviting Atmosphere

An inviting classroom atmosphere helps raise the comfort level of students and parents entering the room. Conference tables are more comfortable than lined rows of student desks. Pregnant students may have trouble fitting into a student desk-chair combination. Chairs around a large table are more conducive to group discussions and the use of interpersonal skills in class. Some teachers prefer to create a home atmosphere by grouping couches, chairs, and end tables in one area of the room.

Educational and colorful bulletin boards help create an inviting atmosphere. Funny and thought-provoking posters also help. Free posters and pamphlets from community agencies may be displayed. Magazine racks holding popular parenting magazines, a variety of resource learning centers, computers, and book shelves of reference and student books entice students to read.

Displays of awards, recognitions for attendance, and student work such as poetry written for class, posters depicting course content, pictures of children, art work, and toys made in class also help the students feel they have some room ownership.

An office area separate from the main classroom is highly desirable. The office area should also be inviting with posters, plants, and pictures, as well as locking files, phone, area resource directory, and references close at hand.

Positive Communication Is Vital

Responding quickly to referrals is high priority for teen parent program teachers. If you can imagine being 14, pregnant, frightened, and having finally found the courage to call, you know how critical it is to respond immediately. You'd want help *now*.

> *When I first started showing, I was afraid to go out in public because I was ashamed of myself. I didn't want anything to do with being pregnant, but it was a fact of life.*
>
> *My counselor told me about the Teen Parent Program and suggested I transfer. When I went to TPP, I felt better. I had no idea there were that many teens who were pregnant. Until I went there, I thought I was the only one.*
>
> Liz, pregnant at 15

How you and the rest of the staff respond to telephone calls is an important part of communicating with potential students. If a staff member is willing, list her/his home phone number in addition to the school phone number on posters, brochures, and other promotional items. Teachers who do this report they don't get a lot of calls at home, but those they receive are likely to be important. A pregnant teen may have the courage to make only one phone call before giving up, and that one effort may not be made during your working hours.

When pregnant or parenting teens call or visit to ask about school services, it's important to respond warmly and with sensitivity. Of course you'll make them feel welcome and wanted as you explain the program. Be concerned, and above all, get their name and phone number. If s/he hangs up, you may never hear from her/him again.

You may learn about a student's suspected pregnancy from a third party, a staff member or another student. You cannot assume that all students referred to you for suspected pregnancy will actually be pregnant. Therefore, take precautions when approaching these students. Meet with students in privacy. You might approach it light-heartedly with, "Andrea, is there something you want to tell me?" or "Are you feeling okay?" Andrea may or may not tell you she thinks she is pregnant. She may not be pregnant, or she may not be ready to talk about it yet.

Leave the door open for her to return. "If there's anything you want to talk about later, please come back to see me. I'll be here." You can offer her some information, such as brochures or small booklets, and your office phone number.

Home Contacts and Other Good Beginnings

A home contact for a new or potential student is an important early step. Contacting the student or family at home can convey a desire to reach out to help both the student and family. In fact, home visits and other home contacts may be an important part of a teen's decision to remain in school throughout pregnancy and after the baby is born.

Occasionally, a family might view the contact with suspicion because previous school/home contacts have been problem-centered. Be sensitive to the student's and family's reactions.

If you feel it may not be safe to make home visits in certain areas of your school district, check with someone familiar with the area. You may choose to take someone along with you. Or you could offer to meet the family at a neutral location, such as a nearby fast-food restaurant. (A comment — *if we don't feel safe, what must it be like for the student?*)

Briefly describe your program and explain immediately that enrolling in the teen parent program is voluntary. Be as positive as you can, and describe the important areas of study, such as personal development, prenatal health, childbirth, postpartum and neonatal care, healthy relationships, positive parenting, and career development. Always give the family a copy of your student handbook which describes your program.

When you're talking with potential students' parents, let them know how they can help with the teen parent program. See suggestions in *Organizing TAPP*. You'll think of other ways to involve parents. See chapter 11 for more ideas.

During the first conversation with a potential student, it's a good idea to comment that most of your students are single and a few (if true) are married. You can also comment that most of your students are planning to parent their child themselves, but when/if someone considers an adoption plan for the child, the class *will* support that student. Stress that these are personal decisions, and no one, including staff, tries to make decisions for someone else.

The Enrollment Decision

If your program is an in-school model, the teen can enroll in your class by changing her/his schedule now, or at the beginning of the next term. If you're at a separate school site and the teen would need to change schools, understand that moving to another school can be stressful. Describe your transitioning plan, such as visiting for a day or two, and/or the assignment of a buddy for a week. If there is door-to-door transportation, help make the arrangements.

When a potential student decides to visit the program, prepare your students. Remind them that the first day at a new school usually isn't a lot of fun, and that their friendliness is important.

If you have on-site child care, invite the student and family to tour the center. Suggest that the teen consider enrolling in the child care lab course for credit.

It's wise not to schedule a pregnant student into the child care center, however, until she's at least four months pregnant because of the risk of rubella. While children are expected to have their immunizations up to date when they're in a care center, you want *no* risk of a pregnant student catching this disease from a child. A mother who contracts rubella early in her pregnancy is at high risk for delivering a handicapped baby.

Ask that the student and parent(s) complete the required paperwork immediately. You don't want to keep a teen out of your program (especially if s/he's currently not in school) for lack of paperwork, but once s/he's enrolled, it may be more

difficult to get those signatures. Students enrolling late in
pregnancy may wonder why you must have a signed pregnancy
verification. After all, her pregnancy is quite obvious. Nevertheless, your district or state guidelines probably require that
documentation for good reasons.

The first day in a new class is important. Spend part of the
day going over the student handbook with the new student. In the
process, you will check paperwork and remind the student of any
missing forms to be completed. Ask a specific student to be the
newcomer's buddy during the first few days. The "buddy
system" can help a new student feel welcome.

Your students are likely to be lovely and charming. They will
include very bright young women and men as well as teenagers
who have a difficult time academically. Many will be quite
anxious, if not in a state of crisis, when they enroll. If you find
yourself forgetting this fact, it's wise to imagine "walking in
their shoes." This may help you understand the reasons you need
to spend time listening to and advocating for them. You want to
form close, caring, and personal relationships as well as assist
them in obtaining the best education, academic, vocational, and
parenting, as possible. This is an opportunity to begin building
trust, and to convey mutual respect.

Some teen parent teachers are responsible for scheduling their
students' classes. When this is the case, the teacher needs to
obtain students' school records, including transcripts, in order to
schedule most effectively.

"Organizer" Starts Program

Three years ago Dot Rhodes was a foods and nutrition teacher
in the Upland Unified School District, Upland, California. She
had never worked with school-age parents, except for a few in
her classes, but she was known as an organizer. When the
superintendent, Dr. Loren Sanchez, decided it was time to
provide services for pregnant and parenting teens, he called
Rhodes and asked, "Can you get us organized?"

Pregnant and parenting teens had been enrolled in independent study. They came to school one day each week, and met
with the district nurse and psychologist for 90 minutes. This

weekly session had been offered for about five years, but the alternative school principal wanted the students in school every day. Some of the young parents, who were used to being home all day, were not eager to get back into "real" school. When they learned they would be scheduled into Rhodes' prenatal health or parenting class and into the child care center each day, they were more willing to attend.

For their academics, they generally attended classes in the alternative school although Rhodes had one independent study class for teen parents who otherwise could not get a class they needed. The alternative school provided a daily 15-minute advisory period for students, and teen parents were scheduled into Rhodes' advisory period. She considered this an important part of building rapport among the group.

Because of students' absences due to childbirth, illness, and periodic lack of child care, and because of her individualized approach to teaching, Rhodes created a weekly newsletter, *Hawks Nest Notes.* (The school's mascot is the hawk.) Each issue included information about the week's activities, up-coming events, new babies, assignment deadlines, and any other information she wanted all her students to have. The weekly issue of the *Hawks Nest Notes* was distributed each Monday morning, and when she visited an absent student, Rhodes took the newsletter with her. Some students who were absent had a family member pick up their newsletter. "Especially in the beginning, when we were building our program, it was an excellent way to make students feel involved even when they were absent," Rhodes explained.

Incentives for School Attendance

Attendance tends to be a problem in most teen parent pro-grams for several reasons. Not only must the teen parent miss school if s/he is ill, many must also stay home when the baby is sick. If the weather is bad, they may not think it wise to take the baby out, especially if there is no at-the-door transportation. The young parent may be so tired sometimes that it's hard to gather up enough energy to get her/himself and the child to school.

Add to this list the fact that some teen parents were poor school attenders before they ever became pregnant, and the attendance rate may be disappointingly low.

Rosann Pollock, teacher, Teen Parent West, Deland, Florida, described their attendance improvement strategies. For each day of class attendance, the student earns 25 cents in baby money. The parent store is open one day every other week, and students spend their attendance "money" for things for the baby. Most of the items for sale have been donated. Sometimes they get parent store items at garage sales. Church groups, service clubs, even school staff, may donate things to the store.

Pollock focuses on attendance in other ways, too. As she takes roll in the morning, she's likely to say, "Staci, three days in a row. Let's see if you can make it four."

"Always comment," she said. "Let them know their presence matters."

In addition, one of the teachers meets the bus each morning as the students and their babies arrive. This seemingly minor activity helps the staff tune in to the students' special needs and how their day is starting.

Each nine weeks, four generous attendance awards are presented to students. The program nurse arranged with doctors in the area to donate several car seats. The nurse's mother makes quilts which she donates to the cause of improving school attendance. An artist is available who will do a sketch of the parent and baby.

Wednesday is clinic day for the students. Rather than assume they must miss school, Pollock tells students to come to school on the bus, and she takes them to the clinic in her car. They miss school for a couple of hours instead of a full day.

Frequent speakers and activities also help attendance.

The result of these efforts, Pollock reported, is an attendance average of about 80 percent, significantly higher than the average across the state for similar programs.

Note: Learn your school district's policy on transporting students in personal vehicles. Some districts strongly discourage this practice with a policy of "Transporting students is at your own risk." Your decision about whether to personally transport students may be different if your district supports it and accepts liability than if they don't.

From Postcards to Grab Bags

Pat Alviso, former coordinator of the teen parent programs for the ABC Unified School District, Cerritos, California, agrees that attendance can be a problem. Added to the usual reasons teen parents miss school, the district's two programs include a high percentage of dropout retrievals, as high as 80 percent at Cabrillo Lane, one of the sites. Regaining the habit of attending school regularly may be especially hard for these young parents.

"Offering child care is the Number One carrot to get them there," Alviso commented. Child care is available at both Cabrillo Lane and Tracy High School.

Alviso stresses the importance of phone calls. "Usually we divide students so each teacher has a group. Our aide makes some of the calls, and we try to reach everybody the first or second day they're absent.

"Sometimes the problem is finding the student. When s/he enrolls, I try to get three phone numbers — home, mom's or dad's work, grandma's number, maybe the boyfriend's, whoever might be concerned about her. Sometimes I use the health emergency file to get phone numbers."

Alviso had four colorful postcards printed in quantity, each with a different message. "Where have you been?" "We miss you." "Congratulations!" "We haven't heard from you." Post cards are kept where teachers make the phone calls. They're pre-stamped, so they can address them and send them quickly.

Alviso described their attendance prize system. "If you come all five days a week, you get a chance at the grab bag. It holds Avon samples, McDonald's coupons, and other small gifts. We put it all in a big huge bag. I waltz in with my bag, hold it up so they can't look in, but can feel the stuff. They love to watch the grabbing. We call it our Hundred Percent Club."

Continuing Home Contact

Ideally, you contact absent students by telephone each day they aren't in class. If you can't reach a student, or if s/he is absent more than a couple of days, a home visit allows you to see if a problem exists, and lets the student know you care.

When a student has problems at school or at home, a visit may be advised, but use discretion. Let the family know you care, and that you might be able to offer some assistance, such as providing information or giving the family helpful referrals.

After the birth of a student's baby, a visit either to the hospital or the student's home is a good plan. At that visit, in addition to admiring the baby, offer support, respond to questions and concerns, talk about a time schedule for returning to school, and check on child care arrangements. This home visit may also be an ideal time to teach a lesson, such as newborn massage. Of course, you'll need special training to teach infant massage.

Occasionally a student may feel a strong maternal bonding and not want to leave her child. During the first month after birth, this bonding is extremely important. If a student wants to be out of school longer than her physician deems medically necessary, discuss how much better the future will be for both her and her baby if she completes high school. Child care on campus can soften the impact of the separation because the student is often able to spend extra time with the baby during the early months.

Many of the PEP programs in Texas have developed a unique and highly effective approach to the mother's need to bond with her baby *and* to return to school soon after childbirth. In the past, students were expected to go on home-based instruction for six weeks after childbirth. Usually the young moms would have little contact with their peers or with the school during that time.

Several years ago, the state granted an attendance waiver which, for about six weeks, allows the teen mother to attend school two hours a day, two days a week, instead of seeing the teacher at her home. The home-based instructor can accomplish more by working with several students at school rather than traveling to each home. The young moms provide support for each other, and the PEP teacher has more chance to observe their parenting techniques and to make supportive suggestions.

It's a win-win situation, according to Sue Kaulfus, former PEP Program Specialist. Kaulfus used this approach to utilizing

home-based instruction *at school* because of the high number of
teen mothers who didn't return to school after delivery. "Our
return rate jumped from 68 percent to 97 percent the first year
we offered this plan," Kaulfus reported. See page 128 for an
example of this technique from Seguin (Texas) High School.

Know Federal and State Laws, District Policies

When you work with teen parents, you need to have a broader
grasp of district policy than most teachers generally need. As a
starter, review your school district's marital or parental policy in
accordance with Title IX Education Amendment Act of 1972.
This Act forbids any discrimination on the basis of sex including
pregnancy, parenting, or marital status. If necessary, develop or
revise the local marital or parental policy to be in compliance
with Title IX, and to encourage and support students to stay in
school. See the introduction for more information.

Be sure the teen parent program is described in the student
scheduling handbook. The program description, which may be
part of the family and consumer sciences courses, should indicate that potential program enrollees are pregnant students
and parents.

Know your state law on home tutoring or home instruction.
Also review your school district's attendance and home tutoring
instruction policies. Determine whether those policies need to be
modified to encourage and support students to stay in school.

The teen parent program should be accessible to the student
who becomes pregnant during the school year or who is identi-
fied as a parent and wishes to enroll in your class or program. Is
partial credit available for the student who enrolls mid-term? If
not, what can be arranged within the guidelines? Or what do you
need to do to change the guidelines to adapt to the special needs
of your students?

You need to develop a plan to identify support services for
students, i.e., counseling and agency referrals. Also identify a
key contact for students in each school in the district, a person
who will be responsible for referring students to the teen parent
program as needed, and for offering support to pregnant and
parenting students who don't enroll in the teen parent program.

This person could be a school counselor, a school nurse, a family and consumer sciences teacher, or another instructor.

As you work with teen parents, you need to know others in your community who interact with your students. Know and post the rules and the changes happening with TANF (Temporary Assistance for Needy Families), WIC (Special Supplemental Feeding Program for Women, Infants, and Children), and other resources. Know which dentist will take Medicaid. See chapter 12 for a more thorough discussion of collaboration with community services.

Be sure each student's high school plan has a career focus and a course of study that will enable the student to achieve his/her career goals. Teen parents have an increased need to become job-ready. See chapter 5.

Staff Communication

Whether you work with only a few teen parent teachers or with many, communicating clearly and often with each other is critical. In a large teen parent school, you'll probably have regular staff meetings, perhaps weekly. In a program with only a few teachers, you may rely more on informal communication. You aren't likely to be as effective in helping students, however, if you don't designate specific times to discuss program plans, activities, and non-confidential student information.

In the BETA (Birth, Education, Training, Acceptance) program, Orlando, Florida, in addition to a weekly general staff meeting, Ray Larsen, director, insists on a daily "stand-up" meeting. "I learned about the ten-minute meeting from the corporate world," he explained. "I worked for awhile in a big office with dividers. Each morning we'd all stand up so we could see each other's heads, and we'd coordinate our work for the day.

"The brief daily meeting also works well at BETA," he continued. "We all need to know if some of the kids are going on field trips, if there are exams today, or the WIC counselor is scheduled, etc. If some students got in a shouting match yesterday, we want everybody to be aware of it. We want to intervene before we have a real problem.

"In working with adolescents, whatever your situation, if

you're not thinking together, not communicating with each other, not only do you lose your effectiveness, you also lose credibility with the kids. Your boundaries won't be consistent if you aren't talking with each other.

"Also, the staff doesn't feel they're out there hanging by themselves," he pointed out. "There is security in truly being part of the team. If there is tension, or a situation that might affect the behavior of the kids in our classes, it's important that we all know about it."

This ten-minute meeting can also help teachers "be together" in their offerings to students. Teen parents, like all students, sometimes complain about differential treatment or enforcement by various teachers. Communication among staff members helps minimize this problem.

If you don't think your staff can stick to a ten-minute meeting, and you don't have time for a longer session this time, you might try setting a kitchen timer. When it goes off, the meeting is over. You will be surprised at how much you can cover in ten minutes if that's all the time you have.

Enjoy the Challenge

As you begin your work with teen parents, you will need all the teaching skills you can possibly muster. You need to be knowledgeable about school and community resources. You want to create an inviting learning environment which will welcome your students. Above all, you will be sensitive to your students' many-faceted needs, to their current realities, and to their dreams of the future for themselves and their children.

Whether you are the only teacher in several schools, even several school districts, or one of many staff members in a large teen parent program, you will probably find it to be one of the most challenging *and satisfying* jobs you will ever have.

They need curriculum geared to their special needs.

CHAPTER 4

Developing Curriculum that Works

Early teen parent programs tended to focus on prenatal health and parenting with little emphasis on other academics or work-force preparation. When I (Jeanne) was hired to start a program in a small school district in the early 70s, I was told to prepare curriculum for only two classes, health and consumer economics . . . and the students were scheduled for their entire day with me. I soon realized, of course, that the "little red school house" approach was required because my students also needed their social studies, English, math, and science along with parenting.

Today you're less likely to be expected to teach all subjects. If you're teaching teen parents in civics or geometry, you'll teach as you would non-parents — *except* you know your students have an even greater need to continue their education because they have already taken on the adult role of parenthood. If you're an academic teacher, you'll use the best curriculum and teaching methods possible as you help young people learn. You'll also

want to make the curriculum as relevant as you can to the
realities in the lives of the young parents you're teaching.

Special Curriculum for Teen Parents

Curriculum specifically for pregnant and parenting teens,
however, generally refers to resources and strategies to meet the
special needs they have because of early parenthood. Helping
your students develop competencies in these special areas is your
challenge.

First, you must have an understanding of what your students
need to learn. That, of course, will vary greatly from student to
student. In one class you may have newly pregnant teens, some
who are parenting newborns, and others whose children are now
toddlers. Some may have part-time jobs and/or be enrolled in an
occupational training program. Others may not have begun the
process of career planning.

Some of your students may live with their parents or other
family members and have a lot of emotional, financial, and
child-rearing support. Others are in a supervised or newly-
married living arrangement away from other family members
with little or no family support. Others may be in foster care, or
even homeless.

Developmental processes are especially important to pregnant and parenting teens. Becoming a mature adult is a process.
So is becoming an effective parent. Becoming a productive
worker is yet another process. Programs geared only to one
semester of pregnancy-related instruction cannot effectively
meet these needs. At least for younger teen parents, a minimum
of two years in the teen parent program is often advisable.

The knowledge and skills, sometimes called *TEKS* (*Texas
Essential Knowledge and Skills*) or *competencies* (Ohio), developed for pregnant and parenting teens are different in many ways
from those needed by teens who are not parents. Basically, teen
parents need curriculum designed to help them become competent in the adult living skills they need *immediately*. In this chapter we refer to this knowledge and these skills as *competencies*.

It is important to identify the competencies that pregnant and
parenting teens need to master. Extremely helpful is a list of the

knowledge and skills they need to know and be able to do. Two types of competencies should be developed, *process* and *content*.

Process competencies are life-long living skills needed by every teen parent. Process competencies should be taught independently and should also be integrated into the content competencies. Examples of process competencies are:

- Problem solving
- Management of resources such as time and money
- Social skills (relating to others)
- Leadership

Content competencies are subject-matter specific knowledge and skills. Many competencies are needed to meet the wide educational needs of pregnant and parenting teens. Some teachers develop their own, but this takes a lot of time and is limited by the resources, knowledge, skills and biases of the teachers involved.

Some schools convene a local panel of experts to identify competencies. Members of the panel need to be knowledgeable about the needs of teen parents. This strategy provides a variety of perspectives, and usually will mean local acceptance of your competency list. However, it is difficult to convene a panel for the length of time (two days or longer) it takes to develop an adequate list of competencies.

A local panel can verify a teacher-developed competency list. Or you can use one developed by others. The GRADS program in Ohio has developed a competency list, the *GRADS Ohio Competency Analysis Profile (OCAP)*. The development of the competency list involved many steps.

First, a literature search and review was conducted. Curriculum specialists used the findings from the literature review to draft the initial competency list. Secondly, a panel of GRADS teachers reviewed the list and made changes. Next, a state-wide panel of experts was convened to edit and verify the competencies.

The competency list verified by the panel of experts was professionally edited and published. This list, titled *GRADS Ohio Competency Analysis Profile,* can be purchased. See the

Examples of GRADS Competencies

Broad category **Personal Development**

   Competency: Analyze factors contributing to the
development of self within the family unit.

   Competency Builders

* Identify characteristics of a healthy family.
* Identify life events affecting families.
* Identify common family traditions and cultural patterns.
* Evaluate effects of family patterns on pregnant/parenting
  teens.

Broad category **Parenting**

   Competency: Analyze legal issues related to parenthood.

   Competency Builders

* Identify the legal obligations of mother, father, grand-
  parents, schools, and community agencies.
* Analyze uses for and importance of birth certificates/
  documentation.
* Define *parentage, child support, visitation,* and *allocation
  of parental rights and responsibilities.*
* Define *guardianship, minor status,* and *power of attorney.*
* Identify resources for obtaining family legal counsel.

Broad category **Economic Independence**

   Competency: Assess school-to-work needs.

   Competency Builders

* Identify importance of completing high school education.
* Identify obstacles to completing high school for pregnant/
  parenting teens.
* Develop a plan for overcoming obstacles to completing
  high school.
* Identify reasons that people work.
* Interpret the needs of employers and employees.
* Identify factors that influence work ethic.
* Identify skills valued by schools and employers.
* Identify the importance of lifelong learning.

Reprinted from *GRADS Ohio Competency Analysis Profile*

bibliography for the address. Broad areas covered in the *Profile* include adolescent development, pregnancy, parenting, health and safety, relationships, and economic independence. For examples of the *GRADS OCAP,* see opposite page.

Writing curriculum to accompany the competency list is a task you can do, or you can purchase one that is already written. An exemplary curriculum is the *Adolescent Parent Resource Guide (APRG)*, written to accompany the *GRADS OCAP.* All of the teaching and learning strategies suggested in this chapter are incorporated in the *APRG.* Additionally, relevant research and other information for teachers are included.

For an example from the *Adolescent Parent Resource Guide* of learning activities for one competency, see the appendix, pages 259-261. Notice that many of the teaching and learning strategies are used in this one competency. The *Resource Guide* is set up so that independent and group learning activities are on facing pages.

Another exemplary curriculum is the *Teens Parenting Series,* consisting of text books, workbooks, Comprehensive Curriculum Notebooks, videos, and games.

Developing Learning Strategies

To meet your students' diverse needs, develop several learning strategies for each competency. Strategies for the process competencies should be developed separately, as well as integrated into the strategies for the content competencies.

When you develop processing questions which integrate the process competencies into the content items, you also help students learn to develop reasoning and critical questioning strategies for themselves. Examples of processing questions are:

- Of all the sources of parenting information, which are you most likely to use? Why?
- How do you know if a resource is reliable?
- Why is it important to consider whether or not a source of parenting information is reliable?
- What are the consequences of using unreliable information when making parenting decisions?

Lecturing is the least effective teaching method for most teens, including young parents. Most effective is when teens are actively engaged in their own learning. You can actively engage students by providing structured opportunities for hands-on learning, self-directed learning, group interaction, and home and community learning opportunities.

For each competency, develop strategies that can be used for both group and individual instruction. Group activities should be used often in the classroom, as students need opportunities to work cooperatively in groups and to "build community." Groups might consist of two students within a class, or all students in your classroom.

Individual activities can be used in the classroom and as out-of-class assignments, and can also be used by students who are absent from school for periods of time. At times, you may have students doing both group and individual activities.

See pp. 84-85 for an example of individual and group activities from the *Discipline from Birth to Three Comprehensive Curriculum Notebook.*

Develop a system for tracking student completion of competencies. Be prepared, too, to assess and evaluate student demonstrations of learning in multiple ways, and to assign grades and credit. Your students will respond best if they know from the beginning what is expected of them.

Keeping track of all the different learning going on will be a challenge. Many teachers have students keep individual logs on which they record completion of each task or competency mastery and the teacher signs it off.

Student Activities

When you integrate many different strategies into your curriculum, you're more likely to maintain your students' interest and facilitate more learning. While it's not necessary to integrate all of the following strategies into each competency, it's best to include several in each broad unit.

Obtain a variety of resources including handouts and activity sheets for student use. For many competencies, you can use resources developed by others, such as books, videos, games, posters, and other materials. The *Teens Parenting Comprehensive Curriculum Notebooks* (Morning Glory Press) include a wide variety of activities. Videos and games are also available within this curriculum. (See the bibliography.) For other competencies, you may find few, if any, adequate resources already developed, and you may need to create your own.

Students can use these resources for learning activities, and also to develop **notebooks, learning logs**, or **portfolios** that become personal resources. Some young parents report using these resources long after they are out of school.

Encourage students to take useable notes each time you have a speaker, and to keep those notes in their class notebook. Keeping a journal can be a valuable learning tool, and the journal may also be kept in the notebook — or the student may prefer a separate composition booklet.

If you check students' notebooks frequently, at least every few weeks, you will be able to determine each individual's progress. Independent study assignments need to be coordinated with classroom activities. These can help students make up missed credit and, even more important, learn at least part of the material covered in the class.

Action projects provide students with opportunities to work with the teacher and family to plan, carry out, and evaluate home or community projects that demonstrate classroom learnings. For example, a student might collect important legal documents such as birth certificates, social security cards, and immunization records. Choose or create a safe place to store these documents such as a notebook, baby book, folder, a decorated box, or a locking plastic bag. Organize the important documents according to the plan.

Beyond the Classroom

Student leadership opportunities, community service projects, and involvement of students' extended families are valuable learning strategies.

Student leadership activities help students grow. Pregnant and parenting teens need opportunities to develop family, school, and community leadership. They need opportunities to take

Developing Curriculum that Works

Yelling, Spanking Don't Help

1. **Activity.** Child Guidance Techniques chart, page 85. Give each student a copy and ask them to respond to the questions.

2. **Handout.** Give each student a copy of Yelling and Spanking Don t Help. Discuss; remind students to put handout in their notebooks.

3. **Class Discussion.** Discipline Situations, p. 86. Give each student a copy, then discuss in class. You might ask students to role-play the situations described. Then suggest they choose a discipline strategy from the Child Guidance Techniques chart (#1 above) suitable for each situation as it is role-played.

4. **Debate.** Resolved: Spanking children generally does not improve their behavior.

5. **Case Studies.** Joanne, pp. 89-90, Raylene, p. 93, Guadalupe, p. 99, text; discussion questions, page 87, *Notebook.* Or ask students to take turns reading the quotes in the chapter. Give them an opportunity to discuss each one.

6. **Journal.** Suggested starter: My favorite time with my child is . . . because . . .

7. **Writing Assignment** (Workbook). Write a paragraph in which you explain how your feelings influence how you discipline your child. Include examples of discipline problems that might not have happened if you had been feeling better.

Excerpt from Discipline from Birth to Three

8. **Class Discussion.** What does setting limits with respect mean to you? Ask students to discuss specific examples. Have some examples ready to get them started.

9. **Writing Assignment.** After the above discussion, write an essay on Setting Limits with Respect.

10. **Quiz.** Chapters 5 and 6, p. 89.

11. **Toy Making.** Make a **Pull-a-Cloth toy**, p. 88. If students supply the coffee cans and lids, perhaps a local fabric store would donate the different kinds of cloth needed for this toy.

12. **Parent/Child Assignment.** Show your child how to play with the Pull-a-Cloth toy you made in class. Report on your experience in your journal.

ENRICHMENT ACTIVITIES

1. **Research** (Workbook). Ask each student to ask at least five parents of children under three how they feel about spanking. Were they spanked when they were little? What do they think spanking teaches a child? Compile results in class.

2. **Field Trip** (Workbook). Take your class to visit a childcare center. Tell students to observe the methods of discipline used by the caregivers. Do they see mostly positive discipline? Or is there a lot of scolding? How about other forms of punishment?

reasoned action for the well-being of themselves, their children, and others.

School leadership could be as simple as inviting a guest speaker to come to class to talk about prenatal health or other topic of interest to your students. A family leadership activity might involve developing an action plan for obtaining a child's immunizations at optimal times.

Service projects provide students with opportunities to make meaningful contributions to their communities. These projects can help students develop personal values and build upon their strengths.

For example, with coaching from the teacher, students could plan and carry out a community education project about the shaken baby syndrome. They could plan multiple approaches including sponsoring a poster contest at school, developing a brochure for health clinics to distribute, developing public service announcements for broadcast by a local radio or television station, and making presentations to fifth and sixth grade students about the harmful effects of shaking a baby.

Parents of pregnant and parenting students should be offered opportunities to be involved in school and in the learning processes. Generally, **parental involvement** enhances outcomes for students. Provide opportunities for parent involvement in the classroom as well as intergenerational learning with lessons that students take home. Some parents of pregnant and parenting students will make good use of the opportunity to participate. See chapter 11.

Actively Teaching Competencies

Brenda Egan, GRADS teacher, Carlsbad High School, Carlsbad, New Mexico, reported that for several years a nurse focused on prenatal health and parenting in the class for teen parents. The program evolved into a GRADS class, and, according to Egan, job skills, career awareness, and more parenting information were brought into the curriculum.

"The competencies seemed overwhelming in the beginning," Egan recalled. "Then I realized I couldn't do all of them immediately, and that I needed to break them down into what I'd do in this class and what I'd do in the next one. The progress record chart for the *GRADS Competency Analysis Profile* helps. At the top you put all your students' names, then note each student's mastery of each competency.

"I chose books to use that fit the competencies. I use a series *(Teens Parenting)* written for school-age parents. I have a couple of child development books, but they stay on my bookshelf. They're too textbooky, and it's easy to get bogged down in them. I use them as references.

"Our big *Adolescent Parent Resource Guide* gives us all sorts of strategies for teaching the various competencies. I teach to make sure we cover those competencies. For example, the pregnancy component can be used as a checklist. I write in the assignment, what they did, and how I know the student mastered it. I can look at that checklist and know they know about labor and delivery, the Apgar score, etc."

Since some teen parents move around a lot, class enrollment tends to be somewhat fluid. Egan commented, "I have a lot of students who float in and out. They may be here, move or drop out, then be back next year. If she comes back, I can pull out that folder and know where she is. If the student moves to another school district with a GRADS program, I send a copy of the checklist to the student's new GRADS teacher."

Egan also stressed the need to be prepared to provide work for homebound students. The *Adolescent Parent Resource Guide* is designed to meet this need, too. For each competency, independent learning strategies are included as well as a wealth of group activities.

The *Teens Parenting* series (Morning Glory Press) Comprehensive Curriculum Notebooks also include many assignments suitable for working at home as well as in class. Young people tend to learn better in groups, but if the student is at home alone, you provide the best independent learning assignments possible.

Sheila Maggard, Ohio Valley Vocational School, West Union, Ohio, another GRADS teacher, uses both kinds of strategies with her students. "We work together on the competencies whenever possible, but I try to do things independently with them. Depending on whether they are six months pregnant, parenting a six-month-old, or parenting a three-year-old, they have very different needs," she commented.

The key word for you is *organization.* You are a facilitator, a leader, and a manager. Be prepared for all types of learning needs, from the newly pregnant student to the student who is parenting a three-year-old, and from the young teen who is just beginning her/his career planning to the older teen who must soon join the work force.

Be ready for the student who attends your class every day, as well as for the one who must be home on bed rest for three months during pregnancy or those who are often absent for other reasons.

Preparing Individual Learning Activities

Because of the diversity of students and situations in your program, your students will learn best with a wide variety of learning activities. Be prepared to facilitate student learning in large groups, small groups, and individually. When students attend your class, their learning is often enhanced by working in facilitated groups, particularly in cooperative learning clusters.

There are a variety of occasions, however, when group learning is not possible or desirable, and students need individual learning activities. As you design individual learning opportunities, you can utilize a wide variety of learning strategies just as you do when you're facilitating group learning.

"Read the book about prenatal care" is, for many students, a non-productive activity. However, this can be expanded into a simple project. "Read this book about prenatal care and respond to these questions" can enhance student knowledge, particularly if the questions require students to go beyond technical information. Questions can involve case studies, and can ask students to consider various options and alternatives, and to view situations from the perspectives of others.

A project can be complex. "Use multiple resources to develop and carry out a prenatal care plan. Document the completion of each part of your plan. Reflect in writing on at least three parts of your completed plan. Share your completed plan with your teacher, and with the newly-pregnant students in your class."

Students can do some of this individually, and some in groups. This project requires students to use multiple resources, to do multiple activities over time, and to take a variety of reasoned actions. It allows them the opportunity for self-assessment, and for multiple assessment conferences with you.

If you prepare resource guides for independent study students, remember that a variety of assignment activities is important. If you include special writing assignments and open-ended questions (as is done in the *Teens Parenting* Series Workbooks), the student's writing skills will improve. Best of all, comments on the study sheet often start a dialogue between student and teacher which might not have happened otherwise.

Generally insist that the student answer questions in complete sentences. Many students need lots of help in learning to write coherently — and those who write well already won't find the complete-sentence requirement too difficult. In addition, include creative writing assignments on the topic being studied.

Instructive videos can be used independently. Unique projects can increase the student's interest. For example, if he's studying home safety, ask him to crawl through his house on his hands and knees in order to check for hazards from a crawling child's viewpoint. Regularly assigning activities in which the parent interacts with the child is important for any teen parent student, whether working with a group or independently.

Assign activities with other students when possible. For a unit on infant feeding, for example, ask the student to interview a breastfeeding and a bottle-feeding mother, then compare their situations.

If you work with students whose only connection with school is a periodic (perhaps weekly) appointment with you, can you devise a way to meet with several pregnant and parenting teens together? Peer interaction can be a valuable addition to an independent study program.

On Being Relevant

Relevancy is important in teaching. Students learn better if they feel the material is relevant to their lives. As you plan curriculum and develop lesson plans, know that parenting is foremost in many of your students' thoughts. They will learn more if they can apply the learning to their daily lives.

Students who say they don't like to read may become absorbed in fiction to which they can relate personally. If you're teaching language arts, or you simply want to help your students learn to read and write more effectively, include plenty of resources on pregnancy, parenting, and intergenerational living. For reading, you can find good novels which focus on pregnancy and parenting during the teen years, such as *Make Lemonade* by Virginia Wolff (2003), *Imani All Mine* by Connie Porter (1999), and *Detour for Emmy, Too Soon for Jeff,* and *Baby Help* by Marilyn Reynolds (1993, 1994, 1998). (See Bibliography.)

One teen parent teacher in a self-contained classroom developed a teen parent English course. Students were given a choice of books to read which related to pregnancy and parenting, some fiction, others non-fiction. She used a variety of study guides, activities, and projects to be completed along with the reading. In addition to reading, students were required to complete an open-ended journal in which they wrote regularly. Sometimes she suggested topics; other times, students came up with their own.

Reading to one's child is a critical part of effective parenting. If the parent doesn't read well, reading picture books to the child offers reading practice without suggesting the "baby" books are assigned because the student can't read well. The child learns from listening to mom or dad read, and in the process, the parent's skills improve.

Shared Beginnings® from Reading Is Fundamental® (RIF) is an activity-based family literacy program for teen parents and their children. RIF has developed materials to help a teen parent guide her/his child toward reading. See the appendix for address.

Evaluating Resource Materials

To be a facilitator of student learning is different than being a traditional classroom teacher who imparts knowledge to students. You need to have the budget and the freedom to build extensive classroom resources and learning centers. Work with your school librarian, who probably has a budget to purchase resources. It is a good learning opportunity for students to use the school library for some of their resources.

How do you determine the usability of materials? First, you need to establish criteria, then evaluate prospective resource materials using these criteria. Consider:

- **Reading Level.** Many pregnant and parenting students have below-grade level basic skills. Many read at the fifth grade reading level or below. Learn the general reading level of most of your students, then select classroom sets of materials at approximately this level. Select other resource materials on the same topics that have higher and lower reading levels so you can accommodate and challenge most students.

- **Relevancy.** Pregnant and parenting students like to use materials that are relevant to them. Often, they prefer materials that focus on teens rather than adults. For example, a book on parenting that is written for adult parents will not correspond to many of the experiences of teen parents.

- **Attractiveness.** Resource materials need to be attractive and reader friendly. A section of hard-to-read type with no graphics, no matter how well written, is not likely to encourage reading. Students generally learn more from colorful, well-illustrated resources.

- **Affordability.** Most teen parent programs operate on small budgets. Usually, you need to purchase materials that are reasonable in price, especially if you want to purchase in adequate quantities. Buy from reputable companies or organizations with reasonable prices or who offer special prices or quantity discounts for your program.

When Nancy Buzzell, adjunct child development professor, Taft, California, started teaching a daily class of teen parents from the high school, she previewed a set of texts in her class and found them too difficult for her students. Buzzell tried to use them for two days, and realized it wasn't going to work. She found parenting texts designed especially for school-age parents, took a sample to her dean, and said, "May we reconsider the text for this class? They need a text relevant to their daily lives." The college provided the texts which were developmentally appropriate for the students. In addition, Buzzell utilizes relevant articles, newspaper items, guest speakers, and projects in her teaching.

Where can you obtain resource materials with appropriate reading levels, that are relevant for pregnant and parenting students, and are affordable? Three resources are Morning Glory Press, MELD, and New Futures, Inc. Each specializes in resources for this special population. See the bibliography for more information.

Developing Assessment Strategies

Instruction and assessment are no longer viewed separately. Assessment is a way of providing students with frequent feedback on their performance as they progress through the course or program. An effective assessment represents measurement of meaningful goals, facilitates learning, is valid, reliable, multi-dimensional, and is easy to use. Teachers of parenting students need to become good managers of assessment systems.

Alternative and authentic assessment strategies, rather than conventional or traditional strategies, should predominate in the assessment of the students in your program. Conventional or traditional assessment generally refers to a quest to discover the *content* students have mastered *after* a unit of instruction, using timed paper/pencil testing (multiple-choice, true/false, matching, short answer).

Alternative assessment requires students to demonstrate knowledge and skills in ways other than the conventional methods. **Authentic assessment** engages students in applying knowledge and skills in the same way they are used in the "real world" outside school. It is performance-based, and requires a student to go beyond basic recall and demonstrate significant, worthwhile knowledge and understanding through a product, performance, or exhibition. The assessment consists of an authentic task and a scoring rubric that are tied to an outcome or major concept, and are made clear to the student from the beginning of a unit or lesson.

Assessment systems need to incorporate a variety of alternative and authentic assessment strategies in addition to the traditional paper/pencil tests:

- **Product/project assessments**. A student project results in a product related to the curriculum. The project is assessed, and the processes used by the student(s) can also be assessed.

- **Performance assessments and exhibitions**. Provides students with opportunities to demonstrate their understanding and to thoughtfully apply knowledge, skills, and habits of mind (such as higher-order thinking skills or problem-solving) in a variety of structured and unstructured situations. These assessments often occur over time and result in a tangible product or observable performance.

- **Process skills assessment**. Assessing a student's skills in progressing through a series of actions or operations, such as thinking abilities, applications of procedural knowledge, and interactions with others.

- **Conferences and interviews**. Face-to-face sessions, formal or informal, where students can get qualitative feedback on their ideas concerning products/projects, performance, and/ or process skills — whether in the planning, development, or final stages.

- **Decision-making matrices**. A device that allows an individual to structure the analysis of a problem and to delineate and weight the factors involved.

- **Graphic organizers**. Mental maps that help students make their thinking visible — to develop a "mental picture" of a concept or issue. They represent the process skills of sequencing, comparing, contrasting, classifying, inferring, drawing conclusions, problem solving, and thinking critically.

- **Class or group discussion**. Involves preparing sufficiently for and participating in an informed and thoughtful way in class discussions.

- **Journals and learning logs**. Can be used to assess the reflectiveness of student responses regarding process skills and student abilities to plan, monitor, and evaluate their own work.
- **Observations**. Formative assessments that focus on specific behaviors, process skills, communication skills, or any other skill. Observations must be objectively documented, often using a checklist.
- **Portfolios**. A purposeful collection of student work that exhibits the student's efforts, progress, and achievement in one or more areas.
- **Questioning**. Can be an effective process assessment tool during discussions, debriefings, conferences, or reviews of journals and learning logs. Effective questioning techniques are important.

Evaluation strategies can include:

- **Rubrics**. A scoring rubric consists of fixed scales related to a list of criteria describing performance. Each scale is composed of anchors that describe the various levels of performance complexity. See the rubric example on page 134.

- **Scoring sheets**. Present the elements to be assessed and provide space for indicating the level achieved. These are less objective than rubrics, which clearly describe performance at various levels throughout the range.

- **Checklists**. Often used with observations, and can be similar to scoring sheets. The checklist must list observable skills and processes. Checklists can be used by teachers, by students in groups, and by individual students.

- **Tests**. Testing can be done in a variety of ways, from traditional paper/pencil tests to oral tests and demonstration tests.

This list is a brief overview of alternative and authentic assessment strategies. For more information and for examples of each type of assessment, see *Alternative Assessment: A Family and Consumer Sciences Teacher's Tool Kit* (1996).

What About Grading?

Student grades still need to be assigned. You need to determine the quality and quantity of work that students need to do for the different grades. Make these determinations before students enter your program, then clearly communicate the class requirements and grade standards to each student as each grading period begins. When students know from the beginning what is expected of them, they are better prepared to meet your expectations.

Establish benchmarks for credit. Students enrolled for the entire semester and who complete the required work will receive full credit. If the student enrolls three weeks later, that student will have additional work to complete for full credit. Since you are likely to have new students enrolling throughout the semester, develop an equitable method of integrating these students into the group.

No Need to Reinvent the Wheel

When I (Sharon) was hired in 1974 to teach in a program in Ohio for school-age mothers, developing curriculum was one of my greatest challenges. I struggled daily with the questions, "What do teen parents need to know and be able to do? What resources are available and what learning strategies should I use to best meet the needs of my students? How do I assess their learnings, and how do I assign credit and grades?" I found no resources or materials focusing on teen parenting to help me.

We know that you, too, face some of these same challenges. Fortunately, there are many resources available today to help you meet your curricular needs. You should *not* have to reinvent this particular wheel. Ask your district to provide the funds for you to purchase curricular materials and resources so that *your* most valuable resources — your time and energy — are available for the other demands of your program.

Non-traditional work often means higher income for a woman.

CHAPTER 5

Preparing Teen Parents for the World of Work

*There's nothing in this world, not even the baby, that will guarantee he'll be with me the rest of my life. My mother wants to divorce my father, but she has no job, and she has six kids. That's why she puts up with him. I **have** to finish school.*

Karina, 16, mother of Saulo, 7 months

When I knew my girlfriend was pregnant, I was scared and I felt trapped. Then once the baby was born, I'd look at her and think, "Just look at what you brought into this world." Looking at that baby gave me the inspiration to get up, put some clothes on, and go out and look for a job.

That's what keeps me going with my part-time job and going to school. That kid will kick you out the door to get a job.

Louis, 19, father of Serina, 1

All parents must provide financially for their children. When compared to adult parents, teen parents are more likely to face obstacles to doing so. Teens generally have less education, fewer skills, less work experience, fewer financial resources, and added difficulty balancing work, school, and family responsibilities.

Single head-of-household families begun by a teen mother are more likely to rely on public welfare than those started by women age 20 or older, but the Personal Responsibility and Work Opportunity Reconciliation Act of 1996, Federal Public Law 104-193, set a five-year life-time limit of public assistance for most families. For school-age parents, the emphasis of this law is on staying in school and remaining in a living situation supervised by an adult. For other parents, the emphasis is on temporary public assistance and work.

The eligibility requirements for teen parents to receive federal Temporary Assistance for Needy Families (TANF) are complicated. The requirements do not apply to all teen parents in a uniform manner. Rather, certain characteristics of the teen determine the applicability of the law. For example, the rules change, depending on the age of the teen parent, the teen's marital status, and if the teen is the head of the household. Ineligibility because of failure to abide by the federal laws is limited to the teen parent, and does not extend to the child. The teen's child is still eligible to receive benefits through a representative payee.

States have a great deal of autonomy in interpreting and implementing TANF. Check with the Human Services Department in your county or state for information.

Why Prepare for Work?

Most young parents will need to work, some while still attending high school, so workforce preparation is a critical component of any teen parent program. If parenting skills alone are emphasized with little or no focus on work, your students may learn that parenting alone, and not paid work, is all that really matters. Students must understand that both parenting (to provide love, guidance and emotional support) and paid work (to provide financial and material support) are crucial in developing a stable, self-sufficient family unit. When career development and work become a formal program priority, when staff actively support the priority, and when adequate child care and transportation is available, student participation increases dramatically.

The income prospects for teen mothers, particularly single teen mothers, is bleak. Single female heads of households earned a median family income of $17,443 in 1993 compared to $26,467 for single male heads of household, and $43,005 for married-couple families *(Equity Issues,* 1996). Forty-seven percent of white female-headed households and 72 percent of African American female-headed households live in poverty, according to *Working Women Count (*1994).

Similarly, the fathers, both adult men and school-age boys, of babies born to teen mothers are less likely to be employed. If employed, they are likely to have substantially lower incomes than fathers of babies born to older first-time mothers. They are less able to provide financially for their young families. If they are not married to or living with the teen mother, they are less able to pay child support *(Kids Having Kids).*

The more education a woman has, the greater the chances she will look for work. Women and men with specialized technical training are likely to earn half a million dollars more in a lifetime than someone working at a low-skill, minimum wage job.

With more families living in poverty — especially female-headed families — we need models of education and workplace support that help teen parents and their families rise out of poverty and become economically self-sufficient. Ignoring this need will push more teen parents and their families into continued poverty.

School to Work

Partnerships with employers can help open up the educational system so all students have career-focused educational opportunities that are structured around career clusters or paths. Such partnerships can create access for students locked out of the traditional routes to academic and economic success. It can introduce students to a range of future employment options, including but not limited to careers in technology. It can provide teachers and students with a better understanding of the demands

School-to-Work Components

School-based learning includes
- hands-on learning
- high academic standards
- career exploration/planning
- career clusters
- integration of academics and vocational/technical education
- student credentialing
- project and problem-based curricula
- new schedules and teaching approaches
- evaluation of knowledge and ability
- curriculum developed with employer input
- pathways to higher education

Work-based learning provides
- real world experience
- reinforcement of academic lessons
- job shadowing
- internships
- workplace mentoring
- cooperative education
- service learning
- youth apprenticeships

Connecting activities lead to
- community-wide partnerships
- students matched with employers
- improved connections between education and business
- increased participation of employers and labor
- school-employer staff exchange
- job placement, continuing education, and further training assistance
- assistance to integrate school-based and work-based learning
- placement to work or college

and excitement of the workplace. And it can provide opportunities for students to enter and succeed in higher education.

States and localities can build school-to-work systems upon existing successful programs, such as youth apprenticeship, tech-prep education, cooperative education, vocational-technical education, career academies, and school-to-apprenticeship programs.

Active and continued involvement of schools, parents, businesses, organized labor, community organizations, community colleges, and universities ensures that students and workers become continuous learners.

Your school-to-work program needs three basic components — school-based learning, work-based learning, and connecting activities. See opposite page for a list of possibilities for each of these components.

School-to-work is for *all* students, males and females, from a broad range of backgrounds and circumstances. Schools need to pay particular attention to the needs of individuals within specific groups — students who are female, are of color, have disabilities, speak a language other than English, or are teen parents. Training and technical support for teachers, employers, mentors, counselors, and others should include strategies for counseling and training these students for high-skill, high-wage careers, including non-traditional employment.

A successful school-to-work system for teen parents contains many elements. Most elements are essential for the success of all students, but some are specific to teen parents:

- Non-traditional career exploration and options
- Child care and transportation assistance
- Non-traditional teacher and role models/peer role models
- Community and parental support for mentoring or job shadowing in non-traditional fields
- Advisory committee representative of the school population
- Collaboration with community, business, and education
- Early intervention for at-risk students
- Parental involvement in career planning and school outcome
- High expectations and financial incentives for students

- Planning that includes all students
- Varied instructional methods
- Gender-neutral language
- A safe working/learning environment, free of harassment and violence

A school-to-work system that contains these elements is likely to meet with success for many teen parents. For more information, contact the workforce preparation director in your local school district or the State Department of Education.

Schools need to focus around career paths and clusters, and to have career-focused educational opportunities for all students. Students without this career focus will not be prepared to compete in the skilled work force of the 21st century.

Understanding the Work Ethic

So how do you prepare your students for workforce participation? It can be a challenge!

You may have some students who lack understanding of the work ethic. The student with no working model at home may have a hard time understanding the importance of such seemingly simple things as going to work every day and getting there on time, of being pleasant and helpful to demanding customers, and of getting along with co-workers. You may find your students need help in learning and internalizing these employability skills as much as they need technical training. Until these skills are mastered, some will experience little success, and therefore little satisfaction, in their work.

A workforce preparation component that will meet all your students' needs will be difficult. When you teach parenting, you know most, probably all, of your students *want* to be good parents. They love their children, and you will see positive results from your teaching.

However, not all students are interested in becoming job-ready. Some are, and will understand clearly the need to prepare for jobs that will pay enough to support their families. Often because of their child, they have already developed a work ethic, a desire to succeed in the world of work. They are ready for serious job training and job placement.

> *I started working in a nursing home doing dishes when I was 14. Now I work in a medical clinic as a nurse's aide. I help with X-rays and other procedures, and I love doing it. I want to be an RN (registered nurse), and I'm starting my training this fall.*
>
> Erin Kathleen, 17, mother of Jenny, 3 months

> *If you're a teen mother or father, you don't have time to think about yourself. This is no time to be a cop-out. There's no time to say, "I can't find a job." Once you decide you're pregnant, or your girlfriend's pregnant, and you decide to have the baby, you have to discipline yourself. You have to do everything possible for your child.*
>
> *Just look at that child and say, "I'm going to do everything I can to take care of you the best I can."*
>
> Elijah, 19, father of Caelyn, 2 months

But some teen parents have little immediate hope of becoming self-sufficient. Caring for a child and getting to school is difficult. Being pushed into the workforce too quickly can be a speedy ticket to continued defeat.

Your challenge is to meet each student where s/he is on this continuum. Learn about school-to-work possibilities and incorporate the components that will help *your students.* Interpret that list of school-to-work learning into your students' needs. For some, this means learning the basic skills first, along with coaching in such things as communication skills, reliability, appropriate job attitudes, and other work ethic basics.

Workforce preparation is crucial for *all* your students. Some will need a great deal of help to become ready for even a minimum wage job. Others will be ready for employment, move on to higher education, or both. Each young parent, wherever s/he is on that continuum, needs your help. It is a daunting challenge.

Testing for Basic Skills

As you develop strategies to help your students become economically self-sufficient, you will be designing quite different programs for the seventh grader and the high school senior. Even more important, you will provide widely different assistance for the student who reads at a third grade level than for those achieving at grade level.

First, do all you can to help those below grade level, either within your program or through referrals, to improve their basic skills. You may also need to help students make occupational and career choices that match their skill level. At times you may suspect that a student has an undiagnosed learning disability. In this case, suggest that the parent/guardian ask the school psychologist to test the student.

Workforce preparation involves building that foundation of basic skills first for students who lack this critical element. Putting students without basic skills directly into specific job training is likely to be a formula for failure.

Jan Figart, executive director, Margaret Hudson Program, Tulsa, Oklahoma, pointed out that the student's prior grade point average may tell you very little about his/her mastery of those all-important basic skills. "Instead, you have to look at their standardized test results," she explained. "These may be available from student testing in a prior grade. Or you could use the Test of Adult Basic Education (TABE). This is a validated test for middle and secondary school students.

"Most work places, whether service opportunities or light industry, need employees conversant at sixth grade level and with eighth grade reading skills," Figart said. "If you have a student who reads at the second grade level and you try to place him/her in a job, s/he is doomed to failure.

The student in need of these levels of education requires a heavy emphasis on the school learning in a competency-based curriculum. You focus on remediation or applied education. For the student who has the basic skills, you offer more of the work-based learning.

"At Margaret Hudson, we try to create situations in which students see the school as a step toward independence," Figart commented. "We try to minimize the things they are given and focus on the things they earn. We have a clothes closet, but the students are responsible for it. They wash the clothes, they handle the layaways, the receipts. It's a gold credit room. The student earns gold credit by being on time at school, completing assignments, doing community service. This reinforces the capitalistic system. By putting students in control, they acquire business skills. Some are in charge of marketing, others handle stock.

"School-to-work preparation is not a class, it's a belief," Figart concluded.

School-to-Work Possibilities for Teen Parents

School-to-work can be successfully implemented in teen parent programs. All three basic components — school-based learning, work-based learning, and connecting activities — are essential.

You may not be able to include all elements of the three components. Perhaps you can't offer occupationally-specific classes or programs. When you plan your school-to-work system, link with other partners, such as career centers, that can provide these elements for your students.

When you link with a career center, offer to provide instructional and support services for the teen parents attending school at their campus. The career center may need your program services as much as your students need theirs.

A resource to help you address the school-to-work competencies with students is "Economic Independence and Employability Competencies" (*GRADS Ohio Competency Analysis Profile*, 1996, pages 16-19). Teacher background information and student learning activities for the *GRADS OCAP* are in the *Adolescent Parent Resource Guide*.

Short-term programs. Vocational-technical education in short-term teen parent programs, one or two semesters, can focus on work socialization, expansion of career awareness, and reinforcement of the message in the parenting curriculum that good parents provide financially for their children. Critical to such an approach would be active longer-term individual career planning. Work socialization and career awareness activities combined with limited work-based learning, such as job shadowing, may be adequate in short-term teen parent programs, if they are paired with active, personalized career planning.

Articulation agreements, individual career plans, and explicit, active support for vocational-technical education planning may be far more important in helping teen parents achieve economic independence than limited short-term job skills training. Making the links between limited, program-based vocational-technical education and related resources outside the program will help teen parents achieve their career goals.

Long-term programs. Many students enroll in teen parent programs for two or more years. In long-term programs where students complete high school and then pursue post-secondary education in large numbers, job awareness, vocational evaluation, intensive counseling, and work-based experiences are important.

In addition, planning around the transition to secondary or post-secondary education, and the development of articulation agreements would enable many students to acquire such training after program completion.

If students tend to drop out or not go on to post-secondary education, occupational training may be needed. Occupational training in many teen parent programs is limited to two to four training areas.

For students with occupational interests and aptitudes not represented, agreements with nearby schools with occupational training programs could enable them to acquire such training for part of each school day.

There are many career-vocational-technical education and training options emerging in a variety of secondary educational settings. Area career centers are but one model. Career academies are school-business partnerships that offer high school students a rigorous academic/technical curriculum, employability skills, career counseling, work experience, enrichment activities, and mentoring, and can be a school-within-a-school. Magnet high schools may have career themes with all courses focused on the career field, such as aviation high schools. High schools may have career clusters and majors.

For more information on these and other emerging models, contact your State Department of Education, division of vocational/technical education or workforce development.

Gender Equity Issues and School-to-Work

There are significant differences in career development between men and women:

- Many people have different role expectations for men and women.
- The husband's career often takes precedence over the wife's career.
- The mother generally takes a strong role in parenting, sometimes without much help.
- Women are more likely to be single custodial parents.
- Women are more likely to experience stress from trying to fill too many roles.
- Women face more barriers in the workplace, including stereotyped expectations, discrimination, and harassment.

Women need to be prepared for the dual roles that most of them will encounter. Teen mothers have taken on dual roles very early in life, and this greatly affects their career development options and strategies. Today, young men, too, may be deeply involved in parenting and in their career. Handling dual roles is difficult *and* necessary for both parents.

Students may hear different messages concerning appropriate careers, depending on their sex, and sometimes on their ethnic group. If you are aware of these differences, you can help teachers, guidance counselors, students, parents, and others change the messages and experiences so that all students have opportunities to enter careers of their choice, careers which will enable them to provide financially for their families.

Computer expertise is critical in many jobs that require high technology skills. In your teen parent program, you can develop computer tasks for students so they learn how technology can solve problems specific to their situations, aid in decision making, and help them achieve their goals. You can also advocate for equal open computer time for boys and girls in your school's computer labs.

The emerging high-technology fields require substantial knowledge and skills in math and science. Males are often pushed more firmly into these areas than are females. Because

the person with the better math and science skills is more qualified for the high technology careers in these fields, males are
more likely to get these jobs. Teen mothers may have low
confidence and skills in math and science, and they may avoid
enrolling in these courses.

You could incorporate math and science hands-on learning
activities in your teen parent program to enhance students' skills
and confidence. You can also advocate for additional tutoring for
students who need to raise their math and science skill levels.

High-Wage and Non-Traditional Occupations

Teen parents need jobs that pay family-supporting wages.
High-paying jobs for high school graduates are usually in
technical fields, or in occupations considered non-traditional for
women. Occupations defined as non-traditional for one gender
are jobs/careers in which fewer than 25 percent of the workers in
that field are of that gender.

Jobs and careers traditionally dominated by men tend to pay
higher wages and salaries than those traditionally dominated by
women, even when the amount of education required for the two
are similar. Career exploration and planning for teen parents
needs to include a focus on high-wage and non-traditional
occupations.

"Statistics show a single mother must earn at least $11 an
hour to support herself and her child. Becoming a day care
provider at $5 or $6 an hour won't work for her," commented
Susan Todd, resource teacher, Pinellas Teenage Parenting
Program, Largo, Florida.

Examples of non-traditional occupations for women include
the technical trades of carpenter, plumber, auto/diesel technician,
math/science careers, and other fields such as law enforcement
and fire-fighting.

Teen fathers can also explore non-traditional careers. Expanding the career options of young men may help them find jobs
more suitable to their aptitudes and interests. Non-traditional
careers for men include nursing, administrative support services,
human services, cosmetology, and education.

It is important that you purposefully help students explore

non-traditional and high-wage jobs and careers. The following case study shows how one teacher used the school-to-work system to help a teen mom explore and prepare for a non-traditional occupation.

Sherry, a tenth grade student who was five months pregnant, was enrolled in her high school's teen parent program. Her teacher, Ms. Smith, gave Sherry an assignment to select a career cluster to explore. Sherry decided to explore careers in the communications career cluster. Her aunt is a telephone operator, so she is particularly interested in this occupation. Sherry is planning to get a job right after high school graduation because she needs to support herself and her baby. In the future, she might go on to college, but not immediately.

Ms. Smith set up a workplace mentoring experience at the local telephone company so that Sherry could explore a range of occupations there. Sherry spent structured time with a telephone operator and an administrative support staff person (traditional careers), and a line repair worker (non-traditional career).

Sherry was astonished to learn she can make twice as much money being a line repair worker as she can as an operator or administrative support staff, with a similar amount of education.

Ms. Smith worked with Sherry to develop a time line that incorporated her personal and family responsibilities with preparation for her career choice of a telephone line repair worker. Ms. Smith set up a visit for Sherry to the area career center so she could explore her educational options, including vocational/technical courses, related academics, a teen parenting program, and child care and transportation options. The guidance counselor at the career center helped Sherry select a course of study that was broad enough to allow her to make changes in her career path.

Since Sherry selected a non-traditional option, Ms. Smith also helped her begin to learn about challenges she

*is likely to face as a female in a male-dominated field, and
to develop strategies for coping with these challenges.*

A caveat: Non-traditional careers are not suitable for all
students. In particular, young women who have been sexually
abused, or are in unstable, unhealthy, or violent relationships
may find that a non-traditional career is hostile, or too difficult or
stressful. They may fare better in a workplace that is predomi-
nantly female. You can help these students explore traditional
high-wage careers.

Some of your students' parents may be opposed to the idea of
a non-traditional career for their daughters. Teen mothers often
receive little family or peer support for non-traditional career
options. Teachers report that parents sometimes ask, "Why are
you trying to put my daughter in that field?"

Perhaps you can influence their families and friends to be
more supportive. Non-traditional careers for women would be
a good topic to discuss in a support meeting for the parents of
your students.

Figart commented that in Oklahoma a single parent would
need to earn a minimum of $8.50 an hour to have the same
standard of living she would have if she qualified for TANF.
TANF assistance will be available only for a limited time, and
students who understand these facts may be more interested in
preparing for higher paying non-traditional jobs.

Featuring Non-Traditional Career Awareness

Patricia Miles, equity coordinator, Orange County Public
Schools, Orlando, Florida, coordinates a single parent program
through the federal Carl Perkins gender equity funding. "I find
that only six of the traditional female occupations offered by
Orange County's four technical centers will pay $7.50 or more
per hour, so we need to explore the non-traditional areas for
women," she explained. "They have to have enough money to
live, give them benefits and job security, plus upward mobility.
We say look at where the income is. The traditional female occupations don't offer these things. Non-traditional occupations do.

"Teen parents have to be aware of the job market, and they

have to get an understanding of who they are and what their interests and abilities are. You have to find a match between those abilities and the job market."

Miles emphasizes "career laddering." Many single parents, she pointed out, can depend on someone else, often their parents, to support them for a year or two. Training for many non-traditional jobs takes one to two years. "With a year and a half of training, they can get a good job and continue upward from there," she said. Truck-driving, for example, is a seven-week program. A parent with a baby probably can't drive cross-country, but she can drive locally.

Getting role models into your classroom frequently can help young women understand that non-traditional jobs could be a reality for them. You can make sure your students know and talk to a woman police officer, electrician, plumber, and others.

Most important is to introduce your students to available careers. What will give them "enough" income? First of all, do they know how much money they will need? Developing a budget is an important step toward career awareness. What will the rent cost? The car? What do you need to earn? Many young people haven't developed these basic understandings.

Another basic step toward workforce preparation is completing an interest survey. There are several tools which are self-administered and self-interpreted such as the Harrington-O'Shea Career Inventory. Ask your career center director to help you choose an appropriate career inventory instrument.

Help each student figure out what s/he would be capable of doing, and what s/he would like to do. It's a little like a jigsaw puzzle. Can they fit together their interests, their capabilities, their income needs, and their personal realities (child care, transportation, family support . . .)?

Miles is developing a "What's My Line" show for students in the BETA (Birth, Education, Training, Acceptance) program in Orlando. Women in non-traditional careers will participate, and students will figure out each woman's occupation by asking them questions. Then each student will choose one of those non-traditional careers and do an in-depth report on it.

She will research the training required, the working

conditions, salary range, and opportunities and challenges in the field. Each will share the report with the other students. "Give them as much information about careers as you can," Miles advised. "Let them explore careers they may not have considered."

Many GRADS teachers in Ohio help students explore non-traditional careers in a day-long seminar at an area career center. One part of the day involves a panel of workers in non-traditional careers. In another part of the seminar the students have hands-on experiences in career areas that are non-traditional for them. The vocational/technical teachers design brief lessons specifically for this day. Students often make a product they're able to take home. In one carpentry lab, students constructed an exercise step which they could use to do physical exercises at home.

You may find your female students don't show much interest in non-traditional work. Or, if they do, they may think working with a lot of men would be a problem. Miles described the support groups she coordinates. "We talk about male bonding, about sexual harassment, and how you deal with it," she explained.

A support system can be developed in several ways. The teen parent program itself may be the best support system. Also look for women in non-traditional jobs to mentor your students.

Developing Partnerships with Parents of Students

Students' parents are likely to have more influence over their career selection and education than are their teachers. Your students are socialized by the work attitudes and behaviors of their parents long before you see them. Teen parents whose own parent(s) have a strong history of workforce participation are more likely to become actively involved in the work force themselves. Students whose parents have a poor work history may need extra coaching in the art and skills required for satisfying and productive workforce participation.

Since the majority of teen parents live in families with low and poverty-level incomes, many of their parents may be unemployed or under-employed. They may have low basic skills and few employability skills. Invite parents to participate in career development and workforce preparation learning activities at school and at home.

Consider actively recruiting the parents of your students into the adult basic literacy education and adult occupational training programs in your district. When parents can say to their teens, "Look at me. If I can do this, you can, too," then the parents have greater opportunity to affect positively the work attitudes and behaviors of their children.

Additional Considerations

Other circumstances or situations can have a major effect on your students' success in preparing for the world of work.

Teen parents may become very attached to you and other staff, and the emotional costs to the teen of leaving the program can be high. This can make it difficult to transfer to another school, such as a career center. For this reason, it's worthwhile to design linking activities to ease transitions — or consider locating a teen parent program in the career center.

Teen parents need the same career options as all other students. It is a disservice to them to channel them into occupational child care programs simply because they are parents.

Many schools or programs insist that all students adhere to strict attendance policies. These policies and practices may unfairly (and even unintentionally) adversely affect pregnant and parenting teens. Teen parents can be exhausted by parenting and school responsibilities, and sometimes need adapted attendance practices, even if this means it takes them longer to finish high school. Students might be given the opportunity to receive credit for classes based on performance outcomes, without a specific amount of time in class required.

You may find an instructor in an occupational training program advising a pregnant student to drop out because of the possibility of harm from toxic and hazardous chemicals. This concern might come up in such programs/classes as horticulture, hospitality, auto body, auto mechanic, welding, health, and cosmetology. You may hear, "How do we keep pregnant students in these programs without endangering them?"

It is important that the safety procedures that have been

implemented regarding the use of toxic chemicals ensure safety for *all* students including those who are pregnant. Inappropriate handling of chemicals by pregnant students has the potential of harming the unborn child. Inappropriate handling of chemicals by any student has the potential of harming any body system, including the reproductive system. The issue should be, "What should we do about safe handling of chemicals by all students?" rather than "What will we do with these pregnant students?"

Pregnant students need equitable treatment. Pregnancy should be treated as a temporary medical disability, not as a permanent condition. Some occupational training programs need to make adaptations for a variety of students with temporary medical disabilities, whether due to pregnancy or a broken leg. For example, in a building trades program, the task of carrying shingles up a ladder cannot be carried out by either a student who is pregnant or a student with a broken leg. Equitable adaptations need to be made in both students' educational programs.

Be alert to other challenges facing some teen parents. For example, most job training programs for teens don't include a breast-feeding consultant as a resource. When you're working with teen mothers, this may be important, according to Pat Guerra, child care center director, Valley View High School, Ontario, California. Guerra spoke of a young mom who enrolled in a Regional Occupation Program (ROP) for nursing. She had been excited about entering the class, but was crying when she came in to see Guerra a few days later.

"I can't take this," she said. She was breastfeeding when she was home, and while she was in the ROP class, her boyfriend was supposed to give the baby a bottle. He couldn't get the baby to eat, so she figured she had to drop out of the ROP class.

"We called the breastfeeding consultant," Guerra continued, "and she brought the pump we had purchased for our class. She showed the teen mom how to pump milk so her baby could have it while she was gone. And I said, 'If you quit the ROP class, you'll always be in charge of the parenting. Your boyfriend needs the opportunity to develop his own parenting style.' A couple of days went by, and she didn't quit. In fact, she reported, 'He's really doing good with the baby.'"

There may be many reasons a teen parent sometimes feels unwelcome in a school or program. School staff may be openly or subtly judgmental or antagonistic. At times, you will need to negotiate differences and advocate for your students' rights.

Preparing teen parents for the world of work is a complex but important undertaking. On-going instruction and support from you and your program can make a difference. With help and encouragement, many of your students will be able to work toward a satisfying and independent lifestyle for themselves and their families. Schools can be part of the *solution* to the problem of poverty and welfare dependence, not part of the problem.

No matter how hard you try, you probably won't be able to see all your students job-ready by the time they leave school. Those who aren't face harsh times of poverty for themselves and their children. However, you will see some, perhaps many, join the workforce in jobs which start at a reasonable wage, provide health benefits, and allow for career advancement. Even if you teach in an area where few adults have jobs, and you have many students who appear not to understand such work ethic behaviors as promptness, reliability, and other important working skills, you will provide as much job-related teaching as you possibly can. Each time one of your students becomes self-supporting, know that you have helped change a life.

*Teens, mothers and fathers, **want** to be good parents.*

CHAPTER 6

Teaching the Art and Skills of Parenting

Teaching parenting to young parents is one of the most important tasks a teacher may ever have. Young parents who, in addition to continuing their education and obtaining employment skills, become "good" parents are likely to have satisfying lives in spite of early parenting.

Parent education is an important component of classes for teen parents, but not the sole focus. If parenting is the only focus, we run the risk of giving teens the message that they are valued mainly as a parent, and not as an individual. Parenting classes for teen parents need to be balanced between parent education and adolescent development. The adolescent development components can include personal development, adolescent relationships, career and workforce development, problem-solving, communication, and leadership skills.

Teens, just like adults, want to be good parents, but the realities of adolescence make this goal difficult to achieve. This is compounded if the models in their experience are not

particularly good ones. A relevant, participatory parenting
component of a class for teen parents can provide some of that
help. Teaching infant and toddler development to the parents of
infants and toddlers can be a marvelous combination of
academic and practical learning.

When you teach a class made up of teenage parents, you have
the relevance factor under control. Your teaching can help your
students learn important material they will use in their day-to-
day living. Your teaching can make a difference in their lives as
you help them learn to parent their children in an effective way.
The opportunity to effect positive change is enormous.

Parent Is Expert on Own Child

Teaching parenting to parents has one very important distinction from teaching it to non-parents. The difference is that the
parent must be considered the expert as far as her/his own child
is concerned. The fine line between their role as a student and
their role as a parent is hard even for them to define — and it
will be hard for you. But it is a necessary distinction.

As far as their relationship with their child is concerned, a
teen parent is not a student in the usual "teacher teaches and
student learns" sense of the word. S/he is that child's parent, and
to repeat, is the expert on that particular child. Even if the child
is in child care for several hours daily, the child is still probably
spending more time with the parent(s) than with anyone else.

The teacher of a school-age parent needs to remember s/he is
discussing issues with another parent who has strong convictions
of his/her own and who loves this child and wants the best for
this child. This is to the teacher's advantage. Of primary importance to both parent and teacher is the welfare of the child.

How parents view themselves is closely connected with the
quality of parenting they can offer their child. Our most important task as teachers may be to help each student maximize her/
his own development. A parent who is stuck in an adolescent
development stage is likely to have difficulty with parenting.

Supporting healthy development is important in any school,
but it's absolutely essential in a class of young parents. They
need to progress as smoothly as possible through their own

developmental stages *and* acquire parenting attitudes and skills that will support the healthy development of their children.

We need to start where our students are, and accept them fully as the important persons they are now. We may disagree with them, but we don't put them down for their opinions. They may not always be "right," just as the rest of us aren't always right, but their ideas have validity just as ours do.

How would we act if we were teaching a class composed of 25- to 35-year-old parents? If we disagreed with one of our students, how would we handle it? We probably would, first of all, *accept* the parent's attitude/action, then attempt *respectfully* to help him/her change the attitude/action we consider not in the child's best interest. A 15-year-old parent needs our acceptance, caring concern, and respect as much as, even more, than does the adult parent.

Teen Parenting in Family Context

Many custodial teen parents continue to live with their parent(s) for at least two years after their babies are born. Therefore, much teen parenting is done in the context of the family system. As teachers, we need to be sensitive about what this means for our students. Our students are parenting in families with traditions of parenting attitudes, beliefs, and practices, and the teen parents are often expected to adopt them.

When we provide new or contradictory information and suggest that our students change their family traditions of parenting, we may not realize the ramifications. Some families are open to new information and new ways of doing things, and some are not. If the families of our students are closed to new information and ideas, then our teaching could contribute to family conflict.

A very important question is, *"Who is the parent?"* The teens are the biological parents, but other family members, usually the grandmothers, may be the practicing parents. If the practicing parent is the teen parent, the teacher and the parenting curriculum have more potential to contribute to successful outcomes for teen parents and their children than if other family members are the practicing parents.

Teen parents usually want help from their families with parenting, but most teens also want to be the primary parent. Four multi-generational parenting models have been described in teen parent families. These models are 1) teen parent receives little or no help with parenting, 2) teen parent is blocked from effectively parenting his/her child, and grandmother or other close family member is the primary parent, 3) teen parent receives little constructive parenting information, but grandmother or other close family member will help care for and parent the child, and 4) teen parent receives targeted help with parenting and receives constructive parenting information from the grandmother or close family member. Teen parents who receive targeted help with parenting and constructive parenting information are likely to have better outcomes for themselves and their children.

When possible, it's important to meet the parents of our students. We also can have strategies for including the families in the learning processes. Many strategies are possible, such as periodic newsletters, parent involvement in the classroom, and intergenerational learning activities for students to take home. Specific parent involvement activities are included in the *Adolescent Parent Resource Guide* and the *Teens Parenting Series Comprehensive Curriculum Notebooks*.

Involving parents in teaching and learning may enable families to support their daughter or son as they implement new parenting practices. For more information on working with families and ideas on intergenerational learning activities, see chapter 11.

Real-Life Parenting Education

In a high school parenting class for non-parents, you are teaching theory and trying to make your teaching realistic. With teen parents, real-life experiences come first, with the theoretical learning building on the experience. Of course you'll teach good parenting concepts. They will learn from you and from their class materials. They may learn even more from each other.

Empowering students through probing questions is an especially valuable technique. As your students share their experiences and concerns, your role is more resource person and facilitator than the ultimate authority.

You need to use appropriate materials, but you may find the traditional child development textbook is not adequate for your students. Most materials prepared for high school students assume the learner may have a child sometime in the future. You want materials that focus on your students' *current* parenting needs, preferably one written especially for teen parents. You will teach about the various stages of development, nutritional needs in pregnancy and during childhood, discipline techniques, good hygiene, and the many other topics important for this subject. A good resource is imperative. The *Teens Parenting Series* by Lindsay (Morning Glory Press) offers parenting help from conception to age three of the child, and is written specifically to the needs of teen parents. Books, workbooks, *Comprehensive Curriculum Notebooks*, videos, and board games are available. See the appendix for this series and other resources.

Because of their developmental stage, most adolescents have difficulty looking into the future. They are more likely to be focused on today. Teaching them the skills they will need when their children are in elementary school would be difficult. Helping them learn parenting skills they will use during their child's first two or three years of life is far more productive.

If you have enough students, dividing them into three groups based on their stage of parenthood works well. The group for pregnant students would focus on prenatal care and care of the newborn. A second group could concentrate on care and development of the child during its first year, and the third group would be composed of parents with toddlers.

If you have only one class, you may choose to develop the three-ring circus approach. One strategy involves using individualized learning activities, allowing students to specialize in tasks relevant to their child's current stage. Use individual activities sparingly, however. Students working independently much of the time are not learning from each other and can become isolated. Individual learning activities work well for home study, and occasionally in the classroom.

Another method is small group and cooperative learning. The

teacher can facilitate the learnings of all three groups during a class. For example, the group of pregnant students could work together on a project of pricing clothing and equipment for newborns, while the parents of infants view and discuss a video on baby bottle tooth decay, and the parents of toddlers read together about language development of two-year-olds, followed by individual journaling about their own child's language development. Some topics lend themselves well to full class groups, such as legal issues of parenthood.

As they learn more about child development and parenting, students can be encouraged to apply their new understanding to their own child. Because it is difficult for many teenagers to project into the future, activities and writing assignments should, whenever possible, apply to the current stage of development of the young parent's child.

However, if you are working under a pullout or case management approach, you may work with a group of students only once or twice a week. Or you may have independent study students, and have found no way to include them in group sessions. Perhaps you would like to do more than lead a discussion once a week, but your students don't earn credit for this activity. Some teachers assume that students only read and complete assignments when they are required to do so for credit.

You will have some students who are too busy, or they simply don't want to read or complete additional school projects. If you use reader-friendly, relevant, realistic resources, however, you are likely to find at least some of your students want to learn more about parenting even if they aren't earning credit. For these students, develop some learning packets with a strong focus on interaction between parent and child. For example, if your students are interested in discipline strategies, let them check out a copy of *Teens Parenting: Discipline from Birth to Three* or other similar resource. The workbook for this title includes activities for each chapter, and the *Comprehensive Curriculum Notebook* includes many more activities and teaching ideas.

Even without credit, your students may surprise you by being quite interested in learning individually. After all, this is the major route to life-long learning.

Parents as Teachers Can Help

Parents as Teachers is a school-home-community partnership program with headquarters in St. Louis, Missouri. In Missouri it is funded by the state legislature, but may be grant supported in other communities across the country.

Parents as Teachers is a national program that focuses, as its name implies, on parents being their children's first and most important teacher. In school districts in many areas of the country, they work closely with the counselor, the social worker, the crisis counselor, the family and consumer sciences teacher, and others who work with teen parents. Parents as Teachers offers a five-day implementation institute for parenting teachers who don't have much background in teaching parenting. The Parents as Teachers model includes a home visiting component, although this can be designed for working with individual teen parents within the school. For districts with child care, Parents as Teachers staff often work with teen parents.

Karen Hoelker, teen parent specialist, Parents as Teachers National Center, advises teen parent teachers, "When training is available, get it. Also, involve teens in the planning when you organize a group for them. Otherwise you might be following an adult agenda rather than one to which teens relate."

Value of Group Discussions

Students' personal lives cannot be kept separate from their parenting education. Sharing personal problems and joys may be an important part of a parenting course. Encourage a feeling of rapport, perhaps even something akin to family, among your students.

A weekly group discussion facilitated by an experienced, capable, and caring counselor — or by the teacher — can be an important part of a parenting course. While problems cannot be scheduled, if students know there is a designated period specifically for group discussion of personal issues, they may be better able to concentrate on parenting topics during the remaining class sessions.

Some schools have a brief advisory period each morning. If your advisory group is made up of teen parents, you may find this is the best time for student sharing.

Bonnie Thompson, a GRADS teacher in Middletown, Ohio, shared a strategy she uses regularly for group discussion and problem-solving. Thompson meets with her students daily, so students have ample time to cover the learning activities for the competencies.

On Fridays, students who have completed their lessons for the week may do hands-on activities, such as making things for the homeless shelter or for their babies. The students sit around a table and work together. "More group discussion happens on Fridays than any other day. Generally, I learn more about my students than at any other time, and I find they help each other solve their problems," she explained.

Parenting Begins at Conception

While a young woman is pregnant she may find it difficult to look very far into the future, hard to imagine her baby becoming a toddler, then a preschooler. If she can learn about parenting during the early stages in a child's life, however, her child is more likely to have the good start so important for his development. The young father-to-be, too, needs to learn as much as possible about parenting his child.

Parenting begins at conception, and if she's newly pregnant, she may need most of all to talk about the decisions she's facing. Anyone talking with pregnant teens needs to be aware of their own biases. If you cannot discuss one or more of their options — adoption, parenting, abortion — in an unbiased fashion, be honest and suggest they talk with someone who can.

Both young parents may need help in dealing with their feelings. Even if the pregnancy was planned (not true for the majority of pregnant teens), the reality may be difficult to accept. Some teens try to ignore the pregnancy as long as possible. Others attempt to hide it. You can help them understand the importance of dealing with what has happened, making the necessary decisions, and changing their lifestyle as needed.

If she continues her pregnancy, she needs to see a health care provider immediately. If she can start to personalize her baby as a living person, she may be more determined to eat the foods she and the baby need, and to stay away from smoking, alcohol, and drugs. Encourage her to talk about her baby, and to know about its current stage of development.

If she's with the father of the baby, he can be part of her prenatal health plan. Perhaps he can go with her to the doctor. If he is attending a school with a teen parent program or a teen father group, he can enroll in or participate in his school's program. He can also model good nutrition and a healthy lifestyle. Producing a healthy baby is important to both parents.

> *I drink every once in awhile. But when Mitzuko got pregnant, and she couldn't drink, I wasn't going to drink around her. So I left it alone.*
>
> Maurice, 21, father of Lana, 14 months

Ask each of them to pretend to be the baby, and ask, "What does your baby want?" When teen parents can take the perspective of the baby, they may be more capable of making decisions based on protecting and nurturing their baby.

Students may be fascinated with fetal development, and this interest provides a good basis for prenatal care teaching. Ask them to draw pictures of their unborn baby at different stages of development. Suggest that students write a letter *from their child to themselves*. In the letter, ask the teens to pretend they are the unborn child. What do they want "mom" to do so they will have a healthy life before birth?

A pregnant teen is often uncomfortable. She's tired, she's sick in the morning, her back hurts, and she can't sleep well. While she's pregnant, she may find it difficult to envision her baby as a living person. At times, she may resent the baby. Her focus is more likely to be on the changes in her own body, and dealing with those changes may be as much as she can handle.

> *While I was pregnant, I was confused and depressed. I didn't like being pregnant. It was an awful experience for me. Just because I felt so fat, I thought my boyfriend didn't want to be with me. I thought he was there only because he felt sorry for me.*
>
> Frederica, pregnant at 15

You can help her deal with these discomforts through class discussion, reading assignments, and learning activities. Having a nurse on call is an asset. Guest speakers and a field trip to the local hospital to tour the labor and delivery facilities can add to your prenatal care unit.

Last Trimester Concerns

If she continues attending school throughout pregnancy, she is more likely to return after childbirth. Dropping out during pregnancy may result in long-term absence from school, possibly the end of her formal education during her teen years.

During her last trimester of pregnancy, pay particular attention to her attendance pattern. She's probably very tired, and may need special encouragement to continue her academic studies. Is she able to make arrangements with her other teachers to make up the class work she'll miss when she delivers? What does she need to do to obtain home instruction or tutoring for the weeks she will be absent? How can you help her with these processes?

During these last months, she needs to prepare for childbirth. Does she have a coach who will take the preparation classes with her? You need to know about the availability of low- or no-cost prepared childbirth classes to share with her. Private teachers may be quite expensive, but your adult school or local hospital may offer less costly classes. Some hospitals, health departments, or organizations sponsor free classes for school programs.

In the Teen Parent Program at Tracy High School, Cerritos, California, teen moms returning to class after delivery are designated "Queen for the Day" in their prepared childbirth class (physical education class for pregnant students). The new mothers share details of their labor and delivery with their classmates. Still-pregnant teens tend to lose some of their fears of childbirth as they listen. The new mothers often give great testimonials on the value of doing their prepared childbirth exercises.

Infant care is a crucial topic *before* delivery. If a son, will he be circumcised? Will the mother breast- or bottle-feed? She may not get much help with breastfeeding at the hospital. Your teaching about the value and techniques of breast-feeding may encourage her to give her baby this gift.

Many young mothers either already know or learn quickly how to feed, bathe, and diaper a baby. We need to teach the physical care of a baby, but we'll be more helpful if we spend much of our time discussing the emotional and psychological needs of children.

Some teen fathers, however, may have had less experience in the physical care of a baby. It's important to provide opportunities for them to learn these important skills. Otherwise, they and their partners may fall into the trap of assuming the mother is the expert, and, therefore, should take most responsibility for child care. When that happens, everyone loses — the baby most of all.

Before delivery is also a good time to discuss contraception. Don't assume all your students will be sexually active after delivery, but recognize that most will be at some point. Help them understand that a rapid subsequent birth to a teen often shows poorer health outcomes than the first birth. Because young parents love their babies and want the very best for them, the most compelling reason to discourage another pregnancy for at least three years may be that they will be able to give this baby better care.

Home Visits After Delivery

By visiting the student while she is in the hospital or, probably more important, after she comes home with the baby, you can help her get a good start with breast-feeding, newborn massage, and other adjustments to parenthood. Will other teachers in your school provide homework assignments for you to deliver?

This is an ideal time to offer special assignments on new baby care and for journal writing through this important period in her life. She's probably learning far more during this month after birth than she would in a semester of child care classes. Fitting her learning into credit earning is advantageous. *Nurturing Your Newborn: Young Parents' Guide to Baby's First Month* by Lindsay and Brunelli is designed especially for this postpartum homestay. The Workbook is available on disk in a personalized version in which you can insert the new baby's name, then print out worksheets which ask questions about her/his own baby, a nice incentive for a new mom or dad.

Whether it's postpartum depression or simple delight with the new baby, returning to school may be far from her mind during these first weeks. Knowing you care during this time may help her understand the importance of going back to school in spite of her added responsibilities. If she doesn't yet know who will care for the baby when she returns to school, perhaps you can help with her search.

Bonding between mother and baby is extremely important. A young mother who returns to school full-time only a couple of weeks after childbirth may achieve more at school, but she may not have time to bond well with her newborn. She may have to choose between adequate bonding with her baby and maintaining her credit at school. It's a dilemma, especially since some schools have a maximum number of days which may be missed without loss of credit. Work with your district to meet the needs of the young parents and their children.

If you have a child care center on campus and she is bringing her baby to school, perhaps she can spend extra time there during the first few weeks after she returns. Alternative school schedules are more likely to adapt to this plan. Or is a modified school schedule feasible? Perhaps shortened days or alternating days would work. Flexibility is the key, and in some schools, flexibility is difficult to achieve. Again, work with your school and district staff to meet your students' needs as much as possible.

Ann Terry, teen parenting director at Seguin High School, Seguin, Texas, described her school's flexibility on this issue. "Once the baby is delivered, the moms go on home-based instruction. They have a week off after delivery, then come to school two hours a day, two days a week. They may bring their baby. We have a waiver for the attendance requirements so they can see the home-based teacher at school instead of at their home. We find this keeps them in touch with school. Many bring their baby with them, and we can monitor their care-giving. It's cost-effective, and it works well for mother and baby."

About half the PEP programs in Texas follow this plan. Significantly fewer moms drop out after delivery as compared to those who stay home for their home-based teacher appointments.

The bond between a mother and her baby *and* between a father and his child is extremely important. A good child care center and a good parenting class can enhance that bond and, at the same time, help young parents become more knowledgeable about and more skillful at their parenting responsibilities.

Child Care Center — Lab for Parenting Class

Involve the young mothers and fathers in as many experiences with babies and toddlers as possible. If you have an infant center on your campus or nearby, you have a wonderful population to study. Make the most of this opportunity. Get your students involved in observing children and working directly with them.

Meri-lin MacGibbon, Putnam County Teen Parent Education Program, Palatka, Florida, explained, "In our parenting classes, we go into the child care center quite often for activities. I truly feel that kids need hands-on instruction in parenting. Having child care on site can sometimes be distracting, but I think it's real important. Talking about parenting can't be an academic thing — it has to involve the parents and babies together. We expect our child care workers to be informal teachers and role models. We offer training to each worker as she comes in, including techniques for working with teens."

If it's a good developmental center, your students may learn even more from the modeling of the caregivers than they do in your class. When a young mother sees a mature adult whom she likes and respects showing patience and loving concern for a two-year-old child in the middle of a temper tantrum, she may finally realize her own child is not being naughty when he does the same thing.

When the young father observes a caregiver pleasantly helping a young child learn how to use the bathroom (but not at a too-young stage), perhaps he will understand that this, too, can happen without a lot of frustration either for him or for his child.

While young parents will learn the most from studying the developmental stage of their own child, encourage them to observe and work with children at other stages, too. Today's mother or father of an infant will be dealing with a super-active toddler surprisingly soon. They need some preparation.

Collaboration between the parenting teacher and the child care center director is crucial, and Liz Irwin and Pat Guerra, Cal-SAFE Program at Valley View High School, Ontario, California, illustrate this concept. Irwin teaches the parenting class while Guerra runs the center. Both are in the parenting class every Monday.

"We call it Child Care Rap, and it gives Pat a chance to get information to the students and to hear from them without the distraction of the babies being present," Irwin commented. Guerra is an early childhood specialist; Irwin's training is in family living.

When Guerra started directing the center, it wasn't organized as a learning lab. She explained, "Teen parents were sitting around socializing, and I said I'd like to change that." She trained her staff, and they started encouraging the young parents to interact regularly with their babies. Each day the students are expected to carry out activities with their own child or with another baby.

"At first they resisted because they didn't think they wanted change," Guerra remembers. "I said, 'We'll do this slowly.' We had handouts for them, and we gave them a lot of support. We pointed out that they were already 'doing activities' when they talked with their babies or read to them." After each session in the center, each student writes down the activities she carried out with a child. Her credit and grade depend on completing a specified number of activities.

Alternatives for Hands-on Parenting Education

Many schools do not have on-site child care centers for hands-on parenting education. If your school is one of these, you need to determine other ways to provide this practical help for your students.

If there is a school policy of no babies/children on the campus, discuss possibilities with your school administrators. You will also need to work out transportation issues with the families of your students. Here are some possibilities:

One day each week, ask one or two students to bring their

similar-age children to your class. Give all students the opportunity during the school year to bring their children. Plan to observe children at a variety of ages and stages of development.

Partner with a nearby child care center for weekly or bi-weekly field trips. Work with the center director to write joint lesson plans for those days.

Have a bi-weekly or monthly group meeting of all parenting teens and their babies. This may need to take place after regular school hours. Your advisory committee or a community organization might make good partners in this venture. If you have a Parents as Teachers program in your district, the PAT parent educator would be an excellent partner. If you have enough partners in this venture, run a concurrent grandparent group while the teens and babies are meeting.

You'll find other approaches that work. When you do, make it a point to share your ideas with other teen parent program teachers.

Reality-Based Projects

Projects can be one of the most important parts of your parenting curriculum. If students only read and write about children at school, but don't interact with them, their learning is seriously lacking in reality. Your teen parent students have that important reality at home. Encourage as much involvement in relevant projects *with their children* as you can.

Most students retain more new information if they learn at least partly through activities. MacGibbon, quoted on page 127, stresses the value of hands-on-activities, partly because the teen parent program includes students with a wide range of skills. "I try to find at least one activity we can do together for each unit," she said. She described typical activities:

"Sanitation is an important goal. Students sometimes put the child's pacifier in their own mouth and say, 'We have the same germs.' Ask a biology teacher for an agar and petrie dish. Take samples from around the room and rub them across the agar, then tape it up so no one can touch it. Leave it in the room for two days, and bacteria will start growing.

"Your students will understand that there are lots of germs

Parent-Child Learning Activities

Parents of newborns

- Rock your baby for at least 15 minutes. If you don't have a rocking chair, can you borrow one? In your journal, describe your experience.
- Talk to your baby as you feed him. In your journal, comment on the experience.
- Choose a time when your baby is tired and fussy. Try several methods of soothing her.

4-8 months

- Hold your baby in front of a mirror. Describe her reactions, either in writing or orally to the class.
- If your baby is at least six months old, offer him some unsweetened Cheerios. Can s/he pick them up and put them in his/her mouth?

8-12 months

- Watch your baby for 15 minutes and list *all* the things the baby is curious about.
- Finger-paint with your baby.

1-2 years

- Make a book for your toddler using the words s/he knows. Read it to your child.
- Roll up two cotton socks into a ball. Play ball with your toddler.
- Describe three times you gave your toddler choices today. How did you feel about his/her choices?

2-3 years

- Ask your toddler to sort clothes or toys by color.
- Take child on an outing — to a train station or airport, to a park, to a petting farm, or for a walk along the beach or down the street. Describe the outing in your journal.
- Give your toddler a small pail of water and a paint brush. Suggest she paint the house. Watch her, then describe her actions in a colorful paragraph in your journal.

Excerpted from the *Teens Parenting* Workbooks.

everywhere. Remind them that they've had time to build resistance to some of those germs, but their babies haven't. And remember to dispose of these samples properly because they are considered bio-hazardous waste.

"Because hand washing is so important when you're working with babies and germs are impossible to see, I get a big mixing bowl and put flour in it. They stick their hands in the flour. Then I give instructions on washing their hands with soap and warm water so that they remove all the flour from under their rings, fingernails, etc.

"We make puzzles by gluing pictures to poster board. We cover this with clear contact paper, then cut into pieces and ex- plain how puzzles help their toddlers' intellectual development."

As you plan activities for your students, you have two pur- poses. You will find ways to reinforce learning of the topic cur- rently being studied. You will also assign projects which encour- age students to work with their own children. These projects need to be developmentally appropriate for the student's current stage of parenting. Projects for parents of infants would be quite different, for example, from projects for toddlers' parents.

A good parenting curriculum guide, especially if it is written for those working with teen parents, may provide a wealth of ideas for projects and group activities. See the appendix for information about the *Adolescent Parent Resource Guide, Teens Parenting Series Comprehensive Curriculum Notebooks,* and other resources.

Projects can be designed to encourage interaction between the student and his/her own child. The more interaction, the more likely the parenting will go well. They may learn as much about their child's development through playing a game together as they might from reading several pages in a textbook. Ideas for assignments which have been developed out of their lives and their experiences are almost always better than anything offered by someone else. See examples on the opposite page.

Case studies, preferably taken from students' actual experi- ences, can promote learning through discussion. So can readers theater, brain-storming, making baby food, sharing of discipline questions and solutions, role-playing, and other activities. See pages 84-85 for a sample of learning activities from the *Discipline from Birth to Three Comprehensive Curriculum Notebook.*

"My Child" Reports

A good on-going project is to ask each parent periodically to present an oral report on their child's development. Every other month, for example, assign a research project covering their own child. Ask them to do some extra reading on their child's current stage of development. Even more important, encourage them to observe their child closely for a few days. Being expected to take a few notes may make them more observant.

Tell a young father you would like him to report on the games he plays with his daughter, the pictures they look at together, her food likes and dislikes, her sleeping habits, and other daily activities. Ask the father to discuss his discipline strategies and his feelings about his child at this point.

You may have students who insist they "don't give oral reports." Explain that this is their chance to talk about their own babies for at least ten minutes without interruption. If a student is quite reluctant, ask her to report on one specific activity. If her son is eight months old, suggest she give him a container full of small, safe items from her kitchen. Tell her to watch him for 20 minutes, then share with the class his reactions to the play materials. She may find giving an oral report is not as big a problem as she expected.

Students' oral reports on their child's developmental stage is a wonderful way to teach developmental stages to the other students.

Sensitivity to Students' Needs

Sensitivity to students' needs is critical. For example, you may know that research "proves" that feeding solid food to an infant when he's two months old may cause food allergies and stomach upsets. He would probably be better off having only breastmilk or formula. But your student reports that she is feeding her two-month-old child cereal and fruit, and he's doing fine.

At the same time, however, she describes quite a lot of night crying. She adds that he seems constipated. How will you react?

You could say, "Well, of course you have problems. I told you you shouldn't feed that baby cereal while he's so young." But you won't say that. You know how insecure most new mothers feel, no matter what their age. You know that a sharp comment from you would only increase that insecurity.

You might say instead, "Most babies do better with only formula or breastmilk the first few months. Yours may be able to handle the solid food. However, you might try stopping the solid food for a couple of days and see if he sleeps better."

She may be willing to go along with your experiment. Or her reply may be, "My doctor told me to feed him cereal now," or "My mother puts the cereal in his bottle."

Your good judgment will determine whether it's wise to pursue the point. You might suggest that she check with her doctor again and describe the baby's reaction, or perhaps she could share informational materials with her mother. But if you continue to stress the problems associated with too-early feeding of solids, you're risking a break in her relationship with her doctor or, even more risky, with her mother. Besides, the baby may adjust to the solid food fairly soon.

It's a fine line between being sensitive to our students' needs and being so wishy-washy that they learn nothing from us. That fine line cannot be described adequately in words. Our sensitivity to our students makes the difference.

Assessing/Evaluating Progress in Parenting

Many teachers choose not to assess their students with traditional paper and pencil tests. How, then, do you assess competence in parenting skills? While there are some important parts of parenting that can never be assessed, many components can be with alternative methods. For descriptions of a variety of alternative assessments, see chapter 4.

Before students begin work on the tasks that will be assessed, it is critical that learning goals are clearly expressed and performance standards are set. We all find it difficult to perform at high levels when the criteria are unknown.

Some parenting practices are more skill-based than others,

Communicating with a Six-Month-Old Infant Assessment Rubric			
Rating	**3**	**2**	**1**
Criteria and Weighting			
Voice **X 2**	Sounds soft and pleasant; often fluctuates tone.	Sounds pleasant sometimes; sounds loud sometimes; fluctuates tone occasionally.	Sounds harsh or disinterested, often talks loudly; talks in a monotone.
Eye contact **X 1**	Has eye contact most of the time.	Has eye contact about half the time.	Has little eye contact.
Responsiveness to baby **X 3**	Listens to baby almost always; takes turns with baby regularly; responds to baby's attempts to engage in or to end a "conversation."	Listens to baby occasionally; takes turns sometimes; sometimes responds to baby's attempts to engage in or to end a "conversation."	Rarely listens to baby; talks all the time or not at all, with no turn-taking; usually ignores baby's attempts to engage in or to end a "conversation."
Words used **X 3**	Repeats baby's sounds and "words" most of the time; words seem very respectful and caring.	Repeats baby's sounds and "words" about half the time; some words seem respectful and caring.	Rarely repeats baby's sounds and "words"; words seem disrespectful and uncaring.
Total Points: _____ **(27 points possible)**			
Comments:			

such as bathing a baby. When teens are learning this skill, a checklist can help them plan and organize the baby's bath, and can also help them assess their skill development. A checklist identifies steps and processes involved, such as "lay out all needed items before beginning bath," "test water temperature," "ease baby gently into water," "wash face with separate cloth," "always attend to baby during bath," and so on. Students can work together in class to help develop checklists. Checklists can also be used by students and teacher together to assess students.

How do you assess parenting behaviors that are complex and more process-oriented, such as communicating with a six-month-old infant? One way to assess this parenting behavior is with a rubric. A rubric is a set of scoring guidelines — the standards for assigning scores to the student's "work." A scoring rubric consists of a *fixed scale* that describes the standards of performance, a list of *elements* (guidelines, rules, principles, products, performances, or responses) to be assessed, and *indicators/evidence* for each anchor (point) on the scale. See the example on the opposite page.

As always, sensitivity to your student's feelings is important. The "Communicating with a Six-Month-Old Infant" rubric provides the basis for a marvelous lesson, but you may prefer to assess the student's interaction with a child other than her/his own. You don't want to run any risk of interfering with the spontaneity between parent and child.

Rubrics are also good for self assessment. As with checklists, students can work together in class to help develop rubrics. Students need to have copies of rubrics up-front, as this helps them understand the performance standards. Assessment needs to be an integral part of the learning processes.

Teaching parenting to teenage parents is one of the most important tasks faced by those working with this special group. Teen parents who, in addition to continuing their education and obtaining job skills, become "good" parents are likely to have satisfying lives in spite of becoming "parents too soon."

Parenting education can help them achieve that goal.

"I'd like to be a good dad."

CHAPTER 7

Working with
Teen Dads

*A good dad is someone who takes time out of his life to
be there, to keep the family together, to be with the mom
and the baby, to play with them, just be a dad. I'd like to be
a good dad.*

Ray, 15 (Adonna, 16, six months pregnant)

School-age fathers may need your help as much as the young
mothers, and they , too, need your program. School-age fathers
complete an average of 1 1.3 years of school by age 27, compared
with nearly 13 years by their counterparts who delay fathering
until age 21. School programs for teen fathers help them stay in
school and develop job skills and career plans as well as encour -
age them to be truly involved in the life of their child.

School-age fathers are not well prepared to support their
young families or to pay child support. Employed teen fathers
earn an average of $4,732 less annually than 20- or 21-year -old
employed first-time fathers. Dropping out of school is not a

solution for school-age fathers, as this contributes to their lowered future ability to support their young families financially   , according to *Kids Having Kids*.

Self-Fulfilling Prophecy

Teen fathers face many challenges, and often experience much confusion. They are told to be responsible, and this usually translates into providing financial support. Financial support is only one aspect of being responsible. Just as important for the baby is the father   s active role in parenting.

Many teen fathers face extremely negative attitudes from those around them. His baby   s mother may not want anything to do with him. Her parents are even more likely to write him of   f as no good. The press portrays teen dads as uncaring guys out there ignoring their children, yet impregnating again and again.

Elijah, 19, commented:

> *I'm trying to change the stereotype of teenage fathers. It's like all fathers were never there. I feel my child didn't ask to be born. My child deserves a mother and a father, and the mother and father should be equal.*
>
> *I feel like if I laid down with her to make the baby, I should be there. I want to be there 100 percent for my child. I'm sick of everything being the mom and the baby in the media. I grew up with just my mom, and I don't want it to be like that.*
>
> *Spend time with your kid even if you don't have a dime in your pocket. Be there for your kid. Hug him. That's more important than anything.*

Evidence suggests that women who cannot parent their baby because someone else talked them into either abortion or adoption are likely to be pregnant again in a short time. Those who parent their children even as they continue school and job training are more likely to delay the next pregnancy until they're more ready.

We can anticipate a similar phenomenon among young fathers. If he isn't engaged in the life of his child, perhaps not even allowed to see that child, he may see no reason to avoid impregnating again. If he's not allowed to parent, creating a baby may seem unreal to him, something that has nothing to do with sex as he knows it.

What Can Teen Dads Offer?

Fathers and adolescent mothers are marrying at lower rates than ever before. Today, babies born to teenagers generally live with only one parent, usually the mother. Therefore, most teen fathers are non-custodial parents. Regardless of the custodial arrangement, both parents have important roles and responsibilities to fulfill. Babies, toddlers, and older children clearly benefit from the active involvement of both parents.

Of course, there are a few exceptions. For example, some mothers have misused drugs or alcohol during pregnancy, and continue to do so after the baby is born. Some mothers abuse their children. These mothers probably cannot provide healthy mothering. Similarly, some fathers behave irresponsibly or exhibit violent behavior or may be involved in gangs. These fathers often have difficulty providing healthy fathering.

Any decisions to exclude either birth parent from active parenting needs to be based on the best interests of the child. If there is no evidence that suggests a child is likely to be harmed by a relationship with either parent, then both parents should be encouraged and supported to actively parent their child.

Most teenage fathers cannot support their child(ren) financially. Often they are written off because they aren't acting "responsible." Is it possible that some 16-year-old fathers are pushed out of their child's life because they act like 16-year-olds?

> *The hard thing is you're still a kid. You can't deny it. You got yourself into this mess.*
>
> *I wish I had never had kids. There are a lot of things I'd like to be doing now, but I can't change what I've done. I have to deal with it even though sometimes I say, "This sucks." I see my friends who don't have kids, and I wish I were like them.*
>
> *Now I have to think about my baby when I'm walking on*

the street. It feels weird. Before, I didn't have anyone to
think about except me. Now I have to watch out for all
three of us. I was mostly raised to take care of myself. I
understood there wouldn't be anybody there to help me
out. Now I have to think of them. It's hard.

                                     Andy, 17, father of Gus, 5 months

A 16-year-old may have a lot to offer his child and the child's
mother. Both mother and child need emotional support. He can
help with the physical care of his child. Building a strong
relationship with his child is important to him and to his child.
Given the opportunity, many young fathers mature and rise to
the responsibility of caring for the new life they have created.
When dad is pushed out, everybody loses.

Joan Koch, GRADS teacher at D. Russel Lee Career Center,
Hamilton, Ohio, commented, "Teen dads often are a misunder-
stood group. They want to be involved in parenting even when
the relationship between the two parents disintegrates during
pregnancy. Many of the guys seem to be more in shock than
the girls.

"We had one dad who really wanted his child placed for
adoption, but the mother wanted to parent," she continued. "He
had no say about the matter, and was concerned about his child's
future. Soon after the baby was born, the mother married someone else, but the father is still paying child support. He's sad that
he has no contact with his child. We're encouraging him to get
legal assistance because he has a right to spend time with
his child."

Teen fathers generally hear a lot about their responsibilities,
but do they know their rights? Whether or not he is providing
financial support, he can spend time with his child unless a court
has removed that right. Some young fathers are not aware of this
right, partly because those around them may imply otherwise.

He has a right to be with his child, to build a relationship with
his child, and to find joy and identity in that relationship.
Chances are extremely good that he is more likely to be financially responsible later if he has bonded with this child. Experiencing the joys of parenting is a strong step toward handling

parental responsibilities.

He and the child's mother may not be married or living to-gether. They may not even be together as a couple, yet they are *both* parents of this child. Their child needs both of them. A young mother once said, "Don't tell your child his dad's a louse because that makes the kid half a louse." Simply put, if dad is pushed out of the picture, his child will suffer.

Some teen fathers resent the power young mothers seem to hold. Social services tend to discourage the participation of fathers. He may realize that from a realistic standpoint, his rights may vanish if he isn't wanted. If he understands his parenting options, however, he is more likely to tap into personal and community resources to gain skills, earn money, and become a responsible parent. The result will be a child less likely to be dependent on TANF (Temporary Assistance to Needy Families) for an extended period of time. Not only the child, the mother, and the father benefit — society as a whole wins when families are able to become financially independent.

Of course teen fathers have legal responsibilities. These responsibilities vary by state, so you need to be aware of your state's parentage laws. Generally, the father cannot escape the responsibility of child support/paternity by claiming to be a minor. Paternity tests are nearly 100 percent accurate. They can be expensive, although the cost is going down. The male may be required to pay the cost.

Once paternity is established, child support may be court ordered, and that order may include back child support. In some states, the parents of a minor father (under age 18) can be ordered to pay support.

Help from School Program

The father's needs are similar to the mother's. In the past, we focused on parenting skills for mothers and job skills for fathers. No longer is this a reasonable plan. Mothers need job skills as much as fathers — and fathers need parenting skills as much as mothers. No longer can we afford the goal of the dad out making the living while mom takes care of the children. The majority of mothers, even in two-parent families, will need to work at paying jobs. And certainly we realize now how important it is for the father to be deeply involved in parenting.

Ruth Frankey, GRADS teacher at D. Russel Lee Career Center, Hamilton, Ohio, stressed the need for father-friendly curriculum such as *Teen Dads: Rights, Responsibilities and Joys* by Lindsay (2001). "The guys that are coming to the class really want to be involved," she commented. "Sometimes the father denies the baby is his, which I think is simply part of the denial process, just as she denies she is pregnant for as long as possible. Sometimes he comes back after the baby is born and gets involved with his child."

Encourage teen fathers to participate in teen parent classes. Those who do are likely to become much more effective parents.

You start out by assuming he is a good person, just as you start out assuming the teen moms in your program are good people. The extent to which young parents of both genders live up (or down) to our expectations is an amazing phenomenon. A 16-year-old father who feels pushed away from his child and thinks everyone considers him irresponsible and uncaring is likely to *be* irresponsible and uncaring. The 16-year-old father who is encouraged to learn the art and skills of parenting and to participate in his child's life is likely to become more responsible and to be willing to demonstrate his love for his child.

Because of the poor reputation teen fathers often have, you may have to work harder at recruiting them. If most of your teen mom students' partners are not at your school, it doesn't necessarily mean there are no teen dads on campus. Julie Vetica, former teacher of the School-Age Mothers (SAM) program at El Camino High School, Norwalk, California, developed a two-week unit for teen fathers, and decided she would offer it to all teen dads at her alternative school. She told all staff and students that this would be a two-week course, and that teen dads would be pulled out of another class to attend. Within two days, she had 14 teen fathers enrolled in the class, yet *none* were fathers of the babies in the child care center or partners of any of the young mothers enrolled. Their babies and the babies' mothers were somewhere else, either at another school, or not in school at all.

When you look for teen fathers in your school, don't focus

only on the fathers of the babies born to your female students.
There probably are others.

Working with Teen Fathers

A teen father may have various motives for being a part of a
teen parent class . . . or he may not want anything to do with it.
He may have a genuine desire to learn and to be an active part of
his child's life. You may find some of your best students are
male. You may hear, "I never knew my father, and that will
never happen to a child of mine. I want to do everything I can to
be the best father." Don't underestimate this motivation.

In addition to teaching the dads how to handle and care for a
baby and how to read the baby's signs, Joan Koch, quoted
earlier, provides a place where someone listens. "We help them
evaluate the messages they are sending. Do you really want this
macho image? What kind of life do you want for your child?
What are some things you'll have to do to make that happen?"

Sometimes a teen father's motives for being in class may not
be so laudable. He may view his pregnant girlfriend as his
possession and enroll in the class to check on her. This domina-
tion is likely to become unbearable for the young woman, and
may be disruptive to your class.

You may have a "Nick" in your class. Nick felt it was completely his girlfriend Debbie's duty to raise their child, while he
continued to play football, go to parties, flirt with other girls, and
do as he wished. After about eight months, Debbie had had
enough. She started to date someone else.

Nick was upset when he came to see the teen parent teacher.
He wondered how Debbie could do that to him when they had
a child.

The teacher talked with him privately, pointing out some
previous events. Nick kept replying, "That was nothing and she
knew it." The teacher decided Nick needed to get a male perspective, so she arranged for him to talk to a male teacher whose
judgment she trusted, and whom Nick really liked. Gradually
Nick gained understanding of Debbie's needs and feelings.

At times, teachers report problems with teen couples being
together in a parenting class. At other times, they find couples

working well together. Ideally, the parents will learn together, but teen relationships are not always positive. Teachers report problems sometimes develop if the young father focuses on a different girl, or the mother decides not to let him be involved with their baby. If you have two parenting classes, you can avoid some of these problems by enrolling the baby's two parents in different classes. Make these decisions individually for each parenting couple. Just as we don't generalize about "all" teen parents, neither should we generalize about relationships among students.

Some teen parents may change partners often. The young parents, particularly the young mothers who typically are the custodial parents, may be eager to engage their current partners as parenting partners. You may be asked if the new partner can enroll in your program. We suggest that you consider each request carefully. It's not healthy for children to have "parents" who come and go quickly, and it's not even healthy for your program to have students' partners come and go frequently.

Sheila Maggard, GRADS teacher, Ohio Valley Vocational School, West Union, Ohio, stresses the importance of the father's involvement in his child's development. "During pregnancy, the attention tends to go to the girls, but I tell them I have had some student couples where the guy seems to be the better parent. I tell both the fathers and mothers that they are their child's first teacher, and how important it is for dad to be involved, too, even if he and mom are not together any more." Maggard also makes a point of talking with the male teachers at her school, emphasizing the need for the teen father's involvement with the child.

Eleven percent of the GRADS students in Ohio are fathers. In Texas, Sue Kaulfus, former PEP Program Specialist, state of Texas, reports that ten percent of the PEP students are fathers. "It's been a real slow process, getting them pulled in, but it's picking up each year now," she reported.

Discipline Important to Dads

You are likely to find teen fathers concerned about disciplining their children, yet unaware of gentle ways to teach babies and toddlers. You can help them understand that spanking simply doesn't work well as a method of teaching children to behave as their parents wish. Your role is to help your students learn methods of discipline that work much better than spanking or hitting. Jimmy, 17, father of one-year-old Roman, attended a class in which he had a chance to discuss discipline methods. He commented:

> *You know how parents yell and say you can't do this and you can't do that? I don't want to yell or hit my son because I don't think that teaches you anything. When I was little, I got hit. It didn't teach me nothing. If you get hit all the time, pretty soon it don't hurt no more.*
>
> *If he does real bad, I don't blow my top. I think about it first, then talk about it with him, and tell him why he shouldn't do this. When he's a baby, there's no way he should be punished.*

Greg, 17, also the father of a one-year-old, warned against harsh discipline:

> *Males tend to be more aggressive, and around children you need to deal with this. Children don't need this.*
>
> *How do you deal with the frustrations and angers of parenting? Take time out. If you need a break, find someone else to hold your child for a little while. Let things simmer down a bit, and avoid thinking it's a power struggle.*
>
> *It's not a power struggle with the child. He's just exploring his world, testing his boundaries, learning what he can get away with. He doesn't do this to anger or upset you.*

Teen Dads Meet Weekly

Emily Runion, counselor, Washington Alternative High School, Terre Haute, Indiana, is seeing more teen dads than in the past. "They want to be 16 but at the same time, they have this panic that they want to be the dad. They face medical expenses now. In just a few years they will be going to school meetings for their child. They need information to make responsible decisions and support in their struggles to grow up quickly."

As a result of Runion's concern, the Teen Dads Program was started several years ago at Washington High. Through a state grant and additional help from March of Dimes, the group meets weekly under the leadership of Mike Trover, Family Service Association. Trover commented, "Teen dads face the typical stereotype — those guys that get the girls pregnant and then leave them high and dry. I encourage the guys to demonstrate how wrong these people are. They can still be responsible and fulfill their obligations. Most of the young men in my group are constantly in contact with the mothers and their children," he said.

"Primarily this is a processing group where we personalize our discussion topics as much as possible. We have an agenda, but I keep it loosely structured because they always have things they bring with them," he explained.

Trover sees the dads as a neglected population. "I think back to my athletic days when being a team player was all-important," he said. "A team is only as strong as its members, and if you don't have strong team members, you miss a lot. If you overlook the father, you give up a lot of strength and possibilities for the family.

"Some mothers say, 'I don't like him and I don't want my child to know him.' But fathers do have rights. Several fathers in my groups have split with their child's mother but are still assuming responsibility for their child," he concluded.

You'll probably find that many of the school-age fathers of your female students' babies are not enrolled at your school. Some of these young men are likely to need extra support, too. Some teachers organize a weekly support group for the out-of-school fathers of their students' children. Jackie Silver, continuing education, Rochester, Minnesota, realized her teen mom students were often commenting, "He's saying . . ." or "He doesn't understand this . . ."

"We didn't want to be the intermediary," Silver observed. So she sent an invitation through the mom to the dad. She explained that his baby's mom was getting a lot of information on parenting, and asked if he would like to get some of that information. She then listed possible topics. Several young men returned the brief questionnaire, indicating an interest in meeting. The result was a series of meetings on Thursday nights led by the school social worker and a male co-leader. Sometimes the whole group meets together, and sometimes the fathers meet in one room, the mothers in another.

Adult Fathers/Teen Mothers

Young males are only about one-third as likely as females to become school-age parents. Fewer than 60,000 males age 17 and younger annually father children for the first time, compared to 175,000 females age 17 and younger. This means, of course, that the fathers of babies born to teenage mothers are generally older than the young mothers. Fathers, on average, are 21/2 years older than the teen mother, and 20 percent are at least 6 years older, according to *Kids Having Kids*. Generally, the younger the mother, the greater the age difference between the two parents.

The fact that a significant number of the fathers of your students' babies are adult men doesn't change the realities of those who are teen fathers. Your school program is not designed for older fathers or older mothers. It is designed for school-age parents, both mothers and fathers. You truly can make a difference in the lives of teen fathers as well as teen mothers . . . and in doing so, you'll make a difference in the lives of their children.

> *Fathers need to get into classes like this so they can really know about the baby. Some men, when they find out she's pregnant, leave because they don't know nothing about it. If they learn what it's like, they're more likely to stay.*
>
> *This baby will be part of your life until you die, and you need to know what you're doing.*
>
> Agie, 18, father of Mia, 1 month

For help in developing comprehensive services for young fathers, see *ROAD to Fatherhood: How to Help Young Dads Become Loving and Responsible Parents* by Jon Morris (Morning Glory Press, 2002). (See Bibliography.)

Child care is critical if young parents are to continue in school.

CHAPTER 8

Caring
for the Children

Lack of child care is a major barrier to young parents completing their education. Most of us, who have children in our 20s and 30s, have trouble finding quality child care. Getting ourselves and our children to the child care provider on our way to work is *not* easy. For a 15-year-old trying to continue her/his education, it can seem insurmountable.

Some teens have a family member who will care for the child while the young parent goes to school, and the teen parent may feel this is a good solution. The teen trusts grandma or auntie with the baby. In fact, many teen parents say they could never leave their child with strangers, or with anyone other than family.

On the other hand, if grandma takes care of the baby all day, she may feel she's in charge, and the teen mother (or father) doesn't get a chance to parent. Over time, particularly after a "honeymoon" period with a newborn in the house, this arrangement may not work so well.

Many teen parents, moreover, don't have the choice of leaving baby with grandma. Grandma is working, and so is everyone else in the family. Will the teen parent then drop out of school? If there is no child care, there may be no other choice. If we truly want teen parents to continue their education, we must address the issue of child care. Without child care, we are back to the old practice of teen parents quitting school.

"Making It Too Easy"

You may find community attitudes to be punitive and judgmental. If you provide child care, you may be accused of "making things easy for those girls." People sometimes say having child care on campus will make other students want to get pregnant. This is likely to be the case only for those already at high risk for becoming teen parents. Child care on campus, complete with crying babies, dirty diapers, and lots of work, is more likely to help many non-parent students understand some of the difficult realities of parenthood and serve as a deterrent.

Has someone said schools should not be in the social service business? Well, schools *are* in the business of educating young people, and child care for students' children may be necessary in order for the young parents to be educated. Help your community understand that support services including child care can help delay additional pregnancies, provide critical parenting education, and make it possible for young parents to become job-ready.

> *I'd been out of school for two years. I saw something at the store about this school for teen parents. I wrote down the number, went home, and called. I'm back in school now, and they take care of my kids.*
>
> *I need an education for my kids so I can get a good job. If my kids want to ask me something, I want to be able to answer them. I want the best for them. My husband wants me in school, too.*
>
> Sharon, 18, mother of Ricardo, 3, and Monique, 1

School principals tend to have more independence and control than they used to, according to Max Schilling, former Teenage

Parent Program Specialist, Department of Education, Florida. "If they want child care on campus and they're getting a little heat from the community, they know that dies down after awhile," he pointed out. "A lot of times you take some flack from a few rabble rousers, but in time people accept it. Some principals who can't handle the idea of child care on campus are agreeable to having a program for student parents with the child care across the street from the school or a mile away."

If your district does not have a child care center for students' children, do all you can to start a center. In the meantime, are certified family day care services available near your schools? Perhaps school personnel or a community group could provide leadership in making services available to school-age parents.

High quality, developmentally appropriate care for infants is expensive. The staff ratio may be as high as one adult per three or four babies. In fact, one caregiver per two babies is often needed. This is the time child care is most necessary for young parents, but when money is scarce, it is difficult for a district to be far-sighted enough to provide the funding now for projects which may not show cost-effectiveness for several years. Nevertheless, it is more cost-effective for schools to provide quality early care and education for the young children of teen parents than fund remedial education during their school tenure.

Schools wishing to provide child care may be too crowded already. If space is available, funds are needed for renovation. Child care requires a specialized facility with two sinks in the room (one for food, one for the diaper-changing area), fenced play yard adjacent to the child care room, fire doors, and other standard features to meet licensure requirements. Temporary buildings, often called portables or relocatable classrooms, are sometimes used on or near school grounds.

The vast majority of teen parents in the United States cannot pay full fees for child care. Many can pay practically nothing. Most of the cost of child care must be covered by other sources.

Providing a developmental child care center for students' babies and toddlers is, in the long run, truly cost-effective. Young parents who are able to continue their education and become job-ready will soon repay to society, through their taxes,

the cost of the child care services which made their continued
education possible. A fiscally conservative community should
respond quickly to the needs of these young people.

Child care centers generally seek multiple funding sources to
maintain their programs. Possible sources include federal
programs, state agencies, local school districts, local agencies
and organizations, foundations, businesses, grants, and personal
donations. See chapter 13 for more specific suggestions
for funding.

Topeka, Kansas — One Model

An example of collaboration among community resources is
the Parent-Child Learning Centers (PCLC) of Topeka, Kansas.
According to Linda Weidner of Catholic Social Service, United
Way of Greater Topeka was the organizing force that pulled several community groups together to discuss community concern
about early childbearing and the related school dropout issue.

Kansas Social and Rehabilitation Services (KSRS), Job
Training Partnership Act, Topeka Community Foundation,
Catholic Social Service, Topeka Day Care, Inc., Grace Episcopal
Cathedral, Highland Park United Methodist Church, and Topeka
Public Schools formed a partnership to develop a program. A
plan evolved that was modeled after a successful program at the
Alternative Education Center in Topeka.

In the fall of 1991, the first Parent-Child Learning Center
opened at Grace Episcopal Cathedral (located adjacent to Topeka
High School). It was licensed to care for nine infants (birth to
one year) of Topeka High students. A second center opened at
Highland Park United Methodist Church in January, 1992. It was
licensed for eight infants and was located a few blocks from
Highland Park High School.

Programs at the centers are similar. Components include child
care (provided by Topeka Day Care, Inc.), parenting education
(provided by a teacher from the Topeka Public Schools), and
counseling (by a social worker from Catholic Social Service).
Services are aimed toward keeping teen parents in school,
promoting successful school experiences, and enhancing
parenting abilities. In the fall of 1992, the Topeka High site

expanded to provide care for ten toddlers (ages 1-2½ years).

Aspects of PCLC that have been particularly successful include the requirement that teen parents using child care services must spend at least one hour of their school day as a child development or lab student at the center. They receive school credit for doing so, plus have opportunities to interact with their child, observe behavior of other children, and learn new ways of responding to children.

Students at both high schools who are not utilizing child care, but have an interest in children, may also enroll as lab students.

In 1996, an outreach component was added to the PCLC program. This enables a counselor to provide support, information, and referral to expectant or parent students (male or female) attending school, but not directly involved with center services.

Representatives from the organizing agencies meet monthly to review program progress, discuss issues needing attention, and to plan. Student representatives have been invited to take part in these meetings to share their views, give suggestions, and make the group aware of any concerns. Students attending have spoken positively about the program services and staff, according to Weidner. They particularly like spending time during each school day with their infant or toddler, and feel they are learning a great deal about parenting in the time spent with program staff.

Along with successes, difficulties have also surfaced. Because infant and toddler care is expensive, balancing the child care budget is a challenge. Another issue, Weidner pointed out, is the general instability of the population being served. Attendance and behavioral difficulties at school, interpersonal problems in and out of school, and a tendency to consider, if not act on, dropping out of school occur. Almost daily these and other concerns are addressed by PCLC team members who continually develop their knowledge and experience to improve the program.

During the first five years of operation, 135 parenting students were served, and 45 are known to have graduated. Successful semester completion rates (student passes five or more classes) range from 70 to 83 percent. Without the support of a program such as the Parent-Child Learning Center, that may not have happened.

Advantages of School-Based Child Care

Those first two or three years of life are critical in terms of child development. Because they are in a pre-verbal stage, babies and toddlers can't ask questions. Putting them in poor quality child care is a detriment that they carry for the rest of their lives, and a missed opportunity for us. Our most vulnerable population needs the best we can provide.

Child care centers are state or county regulated, and regulations can change. In some states, the child care center licensure laws are different for centers housed in schools than for centers in other locations.

Contact your state's office that licenses child care centers and ask for current guidelines and regulations. Whether you are teaching in the child care center, hoping to start a center, or are teaching young parents who are consumers of child care, it is important to know the regulations under which centers operate. Student parents also need to be aware of these regulations.

School-based child care is often the best solution to the problem of caring for students' children while they attend class. School-based doesn't necessarily mean the school district supports the child care center by itself, however. Many centers are formed through collaboration with churches, girls' clubs, YWCA, YMCA, Healthy Start, Even Start, and other community groups. A service organization might provide scholarships for child care for students' children.

A good developmental child care center on campus offers several distinct advantages. First, of course, it makes it possible for young parents to continue their education and to obtain the job skills they need to become productive citizens.

Second, working in the center with their own child and taking parenting classes helps the young parents learn the parenting skills so important for the child's optimal development.

Third, the babies and toddlers in a good developmental center are generally ahead of their stay-at-home peers in social, emotional, and intellectual development. Illustrating this concept are a number of research projects which have focused on long-term benefits to children who receive high-quality child care during their early years.

There are additional advantages of child care on campus. Staff works mainly with teen parents, perhaps exclusively. They are more likely to understand the unique characteristics and needs of teen parents, and may interact more effectively with them.

In many programs, teen parents can interact with or feed their child. This helps promote the parent/child bonding process.

Children can be observed regularly for development, and staff will discuss these observations with the parents. The daily sign-in chart also offers space for messages between staff and parents.

The child care center lab is the ideal place to model and teach parenting skills.

According to Ann Durusky, New Mexico GRADS co-director, state funding for child care centers in schools is being considered, but the centers must meet multiple educational needs of many students. "The centers need to serve the children of teen parents. The centers also need to serve as a learning laboratory for the teen parent students, students enrolled in parenting classes who are not parents, and the occupational child care students. We need to use these child care centers to meet the needs of as many students as we can."

Establishing Trust in Child Care Workers

Lack of trust in non-family care of the baby sometimes keeps a teen parent from utilizing school-based care — even if this means s/he will attend school irregularly or perhaps drop out. Pat Guerra, director of the child care center at Valley View High School, Ontario, California, stressed the importance of pregnant students working in the child care center in order to get a feel for the care provided.

"First of all," she explained, "they come in and they see what the center is all about. They see it is a great place for their kids. They see how much the staff cares. They pick up techniques of calming a crying baby before they have one. They get great educational experiences before the baby comes. When they get to know us, they decide they want their baby in the center. There are usually one or two new moms a year who are a little wary — I tell them they can come in any time. 'Come in and touch your baby, play with your baby whenever you want.'"

Special Training for Staff

The extra needs of teen parents and their children sometimes seem overwhelming to child care workers. Teen parents are still adolescents. They may exhibit the erratic behavior typical of this developmental stage. They may not always act responsibly. In fact, they may often act like teenagers! Staff members need to be reminded of these facts. It is easy to think that because teens are parents, they should act like mature adults. But it doesn't work that way. You will have high expectations for your students, but you will also understand that they will not always be able to live up to those expectations. Training in adolescent lifestyle and developmental issues is critical for the child care staff.

People tend to think of teen parents as bad parents. Rather, they are parents who need support for their own development, including handling their own feelings. Too often we ignore the grief they are experiencing with the loss of their own childhood. These are important years the parent has lost.

The modeling in the center is extremely important. The staff needs to be vigilant with their words and actions. If a staff member becomes concerned, the concern needs to be expressed without becoming critical or condescending. The staff needs to guide young parents gently yet firmly. Direct criticism is likely to draw a defensive response from the teen.

Combined professional development meetings can be valuable for center staff and program teachers. They can exchange ideas and expertise. Often child care teachers and aides are underpaid, and it is important to treat them as the competent people they are.

Everyone who works with teen parents in the child care center needs to cultivate ample doses of respect for the adult role the young parents have tackled. Becky Roth, infant/toddler supervisor, Taft (California) Infant Center, explained, "They are kids, but they have also taken on a whole new role as parents. I think sometimes people overlook that they are playing an adult role.

"There's a fine line," she continued, "between mothering them, which is what they sometimes want, but not doing too much of it. They like to be helpful and respected. I find it works well to say, 'You know, you did a great job yesterday, and I really need your help again to get this job done.' They respond so much better if they know they are a vital part of the program rather than just being told what to do."

Staffing the child care center adequately without expensive overstaffing is difficult, given the attendance pattern of many teen parents. The Carlsbad, New Mexico, AWARE program has a full-time minimum staff supplemented with "regular" substitutes. One sub is available Mondays and Wednesdays, another Tuesdays and Thursdays, and the third on Fridays. Each has agreed to be available until 9 a.m. At that time they call the center to ask if they are needed. "By then we know if we need them," Susan Siepel, executive director, explained. "This has solved an enormous problem for us, and it gives the individuals flexibility in planning their own activities. It also provides more consistency in child care than we had when we called whichever sub happened to be available."

Establishing Guidelines

Often, staff members find they need to develop written guidelines for center use. The handbooks that contain the written guidelines are given to the parents when they enroll their children. The handbook is important — it provides needed structure for the teens. It also supports the smooth operation of the center. See *Organizing TAPP* for a sample child care center handbook.

Many types of rules and guidelines are best put in writing. Many centers include the child care philosophy, detailed guidelines of health care policies, parents' daily responsibilities, and center visitation. General information includes ages of children served, hours of operation, importance of calling the center when the child will be absent, and names of those who can pick up the child from the center. Also included should be procedures to follow when someone other than the custodial parent will pick up the child. Describe the policy for sharing caregiving information with the staff (such as daily caregiving forms).

Other policies or guidelines to consider, which may or may not be written in the center handbook, are attendance policies for both parent and child, payment procedures, and allowable discipline techniques. For example, one rule probably is "No hitting." If the parents think a spanking or hand slapping is in order, they need to understand it can't happen at the center. At the same time, you help the parents find other ways to deal with anger, other ways to control the child without hitting him/her. Usually, the parents will follow your suggestions because they want to parent in a healthy way.

One more word of caution. State laws that govern child care licensure can be very strict and prescriptive, to protect children. Many states require child care workers and volunteers to submit to a background check to ensure that those who work directly with children have not been convicted of felonies. Students who work in child care centers can be considered by state law to be volunteers. You need to inquire locally with the agency that is responsible for licensure of child care facilities to learn whether background checks of student volunteers are required.

Many of your students will be minors, and any felony records they might have may be sealed. If you ask for a background check, you may receive nothing back from the courts, but this does not totally absolve you of responsibility. If you happen to know, by other means, that a particular student has been convicted of a felony, particularly if the felony is a sexual offense, you have the responsibility to counsel that particular student *not* to volunteer in your child care center. Your other responsibility is to make sure that volunteers are never alone with the children in the center's care, as you are liable for the children in your center.

Certified Home Care Providers

Child care at school offers many advantages — if students can get their children there. If transportation is not available, finding certified day care homes in their neighborhoods may be more feasible. If your students rely on day care homes, a teen parent program staff member could be in charge of contracting with the homes. The staff person could also monitor the homes through visits to see that the quality of child care is optimal.

Family day care is more likely to be available for infants, and it tends to be less expensive than child care centers. Still, the cost may be more than the teen parent can afford.

Too often family day care homes are not licensed, and the

quality of the care given to the children may not be high. Some
home providers feel they cannot afford to pay the fees necessary
for certification. Some schools work with family day care
providers, offering training and on-site visits to improve the
quality of care.

Transportation Issues

Child care opportunities may not be workable because of
transportation problems. How do the teen parent and baby get
there? Is there public transportation? It takes a strong parent to
take a stroller, diaper bag, other baby paraphernalia, and school
books, plus the baby, on a crowded city bus. Whether it's a
school or public bus, the teen parent may have to walk several
blocks to the bus stop. In nice weather, it's hard. In bad weather,
the young parent may decide it's too much, and stay home.

Is subsidized transportation available? In some cities with a
good public transportation system, teens may qualify for free or
reduced rate bus or subway tokens or passes. If your school
doesn't offer transportation to teen parents, look for help.
Perhaps you can find a community group or a church that would
offer the use of a van to transport teen parents and their children
to school and child care. Will a local taxicab company donate
services at low or no cost? Does your Department of Parks and
Recreation have a van that could be used?

In many areas, public transportation is not an option, and the
school may be reluctant to have infants on their buses. Some
districts have a van outfitted with infant seats and seat belts.
Others have seats on regular school buses equipped with seat
belts, and the teens must have their own infant seats.

Florida has blazed the trail for other states by mandating that
home to school transportation be provided for the teen parent of
a child enrolled in child care. If child care is not at the parent's
school, this means picking parent and baby up at home, taking
them to the child care location, then taking the parent to school.

Overcoming Community Disapproval

Several years ago fifteen teen mothers at Stonewall Jackson
High School, Manassa, Virginia, decided they needed on-site

child care for their children. They wrote a petition to the administration. They explained their need for an education, and their
difficulties in providing for their children while they attended
classes. They pointed out that child care on campus would
enable them to perform better at school and, perhaps even more
important, parents who had dropped out of school because of
lack of child care could return.

The petition bombed. People scoffed at the idea of bringing
babies to school.

The district was already offering a program for pregnant teens
at an alternative school. After the teen mothers delivered,
however, at least 60 percent dropped out of school.

A year later a new principal arrived, *someone willing to take
risks*, according to Gretchen Almstead, work and family studies
teacher. The new principal wanted to reduce the dropout rate in
the district, and he realized that having a child was a major
reason for dropping out. He asked Almstead to develop a plan
that would provide child care and teach parenting skills.

Almstead called programs in several states and nearby
Washington, D.C., and learned about various approaches to child
care in the schools. "I read a lot, too," she said, "and I put
together a plan for what I thought would work at our school. I
saw two big needs — a need to help teen parents stay in school,
and the need for an occupational child care training program. I
wanted to merge the needs."

Almstead's program is now a GRADS class. Half of those
enrolled are teen parents and the others are students who want a
career in child care. All teen parents with a baby in the child care
center must take the class and must work another period in the
center. "We call it the GRADS practicum, and we treat it like a
job," she explained.

In addition, the students pay $100 a month for the child care.
"Originally I needed to design this program so it would cost the
school scarcely any extra money," Almstead said. "I figured if
we had twelve children and charged $100/month we would be
paying the salary of the one person hired to be there."

The district is mostly middle-class although it contains some
subsidized housing areas. While the fee may keep some young

mothers away, Almstead says attendance is probably better
simply because of the psychology of "getting what you pay for."

"A big issue here is public approval," Almstead pointed out.
"Child care on campus seldom happens around here, and the
community has a hard time seeing strollers at school. They
needed to think students were paying their way. When people
realize teen moms have to pay a fee, they have to work in the
center, and they have to take the class, the disapproval pretty
much goes away."

Part of the cost of the center is covered by donations from
individuals, churches, and service organizations. Almstead
speaks frequently to civic groups, and several have continued to
support the center. One church donates $500 a year, and a
women's group takes up a monthly collection of needed items
such as cleaning supplies, to donate to the center. Almstead stays
in close touch with the organizations through writing to them and
speaking at their meetings. Supportive churches and civic groups
are also represented on the program's advisory board.

Helping Students Locate Child Care

Provide as much child care information to your students as
you can. Many teen parents don't know about child care options
in their community. Depending on their income, free or subsidized child care may be available. One of your most important
tasks as a teen parent teacher is to become well informed on
local child care options. Even if you have a child care center at a
school, you will have students who are not able or don't choose
to enroll their children in the center. As you are researching child
care opportunities, always ask if the care is available for infants.
Many child care centers take only toilet-trained children, and a
teen parent can't wait that long to get back to school.

Find out about child care available at your school, and about
child care centers and certified family day care providers near
the school. Also ask about their policy on sick babies. Generally,
centers cannot accept children who are ill. Home care providers
are more likely to accept a child with a cold or slight fever. You
might also check with a local children's hospital. Occasionally
a hospital, when beds are empty, is willing to accept, at a

reasonable fee, an ill child during the day while the parent attends school.

Where can teens call for help? Your local Department of Social Services or Resource and Referral Agency may have child care referral listings. These agencies can also tell you whether they offer financial assistance for child care. Learn about other financial assistance available to teen parents needing child care, such as social services, churches, and community groups. Also check on transportation assistance.

In Massachusetts, the Child Care Resource Agencies determine the child care eligibility of teen parents who do not receive public aid from TANF. The Ohio Child Care Resource and Referral Network (CCR&R) has a database in all regions that assists families in their search for child care information. Each CCR&R region offers training for child care providers, and in many communities, CCR&R agencies have developed new collaborations combining Head Start, schools, and child care programs. Your state may have a similar child care resource listing.

The Internet can provide help in searching for child care possibilities. See discussion beginning on page 58.

Teen parents qualifying for subsidized child care cannot apply if they don't know about it. Make sure the information is easily available to students. Preparing a list of child care resources may take only a few phone calls, but it can be a tremendous help to teen parents who find social service calls frustrating.

Bringing Baby to Class

Some schools with separate teen parent classrooms allow young parents to bring their babies to class with them. At the Tracy Teen Parent Program, Cerritos, California, this practice was started when the school's infant/toddler center had no space for the new babies. The TPP teachers and the infant center staff agreed that students should wait until their babies were a month old before exposing them to the classroom environment. At that point, the young mom could bring baby with her to the self-contained classroom.

In addition to establishing guidelines for sanitation, the staff requires young parents to care only for their own babies, i.e., students do not handle other babies in this setting. Generally, space is available in the infant center by the time the child is two or three months old.

Parent Is Child's Advocate

Finding quality child care is difficult for most parents. For teen parents, it may be even harder to be assertive in asking questions and checking out possibilities. You and your students can use a variety of reliable resources to help you develop a list of characteristics of high quality child care. Contact the National Association for the Education of Young Children for a brochure on this issue. See the appendix for address.

The parent *must* be the advocate for the child. This is one of the most important things you can teach. If *your* child is a student in a classroom and you think something is happening that is detrimental to your child, you get over there and you do what you need to do to make it right. This needs to be true of young parents, too. If they feel they have a problem with the quality of their child's care, they need to express the problem and help work it out.

Sally McCullough, former director of the Tracy Infant Center, was very clear on this issue. If a teen mom complained to the parenting teacher about an occurrence in the Infant Center, the parenting teacher was to suggest strongly that the young mother talk the problem over with McCullough. "The mother has to be the baby's advocate," she said.

If you are the parenting teacher, you probably realize that an excellent pool of guest speakers is composed of staff members from the child care center. A center teacher brought an 18-month-old boy to our class once. Class members sat on the floor in a circle four or five feet away from the teacher and the child while she read to him. He was so entranced with the book that he barely noticed us. Students who hadn't realized the power of reading to a child truly internalized the concept that day.

Linking with College Child Care Center

A college child care center is located several blocks from Taft Union High School in Taft, California. Several years ago infant/

toddler care was added to the children's center through a collaborative effort between the high school and college. A grant was written by Leslie Dragoo, the director of the child care center.

The center has a capacity for 300 children including 18 infants and 24 toddlers. High school parents have priority, regardless of the age of their child. Nancy Buzzell, adjunct professor in the Early Childhood division of Taft College, teaches parenting to high school student parents the first period each day. Her salary is paid by the college. The parents leave their babies in the center, walk about four minutes to Buzzell's class, then walk four minutes to the high school. Each young parent returns to the center for one period of lab work every day.

Buzzell says she must communicate with a lot of people regarding her class — high school teachers, high school and college counselors, and, most important, Becky Roth, the master teacher/supervisor of the infant/toddler program. Roth also supervises the high school students while they are on site.

"Our setting is especially good from a college prep standpoint," Buzzell pointed out. "They're here every day, and they're more likely to think this is the place to go after high school."

Help with Planning

In School Together: School-based Child Care Serving Student Mothers by Cahill, White, Lowe, and Jacobs (1991) is a handbook detailing the development of child care programs. It's an extremely useful how-to book which provides information on design, staff, program, funding, and other aspects of providing child care services for school-age parents.

Also see *School-Based Programs for Adolescent Parents and Their Young Children: Guidelines for Quality and Best Practice* by Batten and Stowell (1996) and other publications from the Center for Assessment and Policy Development (CAPD). The Center conducted research in 1994 on strategies to overcome barriers and challenges to providing services in and around schools for teen parents. They are working with several school districts across the country on expanding these services. See the bibliography for a listing of their publications.

Visiting child care centers can be a valuable tool in center development. In addition to seeing first-hand the centers in your area, you can learn about more than 450 programs serving teen parents across the country by reading *Learning Together: Child Care Programs for Teen Parents* by Francis and Marx (1989). Prepared by the Wellesley College Center for Research on Women, the directory provides a wealth of information regarding services offered, funding sources, and contact persons. The *Supplement* to the directory (1991) contains an index of important program features across both volumes on such things as programs for young fathers and vocational education training in early childhood.

While teaching in the teen parent program in Springfield, Ohio, I (Sharon) saw a great need for a school-based child care center. My supervisor raised this issue with the district administration every year for five years. The request was always turned down.

A new minister moved to our town. He decided his mission was to help get a school-based child care center in the district. He connected with other prominent and motivated community people, and the proposal made by this group to the district administration was accepted. There was much work and many partners involved in the venture (including the YMCA), and within a year, a developmental child care center and learning lab began operation in one of the comprehensive high schools.

My school district was willing to take this step only when they saw there was great community support. Maybe there is a person or a small group of people in your community willing to champion such a cause.

Providing for the needs of teen parents and their children is a formidable task, but one with multiple payoffs. If teenage parents continue their education and are helped to become adequate and loving parents, everybody wins — the teenagers themselves, their babies, and society. The price for providing these services is high. The price for not providing them is far higher.

A teen parent may feel the loss
of her teen years as they might have been.

CHAPTER 9

Parenthood May Bring Loss

Pregnant and parenting teens face inevitable loss in their lives. Those who choose adoption or abortion, or who miscarry, are losing their baby, and their lives are forever changed. Teens who become parents are losing their teen years as they might have been. For some teens, these losses occur as a result of becoming a teen parent. For other teens, the losses happened long before the pregnancy occurred.

We can't assume that what we see as a loss for the teen is perceived in the same way by the teen. Pregnant and parenting teens may or may not consider their experiences as losses, and their perception of their experiences must be respected.

Pregnancy — Plus or Minus?

Some teens are happy to be having a baby. Other teens may not be particularly thrilled about it, but may view their pregnancy and parenting as carrying on a family or community legacy, as something that is expected of them. Teens whose pregnancy is planned and wanted, or at least not to be avoided, are less likely to perceive their experiences as losses. For example, they might experience higher status in their family or among their peers, the pregnancy might get them away from a difficult home life, or bearing a child may be the only path they see available to them as a rite-of-passage into adulthood. These teens truly have experienced tremendous losses in their lives, but may not identify those losses or be ready to deal with them. These young parents need a lot of education, support, and guidance. They also need a lot of extra help with parenting their child.

Teens whose pregnancy is unintended or unwanted are more likely to perceive their experiences as losses. These losses can include losing friends and support of family, losing treasured activities (such as playing on the school basketball team), losing respect and status, losing self-respect, losing their childhood or adolescence, losing the chance to go to college, losing the promise of a bright future, and more. You, a trusted teacher or advisor, can help them deal with their changes and losses.

Many Potential Losses

Of all teen pregnancies annually in the United States, it is estimated 14 percent miscarry, about one-third abort, and 52 percent bear children. Of all childbearing adolescents, 97-98 percent choose childrearing and only 2-3 percent choose adoption.

If you become known as the school person to see to discuss a possible untimely pregnancy, you need to have information available about options. What is your state's law and practice concerning parental consent requirements for minors who choose abortion? When might she need to involve the judicial system? Is counseling available? Is she aware that some counseling centers will not discuss abortion? Your role is to help her find the information she needs to make the best possible decision, considering her situation at this time. Parenthood, adoption, or abortion — each may be a choice made by the young parents themselves. Each can also be the result of coercion.

Miscarriage is also a pregnancy outcome that occurs fairly often among pregnant adolescents. A helpful resource for a student who miscarries is *After the Loss of Your Baby — For*

Teen Mothers by Connie Nykiel (1994).

Some outcomes, such as stillbirth, birth defects, court battles for custody, loss of custody, infant death, and more are unexpected, unintended, and usually tragic. Grief, anger, guilt, and other complex emotions often result.

Teen parenthood may bring additional personal losses. Some teen parents experience a loss of the self. You might notice a teen who appears depressed, isolated, overwhelmed, and seems to have few sources of social support. Some teen parents experience loss due to their expectations of parenthood not being met. This might include the loss of a partner who left during the pregnancy or after the birth of the baby, or the loss of attention that was lavished on the teen during pregnancy, then transferred to the newborn baby. Teen parents may also grieve the loss of a loving relationship with their own mothers and fathers, whether a recent or a long-term loss.

Many pregnant and parenting students are survivors of abuse (particularly sexual abuse), neglect, or trauma. According to the *Heart to Heart* program's 1995 report, "There is a direct relationship between sexual abuse and early sexual activity and teen pregnancy. In one survey, nearly 25 percent of the respondents who had been sexually abused reported becoming pregnant by the perpetrator."

In two major studies, one in Illinois and one in Washington state, 61 and 62 percent of the teen mothers surveyed indicated involuntary sexual experience prior to becoming pregnant.

The effects of the abuse, neglect, or trauma on the individual will vary depending upon many things, including the invasiveness of the experience, the duration and severity, the age at which it occurred, the responsiveness of the child's support system, personal coping skills, and more. The abusive, neglectful, and traumatic experiences have the potential to delay or interrupt the development of a child's brain, causing it to be organized in a less-than-optimal or even permanently disrupted way.

Strategies Promoting Personal Growth

Learning activities that promote personal growth can include emotional learning, multiple perspective-taking, empathy development, fiction writing, and more. Learning activities that promote the personal growth of your students are also likely to elicit more positive parenting practices by these young parents.

Emotional learning involves identifying one's own emotions or feelings, and learning to identify the emotions or feelings of others accurately. It is not uncommon for survivors of severe childhood abuse or trauma to have confusion about their own internal states. Additionally, they often misinterpret the emotional states and intended messages of others by misreading or misinterpreting facial expressions, body posture, and verbalizations. They may also have trouble identifying circumstances that may trigger another's emotional responses, especially anger and distress. Emotional intelligence is an important personal attribute for teen parents. Emotional intelligence can help them be more attuned to their children's emotional states.

Other important learnings for teen parents are empathy development and multiple perspective-taking. **Empathy** is sharing the perceived emotion of another, as "feeling with another," and identifying circumstances that may have produced emotional responses, especially anger and distress.

Perspective-taking is the ability to consider a situation from another person's point of view, which requires a recognition that someone else's point of view may differ from one's own. **Multiple perspective-taking** allows a person to view a situation from the viewpoints of many different people. For example, a teen parent might look at a situation from the perspectives of her/ himself, the baby, the partner, friends, or extended family members such as mother, father, or siblings. Increased abilities to empathize and to take multiple perspectives are important to a teen's personal growth as well as to an increase in her/his sensitivity as a parent.

Protecting one's children from abuse, neglect, and traumatic experiences is a very important role of parents. If teen parents received little protection during their upbringing, they are likely to have little knowledge and few skills to protect their own children from harm. One outstanding resource that can help teachers instill protection skills in teen parents is *Heart to Heart* (1995), a curriculum designed to teach teen parents how to protect their children from being sexually abused. *Heart to Heart* also has a strong focus on healthy relationships and promotes the development of healthy support systems. See the bibliography.

Teen parents who are abuse or trauma survivors are likely to have damaged boundaries. They may have a tendency to disclose their abuse or traumatic experiences to inappropriate people, and at the wrong time. You can help them set boundaries, and you can respect them by not probing.

If they share with you privately, you can offer to bring in professional help. Depending on the situation, you may also need to report the abuse to child protective services. Be familiar with your state laws regarding the reporting of child abuse, and also the reporting of statutory rape. Additionally, you'd be wise to confer with a mental health therapist who specializes in survivors of abuse and trauma, so you have an ally when you need one.

What Can You Do to Help?

You have very important roles to fulfill to help school-age parents handle their losses. Unless you have the required training and licensing, you cannot provide therapy for your students, but you can establish a personal relationship and a classroom environment that are respectful, caring, safe, and predictable, so your students have a therapeutic experience. The on-going experience you provide can be just as important, if not more so, as that offered by a therapist.

Brenda Egan, GRADS teacher, Carlsbad High School, Carlsbad, New Mexico, feels a home visit can give the message that you truly care: "If they get behind I try to go by and take their work. I think that's partly why we're successful. They feel somebody cares, and sometimes they kind of get lost otherwise. I pretty much know the family situations of my students, and that makes all the difference. Even if it's just a phone call — 'I missed you today. Can you get back tomorrow?'"

Listen to your students. Sometimes they need to talk, and you can provide a caring ear for them. Mary Jo Guidi, GRADS teacher at Belmont Career Center in St. Clairsville, Ohio, spoke of a young grief-stricken mother whose baby had died. When the student returned to school after the funeral, she didn't want to return to the GRADS class, but she still wanted to meet with her teacher. Guidi and the student found it too painful just to get together and talk. "I thought, 'If we can do an activity, the time together will be easier,' she said. "So I brought in some embroidery. One afternoon each week we got together for an hour and embroidered. She talked about her grief, and we cried together."

Use your active listening skills so they know they are being heard. "I hear you saying . . . Am I right?" Affirm their feelings. "That must have been scary for you." Use probing questions to help reinforce their reasoning skills. "What do you mean when you say . . . ?" "What do you see as your alternatives?" "Is . . . the best action for you? for your baby? for your family?"

Help them solve their own problems. Coach them, guide them, provide resources, tools, and experiences for them. Do not tell them what to do or try to solve their problems for them. Offer to help if a student seems distraught, and allow the student to accept or reject your help. Students have more sense of control when they have choices.

Take quick action during emergency situations, particularly when your students need protection. They cannot be problem-solvers when they feel threatened or scared. Bonnie Beckman, a GRADS teacher in Cincinnati, Ohio, discovered that one of her students had been kicked out of her home and was living on an outdoor fire escape. Beckman took immediate action to obtain temporary emergency housing. Later, she helped the pregnant teen explore her options for long-term housing. The student learned how to access needed community resources, and made her own calls.

Employ instructional strategies that provide opportunities for your students to heal. Helpful strategies include reflective writing, journaling, fiction writing, self-assessment tools, open-ended questioning, and self-disclosure opportunities in safe places. The *Adolescent Parent Resource Guide* has teacher background information and learning activities that help students cope with their losses.

Call a grief counselor and ask for advice. Many hospitals and hospices employ counselors who specialize in loss and grieving.

Ask for recommendations of resources for you and your students. The counselors may be able to provide you with some basic materials. In an emergency, this counselor may be able to help with your students.

Adoption: An Option Full of Loss

If she continues her pregnancy, encourage her and her partner to consider both adoption and parenting plans. Few teens make adoption plans, but if they consider both options, they are likely to feel more positive about the choice they eventually make. If adoption is not seen as a possible option, parenthood is a little more likely to feel like a trap. Those who parent because they feel they have no other choice are likely to have more regrets than if they realized all along that they do have other options. If she feels she has to choose adoption, she may get pregnant again very quickly, hoping to replace the baby she lost.

Those considering an adoption decision are wise to look at the parenting option, too. Looking at all the possible options, talking and writing about the pros and cons of each choice, considering family and personal values, personal goals, and possible effects of each option on each person involved is likely to result in a more reasoned decision.

Some teachers don't talk about adoption with pregnant teens "because no one is interested." Less than three percent of pregnant teens release their infants for adoption, but this does not mean pregnant teens should not know about the subject. They — and the rest of us — need adoption education for several reasons:

- If a student is considering an adoption plan, s/he needs to learn as much as possible about adoption as practiced today.
- Students who know about the love and the pain that go into an adoption decision are more likely to support a classmate making an adoption plan for her/his child.
- Students who are adoptees may know nothing about the difficult choice of adoption, and may think their birthparents "gave them away" because their birthparents didn't love them. Hearing a birthmother or birthfather's story of wanting a better life for their child than they could provide

at the time, and of the grief experienced by the birthparent
after the child was placed may greatly improve the adoptee's
self-esteem.
* Adolescents and their families often are unaware of important changes in the adoption arena, i.e., the strong move
away from secrecy and toward much more openness
between birth and adoptive parents.

Pregnant teens want and plan to be responsible parents. They
are not likely to think being responsible includes handing one's
baby over to strangers and never knowing anything further about
this child with whom they have already bonded.

> *My idea about adoption was that you throw your kid
> into some black hole and you never see him again. Then I
> talked to Sarah (counselor) and my mom, and my views
> totally changed.*

> Eleyna

Today in many parts of the United States, pregnant women
and their partners, whatever their age, can plan and carry out an
adoption process through which they select the adoptive parents,
and hand the baby to those parents, perhaps with a presentation
ceremony. They stay in touch, at least through letters and
pictures, and often through direct contact over the years.
Whether they choose the security and counseling (and, one
hopes, flexibility) of an adoption agency or the flexibility (and,
one hopes, security and counseling) of independent adoption,
they should be able to develop a workable adoption plan.

Developing Adoption-Planning Unit

Usually a teaching unit on a specific topic includes lesson
plans meant to be used one after the other until the course of
study is completed. With adoption education for a class of
pregnant teens, however, offering brief units periodically is more
effective than sticking with the subject for a longer time.

Some teens don't want to think or talk about adoption. Some
are honestly convinced that it would be wrong or emotionally
impossible to place one's child for adoption. They may think

you're bringing up the subject because you think *they* should make an adoption plan. Rather than suggesting you're talking about adoption because they're pregnant teens, point out that we all need to know about adoption as it is practiced today. All of us know someone touched by adoption. They might adopt a child in the future. Or a classmate may be considering an adoption plan and need their support.

Before you start, learn as much as you can about adoption resources in your area. Or ask your students to help with your research. Begin by asking what they already know about the subject. Then help them understand the huge difference between the old closed adoptions and the openness of many current adoption plans. The first session of an adoption unit is best spent discussing these changes in adoption practice.

You may want to offer a brief adoption unit more than once during the year . . . or perhaps individual learning activities on adoption will help pregnant teens understand this option. For a free 8-page handout on teaching about adoption, contact Morning Glory Press. *Pregnant? Adoption Is an Option,* a book by Lindsay (1996), offers a thorough discussion of adoption planning. The first three chapters are appropriate for pregnant students generally, while the remainder of the book provides guidelines for those actually considering an adoption plan for their child.

When you have a student willing to consider both adoption and parenting, guide her to an experienced adoption counselor. Know ahead of time which agencies and independent adoption facilitators in your area appear reputable. Professional counseling is imperative for anyone considering an adoption plan.

If the Teen Parent Loses Custody

Here is a sample situation of how a teacher may handle a student who experiences a loss, in this case, the custody of her baby. Sometimes the parent is court-ordered to attend a parenting class, and she may enroll in your class to meet this requirement. If this happens, you're likely to have a defensive student who believes the *system* is out to get her.

Good listening skills are important in this situation. If the student's story of why s/he doesn't have the child seems unclear, perhaps you can call the social worker for clarification. However, if the student feels that authority figures are ganging up on her, she may become even more defensive. A GRADS teacher reported the following situation:

Karen, a student, comes to class in tears.

Teacher:	*Would you like to talk?*
Karen:	*I don't know. (Another student replies that Karen's baby was taken away from her.)*
Teacher:	*Is that true?*
Karen:	*Yes, that dumb, stupid social worker took my baby away!*
Teacher:	*When did this happen?*
Karen:	*Last night.*
Teacher:	*What was happening when your baby was taken away?*
Karen:	*Nothing.*
Teacher:	*There has to be a reason. What did the social worker say?*
Karen:	*There wasn't a reason! She took her away only because she doesn't like me.*
Teacher:	*Why do you feel she doesn't like you?*
Karen:	*She's always checking on me and she doesn't do that with Theresa.*
Teacher:	*What does the social worker say when she comes?*
Karen:	*Once she said the house was messy, and last night she said my daughter's clothes were dirty and I had just changed her an hour before.*
Teacher:	*Would you mind if I call your social worker to see if anything can be done?*
Karen:	*Go ahead, but she'll probably lie to you because she doesn't like me.*

When the teacher called the social worker, the teacher explained who she was, how upset Karen was, and asked what she could do to help. The social worker, who had never heard of GRADS, was very receptive. She explained that the child was dirty and the house very unsanitary. Karen and her family had been warned several times to clean up.

The previous evening Karen wasn't even sure where her child was. After trying four different locations, Karen and her social worker found Karen's daughter at a house where Karen didn't know the people very well. Karen had been with her boyfriend.

Karen was getting a lot of sympathy from classmates, so the teacher talked with her in private. The social worker had indeed explained the requirements Karen needed to meet in order to have her child returned. Karen was so upset she hadn't listened.

The teacher and Karen worked out an agreement based on what the social worker had said. After six months of following the plan, Karen got her child back. This encounter also produced a good contact at the county children's services office for the teacher. The social worker helped the teacher several times when she needed information for her students.

Role of Professional Counselors

Sometimes school-age parents need professional counseling or therapy. Therapists are trained to help people work through very difficult problems and situations. There are many different specialty areas, so you will need to know many of the agencies and resources available in your community.

You may find you need to talk with a therapist of one of your students. Be sure to follow normal protocol for talking to and sharing information with a professional who has confidentiality privileges. Your student, or the parent or guardian if the student is a minor, must sign a release form granting permission for you and another professional to share information. Learn these procedures before you actually need to follow them. Some teen parent programs ask that release forms be signed as a standard procedure during the enrollment process.

All of us must deal with loss throughout our lives. For some teen parents, loss appears to be all-encompassing. Many of them, partly because of your help, will work through those losses and go on to lead satisfying lives. Your helping role will challenge you. Their challenges are even greater.

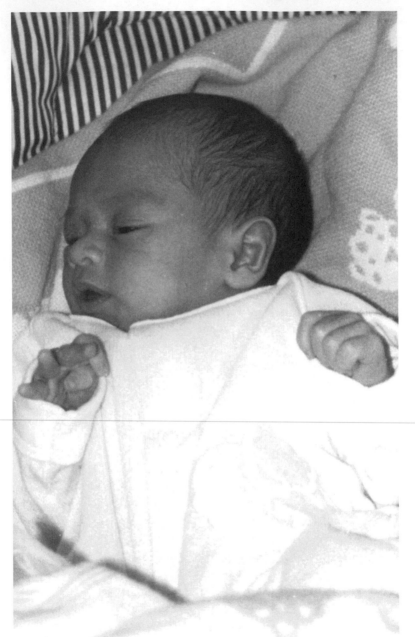

A program objective may be to raise the rate of healthy babies.

CHAPTER 10

Measuring Program Effectiveness

"Why should I measure program effectiveness? Why should I collect and compile data about my program? I need to be spending as much time as I can with my students. Besides, I don't even know where to begin."

Evaluation is a critical but often overlooked task in teen parent programs. Good evaluation takes thought and careful planning from the very beginning of your program. Your school district and/or your State Department of Education has data collection requirements. You may find you need additional data to promote your program successes and as a basis for planning program improvement.

Reasons for Program Research

The downfall of many a teen parent program has been the lack of evidence of program effectiveness. Measuring effectiveness is a critical component for three key reasons. First, it can help you provide information and respond to questions about whether students, the school, and the community are benefiting from the program; secondly, it can guide program improvement; and thirdly, it is an important part of any proposals your program may submit to potential funding sources.

Staff members, administrators, school board members, and the community may ask:

- Why should we fund the teen parent program again next year when we have other pressing educational needs?
- How do we know that the resources devoted to the teen parent program are a good value for our educational dollar?
- Is the teen parent program helping any of our students? I know students who dropped out of school this year even though they were enrolled in the teen parent program.
- What difference does the teen parent program make in the lives of pregnant and parenting teens? In the lives of their young children?
- How do we explain to school district taxpayers that this program is a good investment of their tax dollars?

Responding to these questions with solid data can help you gain on-going school and community support.

Measuring program effectiveness can also be a step toward program improvement. When data is collected in a systematic fashion, it can help identify strengths and weaknesses of the program. It can guide you in the development of improvement strategies, and help you monitor progress.

Because teen parents have so many extra needs, teen parent teachers generally have fewer students than teachers in a regular classroom do. Assuming that your class load is lighter than teachers in more traditional classrooms, teachers may look at your schedule and wonder if you are doing your share. Full-time GRADS teachers, for example, generally have three classes of GRADS students, the state-mandated planning period, and two conference periods for working with individual students and for home and community outreach. Because of the evaluation component, teachers can support the need for this schedule. The average GRADS teacher makes sixty home visits, 101 other parent contacts, and 150 contacts with agencies annually.

Sheila Maggard, GRADS teacher, Ohio Valley Vocational School, West Union, Ohio, points out that evaluation helps validate her program. "It's not just 'Well, we think we're doing a good job,'" she said. "If you have valid data in black and white, it's much better than just a gut feeling. For example, you can prove that the babies are healthier, that the parents are staying in school, and show the exact percentage of male involvement."

Lastly, documentation of the effectiveness of your program is critical to your program's funders, whether it be the school district or local foundations, corporations, or service organizations. When funding entities provide support, they want to know that their investment of dollars is reaping the expected results. It's called accountability, and it is fundamental to any program's long-term financial stability.

What Kinds of Data?

A formal program evaluation is not necessary. Implementing a rigorous evaluation design (which often involves random assignment of subjects to treatment and control groups, identification of an appropriate comparison group, or statistical equation of participant and non-participant groups) may not be feasible. A practical alternative is a performance indicator system (National Center for Research in Vocational Education – 1996). Performance indicators are descriptive statistics that indicate something about the performance of a program.

Ask yourself what you want to learn about the program and your students. Also ask your school administration, your advisory committee, and others what they want to have happen, and the kind of information they need to know that it *is* happening. A variety of questions will be asked, mostly concerned with the following:

- student needs and desired outcomes
- program objectives that are consistent with school mission
- school practices or processes
- school inputs

For each type of question, systematic and representative

information must be documented throughout the school year.

Does your school district have a research and evaluation director who can help you? College interns may be available at no charge to help you evaluate your program.

Measuring Student Outcomes

Student outcomes focus on what your students are doing differently as a result of being enrolled in your program. Performance-type questions you may hear from others include:

- What was the school retention rate?
- What was the graduation rate of seniors?
- What was the promotion rate of students in grades 11 and under?
- What kind of knowledge gains did students have this year, particularly in the areas of parenting and workforce preparation?
- What was the early prenatal health care rate?
- What was the low-birthweight rate?
- What proportion of students had a second or third pregnancy?

Performance measures should be related to your program mission, goals, and objectives. For each program goal and related objective, establish how you will measure student performance. For example, if one of your objectives is "to increase school retention, promotion, and graduation rates," document school enrollment, promotion, and graduation status of students at the end of the current school year.

If another of your objectives is "to have healthy mothers and healthy babies," document events and facts such as dates of prenatal health care visits and birthweights of the babies. If you have as an objective, "to prepare participants for the world of work," document career/work preparation classes and school-to-work activities.

Performance measures will be more accurate if follow-up contacts are made with students during the next school year, or even beyond. For the above objectives, document school enrollment, promotion, and graduation status of students the next school year and birthweights of babies born after the current school year is over. Also document enrollment in career/work preparation classes of high school students, and employment status and post-secondary enrollment of graduates.

Documenting School Practices

School practices (processes) focus on the activities of the teachers and other staff. Practice and process questions may include:

- How much parental (grandparent) involvement did you have?
- How many home/hospital visits did you make?
- How many agency contacts did you make?
- How many student conferences did you have outside of instruction time?
- How many faculty/staff contacts did you make?
- What type of teaching strategies did you use?
- How many agency representatives came to the school to meet with students?

This information is most easily collected by keeping a log of your activities. Log sheets and computer programs can be aids in documenting these activities. One way to log this data is by using a daily or weekly log sheet, on which all of your activities are logged. If you want to track your activities for each student separately, you can log all activities related to a particular student on a student log sheet, and then log all other activities on a daily/weekly log sheet. For an example of these types of logs, see *Organizing TAPP: Useful Forms for Teenage Parent Programs* (1997).

Ruth Frankey, GRADS teacher, D. Russel Lee Career Center, Hamilton, Ohio, admits, "Keeping these records is lots of work, and we probably wouldn't do it if it weren't a state requirement. Contacting the kids after they leave our program is a pain, but part of the reason we keep getting funded is because we have the stats to back up our claims. We know how many we're helping. We know the number of phone calls, parent visits, and student conferences we have had during our conference periods.

"Several other districts have asked for our stats. If people

want to pretend there is no problem, I can't make them open
their eyes, but stats help.

"We have a new administrator who is looking at how we
spend our time. I think those logs justify our two conference
periods — we spend a lot of time trouble-shooting, and we have
the records to back it up."

In spite of the obvious time and work required to collect data,
some teachers are working with teen parents *because* of the data
others collected. LoLita Dawson Pfeiffer, Windover High
School, Midland, Michigan, commented, "A big reason I bought
into GRADS was because of all the data they have for you.

"Our board knows the multiplicity of problems these kids
have . . . because I educated them big time," Pfeiffer continued.
"I gave them lots and lots of information the year we started the
program. Next week I'm doing a full board presentation on the
demographics, who the students are, and the issues they face.
The board realizes the expensive outcome of kids who don't
succeed at parenting and at work. They are willing to battle the
people who question all this money being spent on 24 girls and
two guys. It is expensive, but it has improved our school.

"I think you could sell this to a conservative board because
their thinking is responsibility and pulling yourself up by your
bootstraps. Look at the costs of living on welfare or having
another FAS (Fetal Alcohol Syndrome) baby, and our program
doesn't look so expensive."

In Florida, each school district must submit an annual report
documenting the extent to which each teenage parent program
has met the objectives established by the district. These objectives are based on students remaining in school or earning a high
school diploma, improving parenting skills, and giving birth to
babies weighing 5.5 pounds or more. Some districts have several
program sites. This data is useful for each site, for the whole
district, and, when combined, for the entire state.

Recording Demographics

School inputs are the "givens." They represent conditions that
are difficult to change, such as student demographics, facilities,
and school funds. School input questions you may hear include:

- How many students are enrolled in your program this year?
- How many teen fathers are enrolled?
- How many babies were born? How many second babies?
- How many students were enrolled in each grade level?

The information you collect should be easily observable or easily obtainable from school records, and not require intrusive questioning of students. You will probably be collecting information on such things as gender, grade in school, number who are pregnant during the year, number who deliver babies, number who are parenting only (not pregnant during the year), number who are married, and school programming (i.e., college prep, vocational/technical program, special education, etc.).

Developing a good school program for pregnant and parenting teens is almost certain to help some students stay in school who otherwise would have dropped out. In addition, many teachers report a significant rate of dropout retrieval of school-age parents. Some teens who had dropped out of school before the pregnancy decide to return, at least partly because of the support and encouragement provided by the teen parent program staff. Make sure your evaluation plan includes careful recording of the number of former school dropouts who enroll, and their progress toward graduation and financial independence.

Educating young people is the mission of our school system. If, because of the teen parent program, teens return to school, your district and your community need to know about it. In addition to the value of educating these young people, dropout retrieval represents more school funding dollars for your district.

Measuring Performance and Learning

Performance and learning measures are designed to assess the knowledge and skills your students acquire in your program. Measuring student learning in teen parent programs is a challenge, due to many factors:

- Open enrollment — new students enroll in the program at different times throughout the year.
- Students often study different lessons in the same class (i.e., newly-pregnant students can be enrolled in the same class as

young parents of toddlers; eighth grade students who are
beginning their individual career plans can be enrolled in the
same class as twelfth grade students who are nearly ready to
join the work force).
• A wide range of ages, grade levels, learning abilities, and
support systems are represented.
• Process skills (i.e., problem solving, caring for others,
communication, management, leadership, and building a
future) are not adequately measured with paper/pencil tests.

It is impossible to devise one traditional paper/pencil test to
measure the learning of all students in a teen parent program.
Reliable and valid traditional tests for teen parent programs are
not available. Some reliable and valid instruments have been
developed to measure specific content areas, such as the *Adult-
Adolescent Parent Inventory* (2002: Bavolek), an inventory
designed to assess high-risk parenting attitudes among adults and
adolescents. If traditional tests are needed, you may have to
develop your own. Keep the use of traditional testing to a
minimum.

Assessment of student learning needs to be integrated with all
other teaching and learning processes. This gives you and your
students many opportunities to check on student understanding
and progress. Students need to have alternative assessment
methods available to demonstrate their learning. As defined in
chapter 4, alternative assessment applies to any and all assessments that require students to demonstrate knowledge and skills
in ways other than through the conventional methods. Authentic
assessment engages students in applying knowledge and skills as
they will be used outside of school.

Student exit measures and parent (grandparent) measures
are another source of feedback about the program. These measures are often teacher-developed. Information you might want
to collect from students includes, "What would you like to learn
in this class? What did you learn here? How can this class be
changed to better meet your needs? Using a scale of one to five,
how satisfied are you with this class?" These questions could be
adapted for the grandparent measure.

Collecting Data — When? How?

It is imperative to start collecting your data the first day students enroll in your program. Data that is "re-created" later in the school year is usually unreliable and incomplete. Useful data collection forms include:

- Student enrollment form
- Agency linkage form
- Emergency medical form for pregnant students
- Student and/or daily/weekly log forms for documenting teacher and staff activities, such as student conferences, parent contacts, home and hospital visits, school personnel contacts, agency contacts
- Teacher work sheet for compilation of data

For samples of forms used by teen parent program teachers, see *Organizing TAPP*. If you find that the data collecting system you devised before the beginning of the school year is inefficient or too cumbersome, then change methods during the school year. It is better to have different kinds of records than to have incomplete records or no records at all.

For more detailed information on research and evaluation instruments, see *Handbook of Adolescent Sexuality and Pregnancy: Research and Evaluation Instruments* (Card: 1993). See the bibliography.

Teacher Tips

Good program evaluation takes time, but organization can help minimize the time it requires. Following are some suggestions teachers have shared which might help you.

- I need something I can easily carry around, yet won't lose. I use half-sheets of paper in a small, brightly-colored loose-leaf notebook.
- On your log sheets, make your notes very brief. All you really need is a name, date, and a few descriptive words.
- I keep my records on index cards which I store in a box in my desk. I like things small and brief. I keep one card for each student.

- Two or three times each year, I get out the student enrollment forms for students to review for accuracy. They move
  around a lot, and their addresses can change often. I also ask
  them to review and update the list of contact people. Next
  year, I want to be able to locate them for my follow-up
  contact, and to see how they're doing.
- I place a 'change' form in each student's working folder. If
  they move or when the baby is born, or for any other change,
  they write the new information on the change form and give
  it to me. I like to help students take responsibility for
  notifying us of changes.
- On my emergency medical form, I ask for the obstetrician's
  name and the hospital or medical facility where they plan to
  deliver the baby. Since the emergency medical form in the
  school office does not have this information, I make a copy
  of the completed form on colored paper and take it to the
  office. They are always glad to get this information, because
  they want to know what to do if something happens when
  I'm not here.
- I have students take leadership roles on a rotating basis. The
  student leaders record birth dates, birthweights and other
  information. I find they are very careful with this job.

Compiling and Using Data

Compare your data with other relevant statistics. For example,
keep up-to-date on the percentage of low-birthweight babies
born to teen mothers in your county and in the state. If one of the
objectives of your program is improved health for the babies,
birthweight is one measure. If your rate of low-birthweight
babies is better than the county or state rate, you have a success
story that can be used to promote your program.

On the other hand, if you find your low-birthweight rate is
worse, you may decide you need to push harder for improved
health care for your students, or for earlier enrollment during
pregnancies. You may decide to design better ways of teaching
pregnant students about healthy eating habits during pregnancy.
You might write a proposal for a small grant to purchase healthy
snack foods for your students.

Are your students more likely to return to school after childbirth than is indicated by statistics for teen parents in general? If so, you have another success story.

Success stories are important for a program's health, i.e., continued funding and other support. Anecdotal success stories are great, but singular experiences are not likely to be as convincing as they are when combined with hard data.

Prepare the statistical data in a way that will tell the exciting story of your program in a clear, user-friendly format. Use fact sheets with key points listed with bullets. Show numbers. Show the program's progress toward its goals, and show the return that the community is receiving on the investment in this program. Simple reports and fact sheets can easily be prepared in an appealing way with graphics available on all computers. Reports and fact sheets can "market" both your program results and your message, as well as improve your image. As you prepare your report, think of yourself as the public relations person for your teen parent clients.

Illustrate your statistics with personal stories. When you state the number of student parents graduating from high school, follow with a couple of stories of students who have achieved in spite of difficulties.

Be generous in distributing your report. Of course your supervisor and your advisory council members need copies, as does each member of your staff. Also send copies to school board members, the school superintendent, and the local newspaper editor.

Health and social service people in your area are more likely to support your program if they are informed of its successes. Send them your annual report, too.

You, your supervisors, your community, and your clients want to know that your work is having an impact. When you can show in numbers that you are successful, you are likely to sustain support for your program. And with that support, you can be more sure of making a difference in your students' lives.

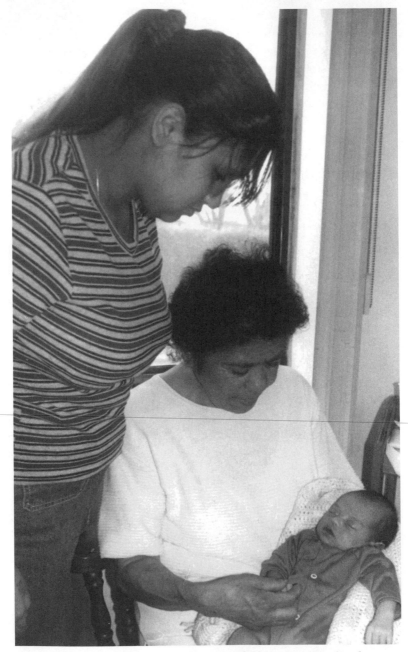

Good program outreach may help her stay in school.

CHAPTER 11

Reaching Out
To Students' Parents

For optimal development, teen parents, like all adolescents, need the continued support of their families. Developmentally, teens in early adolescence (12 to 18 years) are experiencing great change — rapid physical changes, significant cognitive and emotional maturation, sexual awakening, and a heightened sensitivity to peer relations. The psychosocial crisis can be described as group identity versus alienation. Even though the role of the peer group increases, continuing supportive relationships with family members is still an essential ingredient of healthy development

Teen Parents *Need* Family Support

Having a baby during the teen years makes it difficult for teen parents to negotiate successfully the psychosocial crisis of group identity versus alienation. Many teen mothers become isolated and alienated from their friends because it is too difficult to raise a baby and also spend time with friends. Young fathers also tend to be isolated from their peer group. Teen parents need a lot of support from their parents or close family members if they are going to be attached to their peer group and successfully negotiate their own development.

Teen parents also need a lot of support to develop their role as a parent. Teen parents love their babies as much as older parents love theirs. However, the realities of parenting are often much different than the teens expect. Many teen parents do not have the emotional, social, or financial resources to sustain the kind of caring relationship they anticipate with their children. They are likely to develop their role of parent more successfully when they have supportive families.

What do supportive families look like for teen parents? Supportive families will have positive communication and trusting relationships, and will provide emotional, financial, and childrearing support. Some families are more capable of being supportive than others.

You also have an important role to play. In addition to supporting your students in their own development and in the development of their parenting role, you can work with and support their parents and close family members.

Student Differences Signal Family Differences

You will notice differences among your students. Some students eagerly attend your class and learn all they can. Others seem hostile and resistant to many learning activities, or often miss your class. These differences in students could signal differences in their families.

Students who are eager learners generally have one of two types of family situations. Many of the eager learners live with parents or close family members who provide high levels of support. There is positive communication and trust in these families.

The other eager learners are likely to be alienated from their families. These teens might live away from their families, or they might live with them but still be emotionally cut off. You can become an extremely important person in the lives of these teen parents.

Students who seem hostile and resistant are often experiencing conflict with their parent(s) or close family members. If these students learn something different from you than is believed or practiced by their families, they may experience higher levels of family conflict.

Some families welcome your input and involvement, some families view you as an intrusion, and other families do not respond at all. As you keep these differences in mind, you may be able to develop different strategies for working with your students and their families.

Family Responses to a Teen Pregnancy

A teen pregnancy affects the lives of everyone in the family. Pregnant teens and their partners often worry about their parents' reactions to the pregnancy. Primarily, they worry about their parents' anger, but how the baby might affect their parents may be far from their minds.

> *I know my family will be upset when I tell them I'm pregnant. But once the baby comes, they will fall in love with it and everything will be all right.*
>
> Melanie, 17

The responses of families to a teen pregnancy can vary greatly. Many families are initially upset, but eventually accept the situation as they adjust to their new family configuration. These parents will probably go through the typical stages of grief. You might be able to help by supporting the parents in this process.

Many parents react to the news of the pregnancy with shock and deep hurt. They may not have accepted the idea that their daughter or son is sexually active, yet now they have proof.

> *When my wife told me Jamie was pregnant, I went into shock. I felt like I held my breath for thirty minutes, like if I breathed, I was going to explode. I felt betrayed as a father, and I felt a great loss for Jamie because at fifteen she was no way ready to be a parent, yet there it was.*
>
> Toby Erickson

They are likely to experience denial. "This can't be happening to our family." No longer is a pregnant teen likely to be sent either to a maternity home or Aunt Millie's farm in Kansas, but her parents may not want to share the news of this pregnancy. They may worry about the extended family's reaction.

The shotgun wedding response to early pregnancy is seldom chosen today. Parents may experience a lot of anger, however — how could you do this to us? They may encounter depression before finally accepting their new reality.

After Robin told me, I just grabbed her and held her. She and I cried together. Then I went into shock, then to anger, and there was a lot of that. I said things I shouldn't have said. We're an ordinary middle-class family, and we thought we had everything together here. We went to church every Sunday, and we were active in the PTA.

                                                        Don Gray

Throughout this time and continuing after the baby's birth, the teen's parents need support. They need to figure out who they can lean on as they support their child. They need to focus on their daughter's or son's predicament and new responsibility rather than on the neighbors' reactions.

If you can make a home visit during this early stage of pregnancy, you may find the parents as well as the daughter or son need help. As a representative of the school program, your primary client is your student. However, the parents may want some guidance in finding the resources their child needs. Is the pregnancy covered by insurance? If not, suggest they check with the Department of Social Services or ask their doctor where to go for financial aid.

Will the daughter continue to live with her parents? What alternatives are available in your community? What are her parents' attitudes toward the father of the baby? Will the parents support the parents-to-be as a couple? Or do they want the father out of the picture?

If the latter is the case, you may be able to remind them gently that everybody loses if dad isn't around. Is his biggest sin simply that he, too, is very young? Seldom can a 16-year-young man be financially responsible for his partner and child. While it's important that he stay in school, he may be able to work part-time and help pay the pregnancy and baby expenses. He can provide other kinds of support. His emotional support is likely to be important to the young woman. In some states, the parents of a minor father must provide financial support for his baby.

What other help can he provide? Can he take her to her doctor appointments? Is he willing to model a healthy lifestyle for the sake of his baby? That means staying away from alcohol, tobacco, and drugs, and helping her choose the foods she and the baby need during this critical time.

You might want to take a good prenatal health video with you on a home visit or, if possible check it out overnight to your students. Choose one with special emphasis on prenatal nutrition. If parents and boyfriend/husband watch the video, they may become more aware of the needs of this young pregnant woman and her unborn child.

Working with these families can feel like a balancing act. Often you detect family support for the teen, but at times you see conflict. Every family will have its smooth times and its rough times. Take your cues from these families about when they welcome your involvement and when they want some space.

Grandmother's Baby?

Some families "expected" the pregnancy, so it comes as no surprise. In some homes, the baby becomes the grandmother's baby, at least for a few years. The teen parent has little to say about how the baby is raised. There may be great conflict if the teen expects the baby to be hers/his, or if s/he tries to actively parent this child.

Give this teen a great deal of emotional support. However, if you provide a lot of information about parenting that the student is unable to implement, you could be contributing to the conflict in the family.

This situation might be difficult for you because you want to support your student in developing the parenting role, yet you don't want to be a source of stress or conflict for the family. And you don't want to push too hard on this family system, or the grandmother might pull the young parent out of your program.

Linda Miller, former coordinator of TAPP, La Sierra High School, Fullerton, California, mentioned a student whose mother wanted her to stay home and keep the house clean. "The student and I talked about the reasons she needed to stay in school. I asked if she would like me to talk with her mother, or would she rather do it herself. She said she would try to get her mom to understand. She succeeded — she was back in school the next day, and she continued until she graduated."

Occasionally, parents or close family members do not accept the pregnancy or the baby at all. These teens may become alienated from their families, and sometimes must move out. Working with an alienated family is difficult. You may be able to help the young parent find support from other family members. Perhaps you can help her/him connect with a variety of resources in the community so s/he has other sources of support.

Supporting the Parents

Parents need to realize their control is limited. They cannot make the big decision on abortion, adoption, or parenting. They can prevent marriage if either partner is underage, but they cannot require marriage. The parents face much of the financial responsibility, at least for awhile, if the teen chooses parenthood.

If you have a student who might be interested in planning an adoption for her child, but she "knows" her parents would never allow it, help her learn as much as possible about adoption practices today. Perhaps if her parents understand that an open adoption plan may be workable, and that neither the birthparents nor the birthgrandparents need lose all contact with this child, they will be more supportive.

Some parents of pregnant teens might appreciate some good counseling. The counseling needs to help them move from "Ain't it awful" to "This has happened and we'll deal with it the best we can." As one grandfather expressed it:

I'm accepting our situation much better now,
probably because of the support our church has
provided and the caring we've found in the school's

*grandparent support group. I'm not down all the time,
but I still have problems.*

In the grandparent support group in TAPP, Louisville, Kentucky, each meeting begins with lots of sharing, and ends with
the teaching of one skill dealing with communication, nutrition,
or other relevant issue. Participants are asked to practice that
skill during the week and report back to the group.

Connie Graff, Teen Mother Program, Quincy, Illinois, offers a
grandparent support group in connection with her program. She
begins by giving a handout to every parent when students enroll.
She suggests the need for communication between home and
school, and that perhaps the parents would enjoy meeting other
parents who share similar concerns. At her first meeting she
reported, "We had eight participants, a mix of parents of teen
moms, grandparents of teen moms, and a parent of a teen dad.
We felt lucky to have the mother of the teen dad because, when
the conversation started to turn to father bashing, she reminded
us that some teen fathers want to be responsible. The group set
goals that night, and were eager to continue a support group."

The grandparents choose topics, and Graff contacts speakers.
Programs have included legal issues, public aid, three-generation
living, birth control, and other topics. Graff cautions, "Don't get
discouraged if you try this and it doesn't work at first. I actually
planned all this a year ago. The weather was bad, but I still
hurried back to school with cookies and coffee. Nobody came!
But I tried again this fall, and, hey, it worked!"

Brenda Egan, GRADS teacher, Carlsbad, New Mexico, sends
a letter home to the parents of each new student asking if they
need any help. "We were constantly getting calls from parents,
'My daughter is pregnant and we're having a hard time adjust-
ing,'" she explained. "A couple of years ago a student's parent,
who is a teacher, called several times, 'You have to have somebody to talk to who knows what you're going through.' So this
mother helped get our group started. We provide the space and
we participate, but she runs it. Frequently we will give her a
name (with permission) and say, 'They're having a real hard
time. Maybe you could talk to them.' It's working well."

Family — Plan Together for Baby

Families need to plan together for the baby. Encourage your
pregnant students and expectant fathers to talk with their families
before the baby is born. What changes do they see in their family
system because of this new baby? Will the young parent be able
to take responsibility for child care? Will the young parent still
be able to do her/his share of other household tasks? Most
important, who will take care of the baby while the young parent
continues school?

Who picks up the diapers? Who does the laundry? What about
financial considerations? Who pays for what?

The whole family needs to sit down and talk about these
issues. What does this mean for everyone in terms of schedule
changes, habits of the house, sleeping arrangements? All these
things will be changing with the baby's birth. Who is willing to
make these changes? Toby Erickson explained:

> *That nine months changed our lives completely.
> Jamie isn't at all the same person she was. None of us
> are. It changes your whole outlook on what is impor-
> tant and what is not, and some of it is hard to face.
> Part of the change may be harder on the parents than
> it is on the daughter. Acceptance of the reality may be
> hardest on the father.*

Suggest that the family develop a contract detailing responsibilities of the various family members. Consider such topics as
meal preparation and clean-up, laundry, housecleaning, child
care, discipline, financial matters, teen parent's social activities,
rights of individuals, etc.

Also, if the two young parents are not married or living
together, you can encourage the two families to talk about shared
parenting arrangements. Which family is taking on the primary
parenting responsibilities? What plans are being made for
visitation by the other family? How are the financial responsibilities to be shared? If family members can agree on these
issues *before* the baby is born, their lives are likely to go more
smoothly. From your standpoint as a teacher, you know that the

fewer surprises the family faces after childbirth, the more likely your student will be able to stay in school.

When the Honeymoon Is Over

Often there is a honeymoon effect for a couple of months after the baby is born. The family adores the baby, and every-thing may go well for awhile. Soon, however, the newness wears off, and the routine is there. The young mother no longer gets the attention; now it goes to the baby. The grandparents dote on the baby and the young mother is out in left field.

At this point, the teenager may pull away emotionally. She may go see friends and leave the baby with the grandparents. Being parented by the grandparents may seem safe for the baby now, but it can cause a lot of problems. Who is the "real" parent?

Grandparents need to let the young parents take care of the baby. They will intervene if the child's safety is endangered, but they still need to model good parenting rather than taking over. Grandparents have a tendency to say, "Don't do that. Do it this way," and this often triggers rebellion from the young parent.

Parent Involvement in School

Children whose parents take an active interest in the school and the learning processes do better in school. Often, the parents of your students have not had a lot of involvement with their children's education. You have an opportunity to help change this for two generations of students.

Parents are more likely to involve themselves in their children's school and the learning processes if they are invited and feel support to do so. From the beginning, give supportive messages to the parents of your students.

Newsletter to parents. Write short newsletters and mail to the parents at home. Include news about your program and activities, the students, a calendar of coming events, brief parenting tips, and invitations to parents and other family members to come to school. Your students could write the newsletters. Parents generally view newsletters as informative and supportive, especially when they are mailed to the parents at home.

Newsletters are an indirect teaching tool for teen parents and the people they live with. A bimonthly newsletter can offer timely information on issues related to teenage pregnancy, parenting, and sexuality. Pertinent topics may include preterm labor, baby layettes, reading to a child, discipline techniques, grandparenting, prenatal and infant nutrition, holiday travel, nontraditional careers, traits of strong families, anger, communication in the family, stress, and services of community agencies. Short articles addressing key facts and issues on these topics may help a family be more informed.

Publicizing special program events and parent support group meetings can be done in a special section. A format with lots of white space, short sentences, and art work creates an easy-to-read newsletter.

Jean Brunelli, former nurse, Tracy Infant Center, Cerritos, California, edited a monthly newsletter which featured, in addition to articles on effective parenting, items about *each* child in the center. What grandparent could resist reading a newsletter that includes news about her/his grandchild?

Planned family activities. Plan activities at the school or at another site that will bring families together. Families are more willing to attend if food is served, or if there is another incentive, such as pictures with Santa.

Some programs have a family potluck supper at least once a semester. Parents, grandparents, boyfriends, and siblings come. Usually there is a guest speaker or a good prenatal health or parenting video or some other activity planned along with supper. It's a good way to build community in this special population.

Rosann Pollock, Teen Parent West, Deland, Florida, invites former teen parent students to their open house to talk with the current students' parents. The guests are young people who are achieving either though continuing their education or at their jobs, and they talk about their accomplishments. According to Pollock, parents of pregnant teens who *know* their daughter has ruined her life find hope in stories from young mothers who are coping well with their lives in spite of early pregnancy and parenthood.

Some parents may be willing to teach lessons to your class. They might teach about their culture's foods, holidays, religion, or traditions, or they might discuss their jobs, careers, or hobbies.

Intergenerational Learning

You have an opportunity to support your students' learnings by providing intergenerational learning activities. These are learning activities that can be completed by your student and the parent together at home.

Learning activities on parenting are a natural for your program, but intergenerational learning activities can be developed for a variety of areas of study. Examples include adolescent development, pregnancy, labor and delivery, postpartum care, neonatal care, family relationships, workforce preparation, and economic independence.

Students and parents together can view videos, hold discussions, read books, do worksheets, read and respond to case studies, read magazine and newspaper articles, write reports, take photographs, make home videos, watch television programs, and answer questions. Students can also interview their parents on particular topics, and can do reflective writing in their journals for any intergenerational learning activity.

Pam Frazier, a GRADS teacher at Pickaway-Ross County Joint Vocational School in Chilicothe, Ohio, is experimenting with different ways of involving the parents of her students. She does newsletters, has family activities at school, and invites parents to teach lessons. But she says, "The intergenerational learning activities win, hands down. More parents become involved by participating in intergenerational learning activities than any of the other types of parent involvement."

Many perennial problem issues can be addressed with intergenerational learning activities — infant feeding, discipline, toileting, car seat safety, immunizations, finding child care, and more. This could help teens and their parents discuss these issues in a structured, less threatening way. And you won't be as likely to be misinterpreted by your students saying to their parents, "My teacher said you're wrong and behind-the-times because you want me to feed the baby cereal when he's only three weeks old."

A source of help for you with intergenerational learning activities is the *Adolescent Parent Resource Guide*. This guide contains a teacher background piece on parent involvement and intergenerational learning. There are also several intergenerational learning activities included in each of the ten units of study. Additionally, the guide contains learning activity suggestions for teacher home visits.

No doubt many of your students' parents will be too busy or simply not interested in participating in your program to this extent. Even if only a few parents respond, your efforts will be worthwhile. Parents' participation in school programs almost always is a plus for their student son or daughter.

If some of your students' parents are non-English speaking, how can you communicate with them? If you don't speak their language, try to have someone on your staff who does. It's hard to built rapport with a parent if you can't talk to each other.

Encourage the staff person who speaks the family's language to maintain contact with the family, perhaps visit them at home. Some schools develop short newsletters in two (or more) languages so that more family members can read them.

Communicating with your students' families is critical.

Grandparent support group. The grandparent support groups were mentioned earlier as a way to bring parents together for support. These groups can also be educational. Possible problem issues can be raised, speakers can present information, discussions can be held, and participants are likely to learn from the resulting discussion.

Parenting techniques, especially, tend to be family-driven, and you don't want to come between your student and her/his mother. You may hear of home remedies for colic or teething difficulties, perhaps a tea to soothe a baby's stomachache. If these are remedies that are not likely to harm the baby, you don't need to worry about them. You can simply accept different ways of caring for a child.

Yet your student may have some beliefs about parenting that you feel are not healthy for the child. Finding a way to get these messages across without offending takes a great deal of tact and sensitivity on your part.

For example, some families "believe" in spanking children. You may feel that hitting a child is wrong because it's teaching that child to be violent. With this in mind, probably the best way to present the spanking issue is to suggest that spanking does not seem to work very well and explain why. Your students are likely to agree with that statement. Then help them learn more effective ways to discipline.

Share key learning points through handouts. If you can afford to check out books, suggest that your students show their parents some of the things they are learning. Just don't get into a "Your mother is wrong" mode in you teaching. When that happens, nobody wins.

Building Family Relationships

Almost all families aspire to healthy family relationships. Good communication skills help family members share their thoughts and feelings in respectful and caring ways, and listen attentively to others. Trusting relationships are developed when family members set boundaries and limits; maintain appropriate rules and functions, yet change when needed; and make decisions and take actions that are in the best interest of individuals and the family.

Good communication and trusting relationship skills are learned behaviors. School is an appropriate place to teach and reinforce these skills. These skills can be learned and practiced in the classroom, in the child care center, and when working with parents.

The goals within the multigenerational family should be centered on what's best for the individuals *and* the family. How can the development of both the teen parent and the baby be optimized? The teen parent needs to have optimal adolescent development, particularly identifying with a peer group, and optimal development of the parenting role. Teen parents develop best when they have their parents' support.

Your advisory council might help develop a child care plan.

CHAPTER 12

Building School
and Community Support

Does your school welcome teen parents eagerly? Or do you have staff members who seem oblivious to the special needs of pregnant and parenting teens? Do they see no reason to provide special "privileges," i.e., more frequent restroom passes for "those girls"?

Do they verbalize their disapproval of young women who are pregnant too soon? Or of teenage fathers? If so, your school is normal — and the staff needs you to help them better understand the needs of this special population.

For your program to be successful, deliberately build relationships with the school staff. Eliciting support is important whether your program is in-school or a separate school. If you work in isolation from other staff, your students are not likely to achieve as well as they might otherwise.

Pregnancy is a vulnerable time for a woman, whatever her age, and may be for her partner, too. If she's 14, it's much harder. Your school staff needs help in understanding this reality, and especially their role in helping pregnant and parenting teens cope with school in spite of their other responsibilities. Remind them that each time a teen parent drops out of school, we all lose. Through working together, we can prevent a lot of those dropouts.

Your time is limited, and you will never have "enough" time for your students. Working efficiently with other staff people in spite of your time limits is a real challenge.

Help from School Network

Whether your program is an in-school model or a separate school, you need to network. Building and maintaining contacts with other schools who work with your students and other pregnant and parenting teens will help you help young people. You need to promote your program in the school system as well as be an advocate for your students.

In-service presentations are an efficient method of informing all staff about your program. As soon as possible, get scheduled for a short presentation to the faculty. Give program rationale, program goals, and how the program helps students. Explain how the program supports the staff and helps the school meet its educational mission.

Perhaps the school nurse or a friendly guidance counselor can help you. Share your concern about the tremendous importance of pregnant teens attending school throughout pregnancy. Talk about the need for teenage parents to continue their education and of the difficulties they face in doing so.

Brainstorm ways to help pregnant and parenting students. For example, one teacher has a personalized restroom pass made for each pregnant girl. It's laminated, and the student can use it until she delivers.

Share information about the program regularly with administrators, guidance counselors, school nurses, school social workers, teachers, school board members, and other key people. Freely distribute promotional materials such as the following:

• Brochure with program rationale, goals, key components
• Staff information handout with your hours, location, and

phone number
- Referral forms for staff to simplify referring students to you
- Information about your competencies, curriculum, course of study, or other appropriate instructional information
- A report about the effectiveness of your program
- Business card

Cultivate relationships with school staff instrumental to the success of your students and your program. Each key person or group will have different concerns and may want different information. For examples, see the chart on the next page. Building and maintaining support from your school staff is vital.

Is School a Friendly Place?

Pregnant and parenting teens sometimes encounter discrimination within the school. Many school staff have strong feelings about having teen parents on campus. Even though it is not legal officially to discriminate against them (Title IX, Education Amendment Act of 1972), many staff hold attitudes, biases, and beliefs that can make it difficult for school-age parents to be successful in school.

Gloria Parmerlee-Greiner, Boulder Valley Teen Parenting Program, Boulder, Colorado, commented, "At first we were housed away from school. We finally moved to the high school, but that was difficult. Getting acceptance from my colleagues was hard. Not everyone is responsive to a young parent, but over time they see some of these kids succeed, and they get personally involved with some of them.

"You just can't walk in and expect it to happen. You begin to learn which of the faculty are more responsive to special needs, and you do some choosing as to classes parents will be in. You try to do a little matching. We have open entry, which means we take students at any time. If someone shows up in the middle of the semester, we try to find classes where mid-term entry works. It's possible here to earn partial credit for 18 days of attendance in class. I look at a student's transcript and at her graduation requirements, then find classes that will help her. I go to see teachers individually and get their permission to add the student to their roll. If they say no, I find someone else. It usually works."

Tips on Working with School Community

KEY PEOPLE	CONCERNS	INFORMATION DESIRED
Teachers: Particularly • family and consumer sciences • health • vocational • librarian • learning disability • nurse	• Interruption of class • teacher teaching content and not dealing with pregnancy/ parenting issues • student attendance, grades	• Conditions under which you interrupt class (define emergency and schedule) • hall pass use • scheduling conferences ahead with students/teachers • strategies in limiting out-of-class time • referral process • home instruction coordination
Counselors: • Department head/ supervisor • all counselors • secretary	• Work load created by pregnant/ parenting students • scheduling nuisances • home instruction coordination • loss of involvement of students	• How program will relieve their work load and help students • referral process • scheduling and credit concerns • home instruction coordinaton • difference between a teacher and a counselor and limitations thereof • communication regarding specific students, individual situations
Administrators: • Superintendent and staff • principal and staff • secretary • home instruction coordinator	• Dropouts • public image of program • numbers of pregnant/parenting students • legal issues • dollar value, • student attendance, grades	• Number of pregnant and parenting teens • retention and dropout statistics • program statistics • dollar value of program • funding issues • discrimination toward students • attendance • agencies coming into the school
School Board Members: • Particularly individuals identified by administrators	• Public image of program not promoting pregnancy • funding • legal issues	• Retention and dropout statistics • program not promoting pregnancy

Examples of less-than-friendly comments, behaviors, and expectations you may encounter include:

- Statements such as "Rewarding these students with special programs will only encourage others to get pregnant."
- A teen mother is expected to be back in school two weeks after the baby is born, regardless of her health care provider's release date, a clear violation of Title IX, Education Amendment Act of 1972.
- It is an unexcused absence for a teen father to miss school to be at the hospital when his baby is born.
- Teachers give special consideration for the school work of a student with a broken leg, but not to a student with a newborn baby or a sick baby.
- They make comments about "Your student . . . ," rather than "Our student . . ."
- Staff members express hostility or anger.
- You detect an eagerness to drop teen mothers (and sometimes teen fathers) from the school rolls.
- Some teachers and administrators appear unable or unwilling to see how the school failure of a teen mother or father can affect the child's intellectual potential and educational experience.
- Rigid attendance policies may provide no allowances for health problems during pregnancy, childbirth and parental leave, and for sick babies.
- You may see a tendency to blame the teen mother for all that has happened to her ("She made her bed, now she can lie in it"), rather than looking at other contributors, such as previous victimization experienced by the teen, family poverty, poor schools, and more.
- You hear statements like, "She should have thought about that before she got pregnant."
- Teen parents are denied awards or denied induction into honor societies because of their pregnancy/parenting status.
- Attitudes and beliefs still exist that demonstrate the societal double standard that it is okay for young men to be sexually active, but not young women.

If you are the teacher who works most directly with pregnant and parenting teens, attitudes and beliefs held toward the students can be projected or transferred to you. A lack of cooperation from others and comments such as, "Why do you want to work with those students?" can lead you to feel little support from the school staff.

Another frequent complaint was mentioned by LoLita Dawson Pfeiffer, Windover High School, Midland, Michigan. "The people in the building, other students and faculty, say we're coddling our students. But it is not enabling to make the phone call, provide the ride, if at the same time you teach young parents to cope."

Joan Koch, teacher at D. Russel Lee Career Center, Hamilton, Ohio, commented, "There needs to be a lot of communication between the other teachers and myself. If I can help a young parent find child care or listen to her talk about her fight with her boyfriend so she'll be able to do her work in their classes, the other teachers approve."

It is important to build a support network for yourself. Begin early to identify staff in your school who are friendly to your work and your students. You probably will need the support of these allies.

Advocating for Students

The combination of parenting one's child *and* attending high school often creates conflicts for teenage students. The teacher can't solve all these conflicts, but s/he *can* help students tremendously by advocating for them. When Ginger Masingill, director, Teen Parent Center, Deland High School, Deland, Florida, started working with teen parents, her goal was to help them become "super parents." Soon she realized this alone, while important, wasn't going to get them graduated from high school. She explained, "I changed my goal. I became their advocate. I contact the teachers. I pull progress reports. I conference with the parents. I go to the bus drivers, the county people.

"I go to the discipline deans when there is a problem. I suggest we work out a contract for this student who isn't doing well. They're with me as long as we work out a way to make the students accountable. When our students are absent, the attendance clerks call me. If the baby has a temp of 102°, and the mom has no one else to take care of him, I tell them. I also see that she gets assignments from her teachers."

Masingill makes time to tutor young parents as needed. She also sees that teen parents receive the kinds of incentives other students have. She suggests candidates for the school's Student of the Week. Other groups in the school were invited to have pizza with the principal on Fridays. She suggested he invite the teen parents. "He hadn't thought about it, but he was happy to do it," she reported.

You need to be a student advocate as you face circumstances such as these:

• *A guidance counselor is resistive to scheduling students in your class because "their schedules are too full" or they are "college bound."* Help the counselor work out a schedule beneficial to the student, a schedule which will ensure s/he receives needed special services as well as meeting academic requirements. A comparison might be made between teen parent students and working mothers or fathers whose job interferes with parenting tasks. Which is more important? The only possible answer is "Both." You may be able to facilitate a problem-solving discussion between the student and the counselor.

• *Students are "voluntarily transferred" to your separate school for teen parents, even though some prefer to remain in their regular school setting.* Remind the counselor and other personnel of Title IX Guidelines of the Education Amendment Act of 1972. This law, which applies to all states, forbids sex discrimination in any educational institution receiving federal assistance. This includes all public schools and many private ones. If a school operates a special program for pregnant students, the program must be as good as that offered to non-pregnant students. *The school cannot require pregnant students to attend the special program.*

It is imperative that all school staff members understand

this law. A clearly understandable summary of the law and its effect on pregnant and parenting students should be included in student handbooks and in informational materials sent to students' parents.

• *A teacher may be unwilling to give a restroom pass to a student in her class who is 81/2 months pregnant.* Perhaps you can help this teacher understand the physical needs of late pregnancy coupled with an understanding of the importance of the young woman continuing her education during this critical period. Allowing her to go to the restroom is not likely to promote an entire class exodus.

• *A student has missed 15 days of school due to the hospitalization of her seriously ill baby, and the school district policy allows only 10 absences during the semester.* This is a difficult issue in many schools, and two important concepts are involved — the importance of school attendance and the importance of adequately caring for one's child.

School attendance is extremely important, so important that pushing a parent out because of time spent caring for a sick baby translates too often into another school dropout. Attendance rules are not important if the student drops out. Caring for a sick baby, if no one else can or will take the responsibility, is a given task for any parent. Does s/he get credit if the sick baby is left unattended? It is a dilemma and a challenge for all of us who care about teen parents and their children, and who want teen parents to graduate and become productive citizens.

You need to be visible, vocal, and informative. Help others see how your program is an integral part of the educational mission of your school and school district.

Becoming a Resource Expert

Case management, sometimes called continuous counseling or community outreach, means each student has an advocate. The advocate helps students link with the services they need, such as subsidized child care, food stamps, health care, WIC, child support enforcement, TANF, or other supportive services.

The advocate can help pregnant teens get a temporary Medicaid card immediately. The advocate is also there to help students deal with school issues. The student has a consistent person who plays the role of ombudsperson. The case manager assesses the student's needs and helps the student develop a plan (such as a birth plan, parenting plan, adoption plan, school-to-work plan, etc.). The case manager links her/him with the needed services, then checks to see that s/he gets those services.

To be a case manager, you need to be well-informed about community resources. In addition to finding out about public social services and the Public Health Department, know the kinds of services provided by other agencies in your area — employment office, adoption agency, pregnancy testing service, youth counseling group, childbirth preparation class, and more.

You need time to become familiar with local agencies to be able to refer your students to the help they need. This means visiting in person as many agencies as possible, and talking with others by telephone. The school counselor may be able to help identify key contacts. You can also go to the family and consumer sciences extension agent or community agency referral service for help. You need to know about these community resources — and they need to know about you so they can refer potential students.

As you meet with an agency contact, you have a double purpose. You want to know what they can offer your students. Just as important is to "sell" the teen parent program. You want these contacts to understand the services and benefits you can offer their clients.

Start by giving the agency contact your program brochure and a business card. In addition to explaining your services, you need the following information from the agency:

- Services provided
- Eligibility requirements
- Geographic area served (city versus county versus region)
- Costs of services — sliding scale fees?
- Hours? With or without appointment? If no appointment is necessary, the hours the agency is least busy

- Application procedures
- Parking information
- Multiple copies of brochures explaining agency services — to be given to students
- Availability of speakers for class or seminar
- Whether they can provide on-site services
- Contact person for networking purposes

Ideally you will meet with the person(s) directly processing applicants for services as well as the supervisor of the program. Networking with both levels of contacts is helpful.

When you refer a student to an agency, be sure to provide easy-to-follow location information. Perhaps you can create a simple map showing key agency locations. This is especially important in city and suburban schools.

Also, let the agency know that you will be referring students and know they will be well taken care of by the agency. Check with key people at the agency periodically to give them feedback on your students' experiences with their services.

I (Sharon) often receive requests from hospitals and other agencies for a listing of GRADS teachers in their service areas. They want to refer their clients to the programs in the schools. A hospital prenatal clinic director commented to me, "I see a big difference between my pregnant teen patients who are enrolled in GRADS and those who are not. We now ask about school during the intake interview. I want *all* my pregnant teens to be enrolled in GRADS."

Frequent Guests Enrich Offerings

Community resource people can add immensely to your class offerings, and you'll probably find people eager to help meet the special needs of your students. Having other capable people sharing their expertise with your class adds diversity to your regular routine. It also helps your students understand how important they are to their community.

When Liz Irwin was hired to teach the teen parenting class at Valley View High School, Ontario, California, she discovered the practice had been "packet parenting." "Your baby is two so you do this (learning) packet," she recalled.

"The first day I was there," she continued, "I said to the students, 'I'd like to know what you need to be a better parent.'

"They replied, 'Credit. That's all we need.' (They meant course credit was their only reason for being there.)

"I said, 'I can give you all the information you want on toilet training or whatever, but you need to talk to each other and to other people.' When they're off in a corner answering questions from a book, they may be learning, but they can learn so much more from each other. They need both," she concluded.

Irwin stressed that she really co-teaches because of all the community resources she utilizes. Because her classes receive California Cal-SAFE funding, she has money to contract for some of these resources, such as the licensed clinical social worker who is with her students every Wednesday.

The program also has two male counselors who are important, she feels, because some teen moms have had little experience with kind and caring male role models. A lot of group counseling is available to students as well as individual counseling as needed.

A Lamaze teacher comes each week during class, and the YWCA may fund an evening childbirth class at the school. "Even if they don't have to pay a fee, they aren't likely to go to another location for a class, so most of them aren't getting this training with their coach," she commented.

Each Thursday is Girl Scout Day for Irwin's four classes. Girl Scout leaders come in each week and help the girls make things for their babies and complete projects for the community. None of the girls is asked to pay dues. Last year the Girl Scouts sponsored a trip to the zoo for moms and children.

Recently the teen parents were asked to talk with the city council about their program. They spoke enthusiastically about the Girl Scout activity. "The rest of the week we deal with all these big issues, domestic violence, child abuse, rape, this huge awesome responsibility of raising a child," they told the council. "On this day we get to experience the joy of being a mother."

Their Girl Scout community projects have included making blankets for babies who test positive for HIV. They also made items to be used in nursing homes and with sick children.

Other community people and agencies are involved in Irwin's classes. The YWCA has a teen mom program presenter who does a lot of teaching about available resources and also arranges field trips. A drug abuse prevention person presents regularly. The Health Department provides a five-part series, "Street Wise to Sex Wise." Other resources include county adoption counselors, a local domestic violence shelter, and EFNEP (Expanded Food and Nutrition Education Program) from the county extension office.

"These community people validate our students' worth," Irwin concluded.

Someone asked Irwin recently what she would do if she won the lottery. "I'd go home to Virginia and start a teen parent program there," she replied. "That's when it hit me how much I like my job," she confided. "I'd want to do it even if they didn't pay me!"

Promoting School/Health/Social Service Partnerships

Having a good relationship with the health department and social services helps you help young parents. As you talk with health and social service people, encourage them to ask their teenage pregnant and parenting clients where they go to school. If they aren't enrolled, ask them to refer the teen to the local teen parent program. Also ask the worker to contact you so you can contact the student and family. Both the health and social services are important links in school dropout retrieval efforts.

By coordinating their services with yours, health workers can be assured you are also encouraging the pregnant teen to keep her prenatal appointments and to eat the healthy food she and her baby need. You will also insist that babies in your child care center receive their immunizations on schedule, and perhaps routine health checks can be done on site.

In turn, health personnel can stress the importance of school to their teen patients. They can write school releases only as medically necessary, and before doing so, can explore school options which might make continued attendance permissible.

They can offer appointment times that are outside of school hours. Remind them that teens often accept the first appointment time offered, even if it conflicts with school hours. Establishing a weekly teen clinic with late afternoon/early evening or Saturday hours might help.

Invite health workers to visit your class to share their expertise with your students, and perhaps with students' parents. Offer to make a presentation to their professional organization. Share your expertise in working with pregnant and parenting teens together with suggestions for collaborating with your school.

A variety of school-health partnerships have developed in communities across the country. In some communities, health clinics on school campuses have been established. Pregnant teens can receive their prenatal health care in these facilities. Other outstanding school-health partnerships have also evolved.

Mobile unit. Through a partnership between Grant Hospital in Columbus, Ohio, and Columbus Public Schools, a mobile health clinic was developed. The hospital used their own foundation money to purchase and equip an 18-wheel tractor-trailer rig as a prenatal health clinic, and staffed it with volunteer doctors and a paid staff that includes nurses, dieticians, social workers, and a driver. The clinic travels to five inner-city high schools weekly to offer prenatal health care as well as health care checkups for other students. The schools win because students miss very little class time, thanks to the on-site health care services, and the hospital wins because their patients are receiving better and more regular prenatal health care, reducing infant mortality and low-birthweight rates. The mobile prenatal health clinic concept is being considered by some of Ohio's rural communities.

The Early Teen Parent Program Initiative is a result of a Toledo, Ohio, collaboration that includes Toledo City Schools, Toledo Hospital, the Medical College of Ohio, and a few other organizations. The population served is pregnant middle school and elementary-age students. The school district provides a separate school program for these young people. Health care is provided at Toledo Hospital's nurse midwifery clinic. On days the school bus transports the students to the hospital for their prenatal health care, the clinic has a pediatric focus, since the patients are so very young. After the babies are born, health care services are provided by the Medical College of Ohio. Mothers and babies receive medical care at the same time and place.

Well-baby care on site. The county health department provides services twice a month in three schools with on-site day care in the Pinellas County (Florida) School District. Nurse-practitioners conduct health screens and facilitate young parents taking responsibility for their children's immunizations. "If the parent depends on child care with us, the baby's immunizations must be up to date. Otherwise, the baby can't come to child care — and the parent won't be able to come to school. We don't want this to be a barrier to school attendance," commented Susan Todd, resource teacher, Pinellas Teenage Parenting Program.

Nurse practitioners prescribe antibiotics for such common problems as ear infections. They are also available to give pre-natal health check-ups at one of the county's prenatal programs.

Pinellas County TAPP serves 500-700 teen parents annually, according to Todd. Pregnant teens choose between staying at their comprehensive high school or transferring to one of the alternative TAPP locations. Ancillary services (transportation, child care, social services, and health services) are available to all teen parents attending school in the district.

Interagency agreements. GRADS teachers in Defiance, Ohio, have developed interagency agreements with health care providers. Students and their parents (if teens are minors) are asked to sign a release form so the teachers and health care professionals can share important information with each other.

The teachers have influenced the health care community to schedule student medical appointments when they are least likely to conflict with school. The teachers maintain a record card of their students' medical appointments, which is sent with the students to their appointments for verification. The teachers can better monitor their students' health care during pregnancy, and help improve the school attendance rate of students at the same time.

Many innovative partnerships between schools and health care providers are possible. The important thing is that teen mothers and their babies receive optimal health care.

Working with Community Advisory Council

Building and maintaining support from your community is essential. Implementing a strong community advisory council can provide a vital source of support. You'll want to meet at least twice a year, probably more often.

The council can help the teacher plan curriculum and instruction, including validating the competency list and course of study (local curriculum). In many states, the validated course of study must be submitted to the school board for their approval. The council can also help coordinate community and agency support, promote and evaluate the program, and increase public awareness of your services and of the needs of your students.

Advisory council members often become quite knowledgeable about the program and help the teacher learn about available services and community supports. Improved linkage among the schools, agencies, organizations, and businesses should result. The council may help with funding, including the development of grants. Be clear on your program's expectations of the role of the advisory council, and articulate their role/responsibilities to them.

The council needs to be a workable size, about nine to twelve regularly-attending members representing different resources and community networks. Membership can be on a year-by-year or a rotating basis. A three-year rotation works well. When you set up a rotating council, invite one-third of the members to serve a one-year term, one-third a two-year term, and one-third, three years. Each succeeding year, when one-third complete their term, replace them with members who will serve three-year terms.

The first advisory council for the Boulder Valley Teen Parent Program, Boulder, Colorado, was the group of agency people that convinced the school board of the need for the program Many of the same agencies remain on the advisory council — the people change, but the agency stays, according to Parmerlee-Greiner. "Meetings are always held during lunch," she explained. "We find that lunch not only lets them get away from their jobs, but it also allows them to focus on our program. Since this is during the school day, we have babies and parents, regular school going on. This lets them know what we're doing."

Advisory Council Member Possibilities

Individuals

- ¥ School nurse
- ¥ School guidance counselor
- ¥ School administrator
- ¥ School board member
- ¥ Teacher
- ¥ Family and consumer sciences teacher
- ¥ Parent of current or former student
- ¥ Student, current or former
- ¥ Obstetrician
- ¥ Pediatrician
- ¥ Family practitioner
- ¥ Attorney
- ¥ Minister
- ¥ Dietitian
- ¥ Mental health therapist
- ¥ Marital and family therapist
- ¥ Infant massage therapist
- ¥ Workforce preparation specialist

Organizations

- ¥ Adoption agency
- ¥ Business
- ¥ Child care center or organization
- ¥ Children s services
- ¥ College/University
- ¥ Community centers
- ¥ Crisis pregnancy counseling centers
- ¥ Family planning clinic
- ¥ Family service organizations
- ¥ Head Start
- ¥ Health clinic
- ¥ Health department (city or county)
- ¥ Hospital
- ¥ Human services department (city or county)
- ¥ Industry
- ¥ Infant & toddler assessment services
- ¥ Job Opportunities and Basic Skills Program (JOBS) adult parent program
- ¥ Job Training Partnership Act (JTPA)
- ¥ Job Opportunities and Basic Skills Program (JOBS) teen parent program
- ¥ March of Dimes
- ¥ Mental health services
- ¥ Parenting organizations
- ¥ Parents as Teachers
- ¥ Private Industry Council (PIC)
- ¥ Retired Senior Volunteer Program (RSVP)
- ¥ Service organizations, such as Kiwanis, Lions, Rotary, Junior League, etc.
- ¥ Social service organizations
- ¥ Teen/young father organizations
- ¥ Temporary Aid to Needy Families (formerly AFDC)
- ¥ Prepared childbirth organization
- ¥ University extension service
- ¥ Urban League
- ¥ Women s organizations
- ¥ WIC (Special Supplemental Feeding Program)
- ¥ YMCA/YWCA

See the opposite page for a list of possible agencies/persons for advisory council membership.

Support from Advisory Councils

Through their advisory councils, teachers receive a variety of help from local businesses, agencies, professionals, and organizations. Pat Clark, a former GRADS teacher, Eastland Career Center, Groveport, Ohio, remembers an advisory council meeting where members discussed student problems with school attendance. When the council discussed the idea of offering incentives to boost attendance, an executive of a grocery store chain and a member of the council offered monthly donations of items from his chain which Clark used as attendance incentives.

The manager of a marketing company was reviewing the competency list and course of study for the GRADS program in Springfield, Ohio. She focused on the competencies related to school-to-work and economic independence. According to teacher Judy Fletcher, the manager suggested that students serve mentorships at the company's national headquarters offices, then worked with the school administration to set this up. She even funded the transportation for the students.

Income-eligible pregnant women, nursing mothers, infants, and young children may receive supplemental foods from WIC to support adequate nutrition. Several teachers reported having WIC employees on their advisory council. When the WIC representatives realized students were missing a full day of school each month to fulfill the requirements of the WIC program, they decided a change was needed. Each worked out a plan to go to the school one day each month to meet with pregnant and parenting teens on campus. Instead of missing a day of classes, students missed one period.

An attorney learned about the school program for pregnant and parenting teens when she began serving on the community advisory council, and was quite impressed, according to Pat Tucker, GRADS teacher, Grove City High School, Grove City, Ohio. She took the information about the program to the bar association in her city. As a service project, the bar association decided to offer free legal advice to the pregnant and parenting teens enrolled in that program, plus those in 25 other school programs for pregnant and parenting teens in the county.

Linda James, GRADS teacher, Newark High School, Newark, Ohio, reported that a pediatrician who was a member of her advisory council began noticing that teen parents enrolled in the school program were more knowledgeable about the health of their children than teen parents not enrolled in the program. She offered to support teen parents by coming to the school during lunch hour twice monthly. Students are able to bring their lunch to the teacher's classroom for "Talk with the Doc" sessions.

Service Organization Support

Members of Kiwanis International serve on local advisory councils in many schools. Kiwanis International has a national on-going project that focuses on supporting the healthy development of children birth to six. Local organizations have supported programs in a variety of ways. Examples include:

- Provided videos on child car seat safety and childhood immunization for 250 teachers in Ohio
- Purchased and donated car seats
- Funded the cost of retrofitting school buses with seat belts so babies could ride safely
- Purchased children's books for teen parents so they could read to their babies and children at home
- Sponsored "Work Fairs" for pregnant and parenting teens, to support their learning about different types of jobs and careers
- Supported school participation in Reading Is Fundamental® (RIF), a national organization promoting child and family literacy

Susan Scott, GRADS teacher, Worthington High School, Worthington, Ohio, reports that her local Kiwanis not only sponsored RIF in her program, but also built small book cases for storing the baby's books at home. In addition to Kiwanis, service organizations with members who may be willing to serve on local advisory councils include Lions, Rotary International, Junior Service League, Soroptomist Club, and others.

Tips for Success

Successful advisory councils seldom just happen. Planning and continuing attention make the difference. Following are some tips for building success into your advisory council:

- Have one member serve as chair of the council. Work with this person to set up the agenda for each meeting.
- Have an action agenda. Ask council members for help addressing real issues. Ask them to be personally involved with your program. Members are often willing and able to assist in obtaining resources, including financial resources.
- Distribute copies of the agenda for each meeting.
- Teachers should take minutes, write up the minutes, and distribute the minutes to the council members.
- Ask the council to be advocates for the program and the students. At key times, they can be supportive by contacting school personnel, legislators, and others in the community.

An active and supportive advisory council can help you help young parents. So can working partnerships with the public health department and social services. Pregnant and parenting teens should not have to divide their lives into separate compartments for school, health, and social service needs. Through collaboration, we can provide far more support than we can working alone.

When you play the role of catalyst for community support for teen parents, your young clients will progress more rapidly toward that life of self-sufficiency that they want, and that we want for them.

A community service group might provide playground equipment.

CHAPTER 13

Finding
the Dollars

Providing educational and support services for teen parents in schools can be costly. However, *not* providing these needed services is far more costly to the public. In the long run, preventive expenditures can reduce the drain on public dollars for welfare and medical services, special education for the children of teen mothers, and other costly subsidized services.

Teachers as well as administrators need to be aware of the funding available for their programs. This includes "regular" school funding, other local, state, and federal funding for school programs, plus corporate and foundation funding sources. Teachers who don't feel it's their job to plan for funding run the risk of missing out on resources their students need.

With specialized services and a good outreach program, you can expect to retrieve some young parents who have dropped out of school, retain more students in school than were retained before your program began, and see improved attendance for some students. With careful documentation, you may be able to demonstrate to your administrators that your program will actually generate additional funding for the district because of higher enrollment rates and better attendance patterns.

State Funding

All states provide basic school funding to the public school districts in their states. Basic school funding is a specific amount per pupil (K-12), based on ADA (Average Daily Attendance), ADM (Average Daily Membership), or FTE (Full Time Equivalent). Each state determines their own amount per student. In many states, the school districts receive the basic ADA, ADM, or FTE allotment for their pregnant and parenting students, and nothing more. A school district in these states must use local funds or find other sources of funding if they are going to offer any enhanced educational and support services for their pregnant and parenting students.

Some states have recognized that, to be successful in retaining and retrieving pregnant and parenting teens, schools need additional funding for enhanced educational and support services. When states offer a stable, flexible funding base that exceeds the base revenue funding limit, school personnel are able to devote more of their energy and resources to providing services, rather than to searching for funds for their programs. Examples of enhanced state funding include:

Weighted ADA, ADM, or FTE funding for pregnant and parenting teens. Florida, California, and Oregon weight or enhance the basic per-pupil funding for pregnant and parenting teens, giving school districts a greater allocation for these students. An advantage of this type of funding is that there may be no cap on funding or the number of service slots.

For example, Florida provides a teenage parent program cost factor, a weighting of approximately 1.5 for each pregnant and parenting student enrolled in the special program. The additional funds must be expended for educational and support services for these students.

Texas provides weighted ADA funding (2.41) for students receiving pregnancy-related services during pregnancy and the postpartum period. The California Department of Education

Cal-SAFE program provides add-on funding for pregnant and parenting teens in their state.

ADA, ADM, or FTE funding for children of teen parents. Florida provides per-pupil funding for child care and other support (ancillary) services. Each child is given a student identification number, is enrolled in pre-kindergarten ungraded classes as an "at-risk" student, and is part of the school district's student count. No other state funds child care in this way, although California and Minnesota are moving to adopt this model.

Teen parent child care line item in state budget. Line-item funding in the Massachusetts state budget funds child care for teen parents who meet eligibility requirements. To be eligible for child care funds, a teen parent must meet one of these qualifications: 1) receive Temporary Assistance for Families with Dependent Children (TAFDC), 2) receive Social Security income (SSI), or 3) be in danger of needing TAFDC. Eligibility of the non-TAFDC teen parents is based on income, and is determined by the Child Care Resource Agencies.

Eligible teens under age 18 must attend school full-time. Teen parents who are 18 or 19 years old must devote a minimum of 20 hours per week to high school/GED program attendance, work, or a combination of the two. The allocated funds pay for a limited number of child care slots for teen parents. In addition to line item funding for child care for teen parents, Massachusetts also has a line item to fund out-of-home residential placement for teen parents and their children.

Grant funding. Some states provide competitive grant funding for teen parent programs. A disadvantage is that there is a cap on the amount of funds or service slots, or restrictions are imposed on the way the funds can be used. Prior to Cal-SAFE, California grant-funded three separate programs — Pregnant Minors Program (PMP), School-Age Parenting and Infant Development (SAPID) Program, and the Pregnant and Lactating Students (PALS) Program. The limited funding provided overlapping services for some students and no services for others.

Texas offers competitive grant funds for operating Pregnancy, Education, and Parenting (PEP) Programs. Maximum start-up grant is $100,000, and programs receive half their first-year

funding in subsequent years. The local districts must provide
matching funds.

In New Mexico, state funding provides three-year start-up
grants for school districts to implement the GRADS program.
Following the three-year start-up grants, districts are expected to
pick up the costs of the program on their own.

Mary Potter, a GRADS teacher in Clovis, New Mexico, began
her program with a three-year start-up grant. At the end of the
three-year grant, her school district had to decide whether to
continue the program.

Potter had systematically collected data during the three
years, demonstrating that the program was effective in retaining
students in school and retrieving others who had dropped out.
The district administrators calculated that the additional state
ADA dollars coming into the district due to the higher enrollment rate of these students was enough to cover the cost of
running the program.

Vocational unit funding. Some states have viewed their in-
school programs and services as vocational education programs
and have required vocational home economics or family and
consumer sciences certification for their teachers. Ohio pioneered the GRADS program in this way. State vocational unit
funding is intended to fund a teacher, who must serve at least 36
students during the school year. In rural areas, the teacher travels
and serves students at several school sites. The teacher provides
classroom instruction and has two class periods a day for home
and community outreach.

The state of Washington also funds GRADS teachers with
vocational funds, and additionally requires each program to
collaborate with the Department of Family Services to offer
on-site child care services.

If you live in a state that provides enhanced state funding, you
may be able to tap into existing funding streams. If you live in a
state that has no enhanced funding for pregnant and parenting
teens, you can advocate in your state for enhanced funding.

Your best approach is to work with your state department of
education and your state legislature. You can improve your
chances of success if you connect with other teen parent

programs and advocates in your state and present a unified message.

Additional Sources of Funds

School districts also need to maximize other sources of federal and state funding. Sources of federal funds for **child care** for teen parents' children include, but are not limited to:

- Child Care and Development Block Grant (CCDBG)
- Personal Responsibility and Work Opportunity Reconciliation Act of 1996 (welfare reform act)
- Social Services Block Grant (Title XX)
- Single Parent/Displaced Homemaker funds from the Carl Perkins Vocational Education Act
- Title 1 Federal Education funding which can provide child care funds while students are enrolled in Federal Title 1 services
- Even Start federally funded programs which can help with child care if teen parents and their children are also participating in Even Start
- Workforce Investment Act (WIA)

Funds available for **education and support services** include:

- School district general operating funds
- Improving America's Schools Act (IASA)
- Healthy Start
- Social Service Block Grant (Title XX)
- Medicaid
- Enhanced state funds
- Competitive grant funding

Funds for **health care** include:

- Maternal and Child Health (MCH) Block Grants
- Medicaid
- Private health insurers

The Office of Adolescent Pregnancy Programs (OAPP) is a small federal office that funds a few Adolescent Family Life Demonstration Projects. Currently, the programs funded must be community-based and community-supported demonstration projects focusing on pregnancy prevention and comprehensive and integrated approaches to service delivery.

Other state funds may be available. Many states are funding teen pregnancy prevention initiatives, and funds may be available for delaying subsequent pregnancies. At your State Department of Education, the Division of Child Development or Early Childhood Education may have child care funds. Other likely sources of funds include the State Department of Health and the State Department of Human Services.

Other possible sources of state funds that are not as typical include the State Department of Transportation (car seats for babies), employment services (summer youth programs), alcohol and drug addiction services, mental health, youth services (incarcerated youth), women's policy and research, and the supreme court. (Some supreme courts fund education projects related to state laws. They can also help interpret laws for teen parents.)

As this book was being written, the U.S. Congress and the state legislatures were drafting new or modified legislation which would change the state and federal funding programs. As you plan for your programs, stay alert to these changes by reading educational journals and newsletters and checking with your district staff. Your advisory council may also help you obtain current funding information.

Collaboration within School District

If your school district doesn't have a teen parent program, lacks child care, or needs to expand current programs, what can you do? You start by learning as much as possible about available funding *and* you thoroughly document the need for services.

Pat Alviso was hired in 1988 to replace the founding director of the sixteen-year-old Teen Parent Program at Tracy High School, Cerritos, California. An excellent child care center was located on the campus, but the 33 spaces did not stretch to cover the children of all the students enrolled, let alone those of teen parents in the district who were not in school.

Alviso soon realized she was getting a lot of calls from teen parents who needed child care in order to attend school. Alviso started her list. As the list grew, she moved to more serious recruitment.

"I started calling, knocking on doors, putting up signs. I went to the city hall and told them we were looking for pregnant and parenting teens who would like to go to school close to their neighborhood," she reported.

Within a few months, Alviso had 52 names and addresses of young parents not enrolled in school, young people who said they would like to come back to school if they could access child care.

The high school could not provide enough additional money to start the needed second program in the district. The district called a group of school personnel together to plan how best to satisfy the educational needs of these young girls and their children. From this group, Alviso started talking with Dr. Lee Powers, principal of the ABC Adult School.

"Several of us had a meeting," Powers recalled, "and Pat said, 'We need to figure out how to increase the size of the teen parent program, and we don't have any money.' I took them literally and tried to think of a way to do that. The first thing Pat told me was important — that she had 52 names, addresses, and phone numbers of teen parents who had no child care, so could not go to school."

Powers explained that when people come to him with an idea for an adult school class and comment, "I *think* this might work," he's usually not impressed. "But we already had these people, and that made a big difference," he said.

When the next semester commenced, the district had a second teen parent program, this one operating in a former elementary school already partially in use by the adult school. The new program was opened with a mixture of adult and high school funding plus a variety of other funding including vocational education dollars.

At first there was not enough money through the high school to pay for the teachers all day, so they offered a parenting class through adult school in the afternoon. The adult school also helped pay for the child care.

"We also have other sources of funding," Alviso explained. "The Soroptomists (a local service group) wanted to do something in a member's memory. We put up a bronze plaque with her name on it, and they decorated the child care center and gave us a bunch of toys. They also provide a scholarship each year in this woman's memory."

"Sometimes you have to look at it like a puzzle," Powers mused. "You look for ambiguous sections in the Education Code, and you work it out as best you can. It doesn't bother me at all to call people in the state department or contact politicians. You can't be afraid to check with people and ask lots of questions. In California we have marvelous Education Code sections that give advantages to teen parents, but sometimes you have to look hard to find them."

Gloria Parmerlee-Greiner, Boulder Valley Teen Parenting Program, Boulder, Colorado, understands Alviso's strategies. "The first thing I would say is, you can't do it alone," she said, as she described the amount of community help her program has received.

"First you select people for your advisory board who can help find dollars, start child care, provide facilities. Kiwanis helped with our nursery. The shop class built the playhouse using materials donated by the local hardware store. Through a community service grant, IBM bought us a wonderful computer.

"One time we needed car seats for the bus. We wanted them to stay on the bus rather than having the teen parents drag the car seat along with the baby each day. So our advisory chairperson wrote a letter to the newspaper editor, and we wound up with great numbers of car seats, some of them new."

A little extra funding can enrich a program's offerings. Rosann Pollock, teacher, Teen Parent West, Deland, Florida, advises, "We need to beg. Tell everyone what we do. Church groups and other organizations donate money, $40, $100, $5. One church used our program as their advent tree designate. If you have a community college near you, check out the service sororities. They need projects. One gave us a changing table for our child care center. Make a wish and set these people up!" she advised.

Tips from Grants Director

Irene Dardashti, director for grants development, Fullerton (California) Joint Union High School District, stressed that in a school district you start by taking the money that's already available. "Find out first if there are any additional funds," she urged. "Your students may qualify for Title I funds for the educationally disadvantaged based on their income. Do you have at-risk students? You might get funding for special class time for them. Are there leadership stipends that might help?

"Does your school district have additional fund-raising efforts, perhaps foundations or parent-teacher groups outside the system that may provide support for school-based programs beyond the typical needs of reading, writing, and arithmetic? A dropout prevention program might mean special dollars.

"After you've researched the possibilities for funding within the school district, go to local community groups. Does your city have community block grant funds, often based on the economic area, for which your program might qualify? Also check other services within the community to see if an alliance can be arranged. Other programs may have a program to which you can attach yours, or you can look for funds together. If you're looking for a building, an established organization with an interest in this special population may help."

Dardashti moved on to grant writing. "First ask who has access to information. Does your district have a resource library or is anyone receiving a grants newsletter? You probably have access to the Internet. You will find lots of information there on foundations, and even federal and state government funding. Your state may have a web site to use for research from your own home or classroom.

"If none of these are available, find the organization in your community that provides information to people on setting up non-profits and getting funding. You're certainly not alone in looking for funds. Call your state education, social services, and health offices or a local information and referral number and ask for a foundation resource library. Then ask those funding sources if they have any grants or funding scheduled for the near future. Ask to be put on their list for funding information."

Dardashti also talked about corporate and other business funding. "Check with banks that might provide $1,000-$5,000 for a local project," she advised. "Or go to a business, such as Target Stores, that has a neighborhood store close to your school. Many of these businesses have a community giving program. Start out by talking with the manager, and be sure you have written materials about your program needs for the manager's records. This kind of giving is usually one time, like seed money. Then you use that money to leverage other money."

Finally she advised, "You have to have the time to research. Funders appreciate it if you aren't just shooting in the dark. Be knowledgeable about the funding source you're approaching. What do they do? What do they fund?"

Community Funding

What is available in your community for programs for young people? Is United Way concerned about school dropout rates in your area? When they realize that half of the females who drop out of school are already mothers, they may be willing to help you help young parents.

GRADS teachers in Springfield, Ohio, started a mentor mother program. They trained local volunteers who were mothers on how to mentor teen mothers. The project was successful the first year, and after that was funded by United Way through the Big Brothers/Big Sisters program.

Churches and synagogues sometimes provide funding, program support, and volunteers. Church groups are often looking for special projects.

Consider community foundations. Look at their annual reports to learn about their funding priorities, operating practices, timelines, and previous grant recipients.

Is corporation funding available? Many disperse smaller funding amounts through public affairs or marketing departments. Larger funding may come from the corporate foundation associated with their national headquarters.

Some service clubs and auxiliaries may operate with the express purpose of helping youth in their community. They may have annual fund-raising events for this purpose.

Don't forget the individuals who give money to projects they consider worthwhile. And check on businesses that can supply "in-kind" donations such as diapers, toys, etc.

If you're starting a new school program, you might apply for grant funding for prenatal health education, outreach, follow-up and counseling. Some of these can be provided through networking with community services. As you write grants, work toward having your school district pick up part of the funding each year. Then, during the time you're relying on grants, do a thorough evaluation of the impact of the services the grant funded. Income from your grants may decrease, but if you are able to show the value of the service, you can justify the district picking up that funding on a more permanent basis.

Common Mistakes in Proposal Writing

People write a lot of grant proposals that are never funded. What makes the difference between one of these and the ones that win the dollars? First of all, learn to avoid some common mistakes.

The following list was compiled by Sharon Rodine, former executive director of NOAPPP (National Organization on Adolescent Pregnancy, Parenting and Prevention), and is reprinted with permission from *Teen Pregnancy Challenge: Strategies for Change* (1989):

- **Failing to do your homework.** Research potential grantmakers thoroughly. What do they fund? In what amount? When?

- **Not following the application directions.** Whether a foundation or government grant, most groups offering the grants will outline the information they wish to receive from applicants and indicate their time frame. Follow their outline. If you're unclear about something, call them.

- **Project doesn't fit the priorities or focus of the funding source . . . or, the "great contortions act."** This is a trap into which programs can easily fall. We need funding. Funding is available, though it really doesn't fit our main mission and goals. But we come up with a way (through

great mental and programmatic contortions) and a rationale
for applying. Unfortunately, this may serve to cloud your
program's focus and steer it off course on the achievement
of its program goals.

- **Shotgun proposals.** A reminder again to tailor proposals to
  the specific priorities, application procedures, and focus of
  the individual funding sources. It may seem less time con-
  suming to duplicate several dozen identical proposals and
  mail them to multiple funding sources, but your chances of
  being selected with that approach are probably slim to none.
- **Too long and confused.** We've all read really good proposals and really bad proposals, and the difference was appar-
  ent. Often, program providers feel more is better when it
  comes to writing a proposal, but that's not so. When you
  write more than five pages for the body of a corporate
  proposal or ten pages for a foundation proposal, you probably need to edit. Make sure the text of the proposal clearly
  and simply outlines what you're going to do, how you're
  going to do it, and how you'll know if it's been successful.
- **Fuzzy language.** Make your writing clear, concise, and easy
  to read. This is no time to impress someone with the word of
  the day on your desk calendar. Avoid using acronyms,
  terms, or phrases that may be common to your organization
  but not to funders who know nothing about your program.
  Use positive action terms and future-oriented language —
  it's much more appealing.
- **Twisted statistics.** Use all data as accurately as possible.
  Use firm numbers, not subjective or undocumented data
  as facts.
- **Promising more than you can deliver.** This happens to a
  lot of programs. Don't overstate the case in terms of what
  can be delivered or what your program will do. This can be a
  set-up for failure.
- **Inattention to details.** Usually as a result of a tight dead-
  line, little things like page numbers get omitted, or typing
  errors don't get corrected. Proof the proposal yourself, and
  have an objective third party look it over to make sure it's
  clear and reads well.

Grant Writing Works

Linda Miller, former coordinator of TAPP, La Sierra High School, Fullerton, California, spent at least a year planning the program. Her first grant-writing effort, she was told, was good, but not good enough to get funded. She didn't consider her grant-writing time wasted, however. "In the process of writing, I learned a lot," she commented. "I had to make arrangements with all sorts of community organizations to provide services. Those arrangements were already in place when we finally started."

As a supervisor in her district's Recovery Retention Program, Miller was contacting teen parents who couldn't come to school because of lack of child care. She figured if she could make services pay for themselves, the district would approve.

"At first I thought of renting a church nursery," she said. "I was thinking small, one teacher, one class of teen moms. I wrote up a budget and started planning. I contacted various churches, but they said they were using their nursery one day a week and wouldn't rent it. But one church told me they had several rooms we could rent for relatively little money.

"My supervisor said I could use $6,000 from the district as start-up money. That went mostly for cribs, a washer and dryer, a VCR, a microwave, and a dishwasher. Parents at our local preschool donated some equipment.

"I showed my supervisor that we would have enough ADA to pay for the teacher, a nutrition aide, and two or three child care aides. Then I started looking for grants for the rest of the things we needed."

Miller first got a start-up grant from the March of Dimes, only $500, but no strings attached. She applied again to the March of Dimes for a grant to pay for an outreach teacher to work on the district high school campuses. This teacher visits students who are home on bedrest, meets with them once a week after delivery, and checks with pregnant students in the schools.

At the end of the three-year March of Dimes grant, the district allocated money for the outreach teacher.

A couple of years ago Miller said they served only infants and crawlers, but they also needed a toddler room. She discovered

that Target Stores gives community grants. She applied, and
received $5,000 to outfit the toddler room.

Miller continued to apply for and win grants. "You have to
apply for any grant you want the first year it's available," she
stressed, "because after that it's not likely to be available again
for a long time."

The Fullerton program has grown to four classes with about
100 students and 70 babies enrolled. Several parents of babies in
the child care center attend Fullerton High School located two
blocks away.

Having a good mentor is important when you start writing
grants, according to Miller. "Most important is to take the
request for proposal form and answer each question as completely as possible," she said. "You feed back what they want to
know. It's tedious, but it works."

Sharing Services

As mentioned before, funding for child care in Florida is
based on the baby's attendance. Students whose children are
enrolled in child care must participate in or have completed an
approved parenting class.

When a child care center was opened on the school campus in
Port Charlotte, Florida, there weren't enough children of student
parents to support the center. As a consequence, state funding for
the center was inadequate. They decided to open the center to
children of staff, and have them pay for the service through
payroll deductions, according to Chantal Phillips, supervisor of
alternative programs, Charlotte County Public Schools.

"We were leery of doing this, but decided to give it a try, and
it's worked beautifully for us," she explained. "Staff member
parents, in a lot of cases, have been excellent role models for our
teen parents. They share in the struggles of getting the baby
settled in the morning. Sharing child care space also made the
school staff more supportive of our program."

Fundraising — A Necessary Step

Almost no one has enough money to fund teen parent services
adequately. Seldom does a district have desired funding for its

regular education program. Finding extra dollars for teen parents and their children takes creativity and a willingness to look for funding in various places.

Good fundraising means showing that your program is cost-effective, that it is making a difference, and that, by serving young people, it is future-oriented. Good fundraising involves showing the benefits for the participants and the benefits for the funder.

Successful fundraising takes time, planning, and finding the right people to contact the right sources with the right program ideas. In all communities, there are people who know how to raise money, there are people who would like to learn how to raise money, and there are potential sources of funding for your program. Find them; involve them in your program.

Good fundraising means that the funds from the donor will meet *specific needs* of your target population. Funding sources are going to give their money to some program . . . your job is to convince them that yours is the program to fund.

Good program outreach may help her stay in school.

CHAPTER 14

Outreach, Marketing, and Public Relations

Several years ago a teen parent program teacher in Orange County, California, was told by her administrator, "It's best to keep a low profile. Don't remind people of our teen pregnancy problem."

That was good advice *only if* this program's goal was to keep enrollment low rather than encouraging pregnant and parenting teens to continue their education. If, as a teen parent program teacher, you "keep a low profile," you'll miss a lot of young people who need your help. If they don't know you exist, you can't help them. *If you want to help kids, don't have a low-key program!*

Outreach is important for two reasons: to find clients and to build community support for the program.

Drop Out Because of Pregnancy?

Since 1972 it has been illegal to push a student out of school because of pregnancy, parenting, or marital status. Pregnant and parenting teens face the same attendance requirements as other students. In some cases, having a child depending on the teen parent for care excuses the teen from compulsory school attendance. However, if child care is available, the teen parent is expected to be in school.

Many people, however, still believe that it's all right for teen parents to drop out of school. That's the way it was, and that's the way it continues to be. These people need to be reminded that those who don't graduate from high school earn 70¢ to the graduate's $1. Yet only about half of all teen parents graduate from high school. Three-fourths of all single mothers under 25 live in poverty, and most of them must rely on public assistance. *This is happening in your district.*

Over and over we need to spread the word that pregnancy and parenting are *not* reasons to leave school. Marketing your teen parent program can help. An aggressive outreach approach will mean more young people know about your special program, young people who might drop out of school without your help — or young people who have already dropped out of school. Because of your assistance, they may continue their education.

Pat Alviso, former director of the Teen Parent Program in the ABC Unified School District, Cerritos, California, reports that 40-50 percent of their students had dropped out of school before enrolling in this program. About half of this group dropped out after getting pregnant, and the others before they conceived. The coming baby combined with the special services at TPP gets these young people back on the education track.

From its inception in 1972, this program has developed strong and effective outreach strategies. A combination of media publicity, family contact, community speaking appointments for teacher and students, and plenty of program information targeted to school personnel helps spread the word about the services for pregnant and parenting teens. Retrieval of many school dropouts is the result.

Recruiting Eligible Students

Don't assume the young people who need your services will flock to enroll. Effective outreach to potential participants is essential. If there is one pregnant or parenting teen who isn't in your program because s/he doesn't know about it, there's room to improve your outreach.

Bonnie Thompson, Middletown, Ohio, spoke of her first day on the job many years ago. "The first year I was hired to teach GRADS, I got my classroom ready and prepared a great lesson for the first day. To my surprise, no students showed up. I realized I had a lot of home, school, and community outreach to do to get my students."

Satisfied students can be your best source of referrals. They are likely to bring potential students to you, or tell you about their friends who might enroll. Other teens are likely to trust their friends' recommendation.

"Make sure the traditional schools are knowledgeable about the teen parent program," Patrice Hall, assistant director, alternative education, Tucson, Arizona, urged. "Meet with the school principals, school nurses, and counselors. Let them know what's going on. They get information about kids who are pregnant or parenting, but they can't refer unless they have program information."

Radio and television public service announcements (PSAs) can help get your message out. Contact local stations with programming for teens for information.

Reaching teens involves designing a message and materials that will be relevant to them. Program information needs to be presented in a teen-oriented manner and placed where teens will see or hear it. Keep the message simple, clear, non-threatening, and non-judgmental.

One school nurse found a particularly effective spot for teen parent program brochures — inside the door of the restroom in her office. Pregnant students not yet broadcasting their pregnancy tended to be there occasionally. With the brochures she put white envelopes so the student could take the brochure without advertising the fact of her pregnant status.

Develop a poster promoting your program and place it in clinics, doctors' offices, welfare and other social service offices, community centers, unemployment offices, schools (classrooms, counselors, and nurses' offices, cafeteria, physical education

areas), anywhere young people might gather. Put the same
information on 3" x 5" cards and place them on supermarket,
laundromat, and other community bulletin boards.

Students can be immensely helpful with this kind of outreach.
Encourage them to take brochures to their doctor's office and
other public areas. Perhaps a student could design a poster which
could be used with your brochures. Preparing a business card
with program information and leaving these cards along with the
brochures is another effective strategy. It's probably best to say,
"Do you know someone who is young and pregnant?" rather
than "Are you young and pregnant?" If she's pregnant, she may
not be willing to admit it, but she certainly knows the question
applies to her. Most important is that this approach encourages
friends and expectant fathers to get involved, too.

A class brainstorming session on brochure placement may
generate additional ideas for distribution. Such a session is also a
good way to get your students involved in this important
community outreach task.

Teen Parent Panels Can Help

Teen parent panels can be an important part of your outreach.
You may get requests from middle and high school teachers for a
teen parent panel to tell their students about the realities of early
parenthood. A service organization or a church group may be
open to learning more about your program through a student
presentation. Teen parents willing to share the realities of early
parenting are perhaps the best spokespersons to help other teens
hear the reasons to delay parenthood until they are emotionally
and financially ready. If any panel members are under age 18,
you need to obtain written parental permission.

Some schools offer credit for panel preparation and participation. Even students unwilling to "make speeches" in front of
anyone are sometimes willing to share their real-life experiences
of pregnancy and parenting. As they do so, their self-esteem may
improve as well as their speaking skills.

Not only may teen parents be the most believable people to
talk about the realities of teen pregnancy and parenthood, but
their comments also spread the message about the school

program. It's a good idea for the teacher to describe the program briefly before the students start sharing their experiences. As one teacher said, "I talk first, because the listeners get so engrossed in my students' stories that I don't stand a chance afterward!"

In your program description, focus on the fact that some young people still drop out of school because of pregnancy and parenting, especially if they don't know about your district's special services. Point out that those in your audience can help keep a pregnant friend or a young mother from dropping out by telling her about your class. Or they can encourage a young father to enroll in your class and get some of the support he needs with his new role of father.

It is important for you to set boundaries with your students. Discuss the kind of information it is helpful to share. You want them to describe the realities of teen parenthood that include not only their wonderful children, but their baby's sleeping patterns, the financial costs of parenthood, and the challenge of being a teenager, a student, and a parent at the same time.

Allow for questions at the end of the panel's presentation. Tell your students ahead of time and again in the classroom that if there is a question they don't wish to answer, that's okay. Also be prepared to ask questions in the unlikely event the students don't.

One question often asked, and which young people generally don't mind answering, is, "Were you using contraception when you got pregnant? If not, why not?"

"I didn't think I'd get pregnant" is a common reply. It's a thought-provoking comment.

However, not all teachers are enamored with teen parent panels. Some are concerned that their students may be exploited, similar to the ways some television talk show programs today exploit their guests. Your students place their trust in you, and they need to feel safe and protected. Your decisions regarding teen parent panels need to be based on their best interests.

Speaking in public is often a beneficial experience for youth. Some parenting students benefit by telling their story in public. Other students need to share in a safe and protected environment. If public speaking is a valued part of the experience, you could

explore other opportunities for students to speak publicly, such
as in-class presentations or community service projects.

You may choose to accept some requests for teen parent
panels, or you may decide to turn down all such requests. When
making your decision, consider your students and their best
interests. If you decline a request, perhaps you could offer
suitable alternatives such as a video, an adult who was a teen
parent, a presentation by you, or a combination of any of these.

In-School Publicity

Outreach to your school and to other schools in your district is
important. Encourage your school newspaper to include a story
about your program, perhaps something each semester. Suggest
several possibilities for feature and news stories, and stress the
importance of including information in each story on how to
enroll in the program. Also suggest including data you have
collected and student performance outcomes.

Students and families who don't need your services today are
not likely to pay much attention to your program's existence.
The result can be a student not aware of your services when s/he
could benefit by enrolling. Periodic stories in the school
newspaper help build this important awareness.

Some programs even run small ads in the school paper. A
classified ad might raise awareness. Wording could be as simple
as "Know someone who is young and pregnant? The Teen Parent
Program could help. For information, visit Ms. Smith in room
101 or call 234-5789."

Nearly all schools have student handbooks which describe
school policies, activities, etc. Write a program description that
includes enrollment information for your school's handbook.
Include Title IX information, the Federal guidelines which state
that no one can be pushed out of school or denied participation
in school activities because of pregnancy, parenthood, or
marital status.

Susan Siepel, executive director, AWARE, Carlsbad, New
Mexico, has an open house every year in their child care center.
"We advertise it in the paper, and we put flyers all over, includ-
ing teachers' lounges. We invite people who attend our annual

meeting and ask them to bring co-workers. We make a special effort to reach teachers in our high school. It was a major victory last year when a teacher called to tell me she wanted to make sure our annual open house was on the school calendar."

When you plan an open house, invite more people than you think you can handle. Many won't come, but your well-designed invitation can give them information about your program. Giving an invitation to each staff person may result in referrals to your program. Referrals are at least as important as getting district employees to attend your open house.

My principal was shocked one year to learn I (Jeanne) had sent out 1500 invitations to an open house to be held in our classroom. He knew the room would not hold a large group of people. As I expected, only 40 people came, a group we easily handled. However, 1500 people, mostly within our school district, were reminded of the Teen Parent Program. That was my objective.

At that open house, we also generated positive newspaper publicity for the program because we gave a "Rocking Chair Award" (tiny rocking chair charm) to the person most instrumental in obtaining on-site child care for students' children. The local newspaper sent a photographer, and expanded the story to describe other positive aspects of our program. As a result, a young mother who had dropped out of school called for information, then enrolled.

Reaching Out to Community Groups

Publicity includes a wide variety of activities. Other forms of outreach into the community might include you and/or your students speaking to church/synagogue groups, clubs, and other groups of people.

Community groups use lots of speakers. You might prepare a short press release offering your services, perhaps with a couple of students, for presentations on teen pregnancy, parenting, and prevention. Always focus on the positive effects of providing needed services, and on program statistics that demonstrate favorable outcomes for students such as dropout, low-birthweight, and repeat pregnancy rates. In your presentation, you'll want to include suggestions for your audience on preventing too-early pregnancy as well as how they might support your program.

Sometimes even well-planned and well-run teen parent programs lose funding, community support, and teen participants because they do not continuously market their program to each of these groups. If you receive any funding or other kinds of help from city or county agencies, foundations, businesses, churches, service, or other community groups, you must constantly sell yourself and the value of your program's existence to these organizations.

Value of Service Projects

Another community winner is service projects. Teen parents are more likely to be viewed in the community as "takers," rather than "givers." Performing community service projects can positively influence the attitudes and beliefs of the community about teen parents, and may also generate favorable media attention.

The projects could be educational, such as informing the public about shaken baby syndrome, or the serious effects of sexual abuse, or the dangers of lead paint for children in older homes and buildings.

The projects could involve making and giving something. A wall on the pediatrics floor of Akron (Ohio) Children's Hospital is decorated with a quilt that was sewn by students in Akron GRADS classes. Students in the family and consumer sciences classes at Kent (Ohio) High School, including Jeanette Abell's GRADS classes, took home plain Teddy bears purchased by the Salvation Army and "dressed up" each bear. The Salvation Army had 100 very well-dressed Teddy bears to give away for Christmas, and the school's family and consumer sciences classes, including the GRADS program, received favorable media attention. Most important, students can benefit greatly from service projects. "Giving" can provide great internal rewards.

Handling Media Publicity

People don't want to know about programs for pregnant and parenting teens — until their daughter or best friend's daughter is pregnant. If they've read a feature story about the program in their local paper, they're far more likely to remember there's help when they need it.

Send press releases regularly to your local papers and other media. The purpose of a press release is to report news, and you can find news items all around you in a teen parent program. If you have a staff change, it's news. The beginning of a new semester is news, and of course would include enrollment procedures and time. Classroom speakers may be newsworthy.

Be aware of your district's guidelines regarding working with the news media. Know that you can decide whether to accept or decline interviews with the media. You'll probably accept some but not others. A reporter called us once and demanded to know the age of our youngest student. We chose not to talk with him because we felt he wanted sensationalism rather than a positive story about young people continuing their education even as they handled the additional responsibilities of parenthood.

Most reporters, however, are likely to be interested in graduation statistics, especially if those numbers include retrieved school dropouts. They will be interested in community service projects in which your students are involved. If your program is also working toward the prevention of teen pregnancy, let them know.

The best news of all are feature stories about students who are doing well in spite of obstacles. Your community needs to know that, with help, teen parents can move toward their dreams of having a productive life. A positive news story can also add greatly to the featured student's self-esteem.

If you're involving teens in media interviews, prepare them adequately for the experience. An interview can be intimidating for an adult, and extremely so for a young person who may be asked abruptly by the interviewer to share very personal facts about her/his life.

If the student is under 18, you need the parent's written permission for the interview, photo, and/or story. Even more important, you need to be sure the student *wants* to be involved in this way. No student should ever feel coerced into talking with a reporter or providing personal data to the media. Some students may feel more comfortable using a fictitious name.

Directors of some teen parent programs have decided, through experience, to have adult staff members handle all interviews with the media to avoid any unnecessary embarrassment, hurt feelings, or exploitation of the young people in the program. However, some teens thoroughly enjoy media opportunities. They, preferably with an adult staff member also involved, can provide the positive human interest kind of story both your program supporters and the media appreciate.

Cooperating with the news media to produce positive news and feature stories about your program and your students is important. Take care to set clear guidelines for any stories or interviews with students, however. The media isn't often looking for "good news." They're looking for controversy or a story angle that will grab public attention. Don't let your students or program be exploited by the media.

Prepare a list of positive information to share when a reporter calls. Are young people verbalizing a desire to delay the next pregnancy? Are they setting goals for themselves, then working toward those goals? How many young mothers and fathers are graduating from high school with the support of your program? How many return the next year or advance a grade level? Tell the reporter. Have a clear idea of the message you want reported and keep repeating it. Most reporters will follow your direction.

Make sure your data and information are clear and accurate. Have printed fact sheets and descriptive information about the program available for a reporter to use in an article. Practice difficult subject areas ahead of time so you have smooth, genuine responses that are comfortable and appropriate. Working with the media is a learned skill that improves with experience.

When you anticipate your public relations needs in advance, you enhance your ability to respond appropriately in a timely manner. The public is more likely to support your school program when you provide clear and accurate information.

Develop an outreach, marketing, and public relations plan. Your objectives are to recruit school-age parents who need your program's eduational services and to build community support. Thoughtful planning can help you meet both objectives.

CHAPTER 15

Where Will You Start?

Trying to create a road map for teaching pregnant and parenting teens to succeed has been a difficult challenge for us. Actually teaching those teens to succeed is the real challenge.

Chapter 1 provides an overview of a variety of programs for pregnant and parenting teens, but this is only a sampling. Your school district may provide something quite different. Look at the opportunities in your setting and plan how best to help young people where you are.

You probably know about setting priorities. Effective people know the scatter-gun approach seldom works well. If you have a task to accomplish, you plan, you focus on the most important aspects of the task, you look at your available resources, and you work out a feasible approach to moving toward your goal.

Setting priorities is especially hard when you work with teen parents. Their needs are often intense, but the rewards of helping them meet those needs are high. Each time you help a teen parent continue his/her education, prepare for work which will provide financial support for his/her family, and become an effective parent and citizen, we all win.

But where do you start? How will you prioritize your efforts? Which is most important?

- Documenting needs?
- Gaining community support?
- Organizing a program?
- Developing curriculum?
- Recruiting students including teen fathers?
- Providing child care?
- Offering workforce preparation?
- Supporting your students in their many needs?
- Evaluating your program?
- Working with families, school, and community?
- Locating funding?

Many of us, when we look at all those priorities, might be tempted to give up. The challenge is too much.

But of course you don't do that. Instead, you

- Bring others into your circle of strategizing and prioritizing.
- Include teen parents in your planning and in your needs assessment.
- Collaborate with social, health, and community services involved with youth.
- Get started!

If you're just starting a new program, building interest and support in your community is critical. Collect and share local data on teen pregnancy, school dropout, and low-birthweight babies. Help people understand that resources *are* going to these young people already. Providing the services teen parents need to become self-supporting, productive citizens and good parents is caring, rational, *and* cost-effective.

As a society, we cannot afford to have young people dropping out of school with little chance of adequately supporting their families. We cannot afford to have mothers and fathers who parent poorly because they have had no help in learning the art and skills of parenting. We cannot afford to have babies who don't get the best possible start in life.

No matter whether we are focusing on the golden rule or the hard dollars and cents realities, we simply cannot afford to ignore pregnant and parenting teens.

To start a program, you build your case and you have a plan. You form community support linkages, outline a budget, and identify funding sources. In short, you get organized . . . and you end up serving young people.

If you're already working with teen parents, you are aware of their many needs. You probably continually assess where you are with your program, and where you want to go. Even if you feel you already have the most important components in place, you may recognize a facet of your program that can be improved. Perhaps you're doing an outstanding job with parenting instruction, but need to shore up your workforce preparation component. Maybe your child care is high quality and available as needed by your students, but you'd like to do more to engage young fathers. And when was the last time you said to yourself, "Well, now I've got all the funding I need"?

Even if you've been working with teen parents for years, you want to do more. You're always looking for the missing pieces so you can provide the best possible services for pregnant and parenting teens. We hope you find in these chapters some help with your planning.

If you're an experienced teacher, you can also do something wonderful for a new teacher or a new program in a neighboring school or district. You can do for other professionals what you do for your students by reaching out and offering a helping hand. In this way, you can help even more teen parents.

And isn't that your goal?

AFTERWORD

*At this moment, as **Books, Babies and School-Age Parents** goes to press, Jeanne and Sharon may not be particularly interested in thinking about the next edition. At some point, however, they'll be ready.*

As readers, we would all benefit if you shared a potential contribution for that as-yet-unscheduled next edition. Do you have a favorite chapter? Or a story that poignantly illustrates a point in this book? Has your experience in teaching teen parents helped you develop a technique that might prove worthwhile for your fellow teachers "in the trenches"? Or is there a section (other than the Foreword, of course) that can be improved? Write these down and send them to the authors. You will be providing valuable help for others, and I'm sure your comments will be welcomed.

Max Schilling

APPENDIX

Organizations

The following organizations publish materials related to adolescent pregnancy prevention and teen parents. Contact them for information.

Advocates for Youth
1025 Vermont Avenue, Ste. 200
Washington, DC 20005
202.347.5700

The Alan Guttmacher Institute
121 Wall Street, 21st Floor
New York, NY 10005
212.248.1111

Center for Assessment and Policy Development (CAPD)
111 Presidential Blvd., Ste. 234
Bala Cynwyd, PA 19004
610.664.4540

Center for Law and Social Policy
1015 15th St., NW, Ste. 400
Washington, DC 20005
202.906.8000

Children's Defense Fund (CDF)
25 E Street NW
Washington, DC 20001
202.628.8787

Child Trends, Inc.
4301 Connecticut Ave. NW, Ste. 100
Washington, DC 20008
202.362.5580

Child Welfare League of America
440 First Street NW, Third Floor
Washington, DC 20001
202.638.2952.

National Association for the Education of Young Children
1509 16th Street NW
Washington, DC 20036
202.232.8777

Planned Parenthood Fed., America
434 West 33rd Street
New York, NY 10001
212.541.7800

Education, Training and Research Associates (ETR)
4 Carbonero Way
Scotts Valley, CA 95066
831.438.4060

National Adolescent Health Information Center (NAHIC)
Univ. of California, San Francisco
3333 California St., Ste. 245
San Francisco, CA 94143
415.502.4856

National Organization on Adolescent Pregnancy, Parenting and Prevention (NOAPPP)
2401 Pennsylvania Ave. NW, Ste. 350
Washington, DC 20037-1730
202.293.8370

Population Affairs, Dept. of Health and Human Services
1101 Wootton Parkway, Ste. 700
Bethesda, MD 20852
301.594.4000

Program Archive on Sexuality, Health and Adolescence (PASHA)
Sociometrics Corporation
170 State Street, Ste. 260
Los Altos, CA 94022-2812
650.949.3282

The Robin Hood Foundation
826 Broadway, 7th Floor
New York, NY 10003
212.227.6601

Sexuality Information and Education Council of the United States (SIECUS)
130 W. 42nd Street, Ste. 350
New York, NY 10036
212.819.9770

GRADS Adolescent Parent Resource Guide
Sample Activities

Unit 4: Parenting.
Competency 4.4: Analyze legal issues
related to parenthood.

Competency Builders:

4.4.1 Identify the legal obligations of mother, father, grand-parents, school, and community agencies.

4.4.2 Analyze uses for and importance of birth certificates/documentation.

4.4.3 Define *parentage, child support, visitation,* and *allocation of parental rights and responsibilities.*

4.4.4 Define *guardianship, minor status,* and *power of attorney.*

4.4.5 Identify resources available for obtaining family legal counsel.

Individual Learning Activities

a. Collect newspaper articles, watch television programming, and think of personal experiences to make a list of situations that involve legal issues related to parenting. Circle those legal issues you might face as a parent. Share your list with a partner or your teacher and explain how each issue might impact you, your child, your family, or your community. (4.4.1)

b. Read **Legal Terms Parents Should Know** (handout). Write the items on index cards and their corresponding definitions on the backs of the cards. Ask a partner or your teacher to "flash" the cards as you give the definitions. In your journal explain how these terms affect your life. (4.4.3, 4.4.4)

c. Use a computer to search on-line sources for legal terms and definitions as well as legal resources available to you. Print the information you find and share it with other teen parents. (4.4.1, 4.4.3, 4.4.4, 4.4.5)

Processing Questions
- *How many different sites did you find that could provide information about legal terms or issues?*
- *Why is this information important to you?*
- *How can you determine if the source of information you located is reliable?*

d. Review **Sample Birth Certificate** (handout) and make a list of specific pieces of information found on the birth certificate. Obtain a copy of a hospital certificate of birth and compare it with the sample on the handout. Identify the similarities and differences. Use classroom resources or an interview with a legal aid representative to find out information about birth certificates related to the questions below. (4.4.2)

- What is the difference between a hospital certificate and a birth certificate?
- Where do you go to get a birth certificate and how much does it cost?
- Why do you need a birth certificate?
- Does the father of the baby have to sign the birth certificate?
- What does it mean if the father does or does not sign the birth certificate?

_____

Group Learning Activities
a. Read student resource **Legal Situations** (handout).

Processing Questions
- *What are the consequences of these situations for the parent(s)? The children? The extended family? Society?*
- *What legal issues might you anticipate in your life as a parent?*
- *What action can you take now to prepare to face or prevent these legal issues?*

b. Write the terms listed on **Legal Terms Parents Should Know** (handout) on the chalkboard or a poster. Do not write their definitions. Working with a partner, write your own definition for each of the words on the list. Then check your definitions against those on the handout. (4.4.3, 4.4.4)

c. Invite a speaker from a local legal aid society or child support enforcement agency to class to discuss legal issues facing teen parents and information related to the topics below. Make a list of questions to ask the speaker during the presentation. Following the presentation, summarize the major points in your journal. Add names to your directory of community resources that provide help with legal issues. (4.4.1, 4.4.2, 4.4.3, 4.4.4, 4.4.5)

- Legal obligations of mother, father, grandparents, schools and community agencies
- Importance of birth certificates/documents
- Resources available for obtaining legal counsel
- Parentage, child support, and visitation rights
- Allocation of parental rights and responsibilities
- Guardianship, minor status, and power of attorney

Processing Questions
- *What did you learn from the guest speaker that you can apply to your own situation?*
- *Why is it important to establish paternity?*
- *Why is it important to be familiar with legal documents and understand them?*

d. Make a list of legal documents that should be kept in a safe place, such as those listed below. Brainstorm places to keep legal documents and other important papers. (4.4.1)

- Birth certificate
- Social security card
- Immunization records
- Fingerprint records

GRADS
Professional Development Program

Supporting professional development is a major focus of the Ohio Department of Education. The types of professional development opportunities available for GRADS teachers include:

- Yearly conference. One strand of sessions at the three-day All Ohio Vocational Education Conference is planned by and for GRADS teachers. This conference is open to all the national GRADS sites.
- New GRADS teacher training. This is a two-day workshop for all teachers new to GRADS. This workshop is open to teachers from all states.
- Regional inservice meetings. Twice yearly, five regional meetings are co-sponsored by the Ohio Department of Education and GRADS teachers. The teachers co-sponsoring each meeting help determine the agendas.
- GRADS Teacher Leader Institute. Thirty GRADS teachers participated in this two-year institute. The goals of the Institute were
  1. to rewrite the *Adolescent Parent Resource Guide.*
  2. to build a professional community of learners.
  3. to provide professional development for all Ohio GRADS teachers. As the rewritten *Adolescent Parent Resource Guide* was introduced, the Teacher Leaders were the professionals who provided the professional development for all GRADS teachers. The Teacher Leaders were also striving to build professional communities of learners among GRADS teachers around the state.

BIBLIOGRAPHY

The following bibliography, updated in 2003, is divided into three sections. The first two sections contain books, videos, and a few other resources for pregnant and parenting teens. Workbooks and other classroom aids are available for many titles. The third section contains descriptions of resources for professionals.

If the resource is available on Amazon or other on-line bookstore, only the publisher's name is listed. If not, the publisher's address and phone number are listed, but only with the first resource described from that publisher. For most video producers/distributors, one or two representative titles are described. Contact these companies for complete listings.

Prices quoted were current July, 2003, but prices tend to change. If you can't find a book in your bookstore, you can usually get it directly from the publisher. Enclose $3 for shipping per book. See page 287 for an order form for Morning Glory Press publications.

Resources
for Pregnant and Parenting Teens

Anasar, Eleanor. **"You and Your Baby: Playing and Learning
Together." "You and Your Baby: A Special Relationship."** 2001.
"You and Your Baby: The Toddler Years." 2003. 32 pp. each.
Each available in Spanish edition. $2.65 each. Bulk discounts. The
Corner Health Center, 47 North Huron Street, Ypsilanti, MI 48197.
734.484.3600.
*Gorgeous photos of teen parents and their children on every other page.
Each booklet contains helpful information at an extremely easy
reading level.*

Arnoldi, Katherine. *The Amazing True Story of a Teenage Single
Mom.* 1998. 176 pp. $16. Hyperion.
*Written in a true experience/comic book format, it's the story of a young
mom who had dreams, but faced many obstacles in fulfilling them.*

Arthur, Shirley. *Surviving Teen Pregnancy: Your Choices, Dreams
and Decisions.* 1996. 192 pp. $11.95. Teacher/Study Guides, $2.50/
set. Morning Glory Press, 6595 San Haroldo Way, Buena Park, CA
90620. 714.828.1998, 888.612.8254.
*Helps pregnant teens understand their alternatives. Offers guidance in
learning decision-making. Chapter on adoption planning is included.*

Barr, Linda, M.N., and Catherine Monserrat, Ph.D. *Teenage Pregnancy: A New Beginning.* Revised 2002. 151 pp. Spiral binding,
$18.95. Workbook, $4.95. New Futures, Inc., 4919 Prospect NE,
Albuquerque, NM 87110. 505.872.0164.
*Prenatal health book written specifically for pregnant adolescents. Spans
the childbearing cycle from conception through early parenthood.*

Beaglehole, Ruth. *Mama, listen! Raising a Child without Violence: A
Handbook for Teen Parents.* 1998. 224 pp. $25. Curriculum Guide,
$20. Ruth Beaglehole, 2162 Echo Park Ave., Los Angeles, CA
90026. 323.661.9123.
*A unique book. Most of it is written as if a toddler is speaking, explaining
what s/he needs from his/her parents. Good description of emotional needs
of small children. An absolute lack of violence (**no** spanking) is
recommended throughout.*

Bjorklund, Barbara R. *Parents Book of Discipline.* 1999. 272 pp.
$5.99. Mass Market Paperback.
Emphasizes that discipline is not the same as punishment, but is one of the

fundamental ways that parents teach their children to respect others and themselves.

Brinkley, Ginny, and Sherry Sampson. *Baby and Me: A Pregnancy Workbook for Young Women.* 1997. 44 pp. $3. ICEA, P.O. Box 20048. 951.854.8660.
Reader-friendly overview of pregnancy, labor, and birth written especially for teens. Simply written, cartoon illustrations.

————. Illus. by Gail Spratt Cooper. *You and Your New Baby — A Book for Young Mothers.* Also in Spanish: *Usted y su nuevo bebé.* 1996. 80 pp. $3. ICEA.
Simple and complete guide for caring for baby. Written in a format for easy understanding.

————. *Young and Pregnant — A Book For You.* Also in Spanish: *Joven y embarazada.* 1995. 73 pp. $3. ICEA
*Refreshingly simple book on prenatal care directed to teenagers. Provides basic information. Also available in condensed 48-page version, **Promises: A Teen's Guide to Pregnancy.** 1993. $2.*

Eisenberg, Arlene, Heidi E. Murkoff, and Sandee E. Hathaway, B.S.N. *What to Expect When You're Expecting.* 2002. 624 pp. $13.95. Workman Publishing.
Discusses prenatal diagnosis, childbirth options, second pregnancies, twins, Cesarean birth, practical tips on coping with pregnancy symptoms. Step-by-step guides through labor and delivery, postpartum care, breastfeeding.

Fenwick, Elizabeth, et al. *How Sex Works: A Clear, Comprehensive Guide for Teenagers to Emotional, Physical, and Sexual Maturity.* 1996. 96 pp. $9.95. Dorling Kindersley Publishing, Inc. 877.342.5357.
Profusely illustrated, easy-to-read comprehensive guide for teenagers to emotional, physical, and sexual maturity.

Gottfried, Ted. *Teen Fathers Today.* 2001. $24.90. Twenty First Century Books.
Focuses on teen fathers in America and their role in the childrearing process. Real-life stories complement the discussions. Provides practical information such as dealing with the reactions of parents, realities of pregnancy and birth, and taking responsibility for one's baby.

Guidance for the Journey: A Pregnancy Journal. 2000. CD, $100. Booklet, 2002, $6. Face to Face Health & Counseling Service, Inc., Doreen Williams, 1165 Arcade, St. Paul, MN 55106. 651.772.5555.
Software program which produces personalized pregnancy journals.

Harris, Robie H. Illus. by Michael Emberley. *It's Perfectly Normal: Changing Bodies, Growing Up, Sex and Sexual Health.* 1996. 89 pp. $10.99. Candlewick Press.
The illustrations are wonderful, and make it difficult to continue thinking of sex as something we never talk about with our children.

Humenick, Sharon S. *Having a Baby.* 1997. 96 pp. $9.75. New Readers Press, Box 35888, Syracuse, NY 13235. 800.448.8878.
Provides a quick guide to pregnancy and childbirth. Very easy-to-read. Provides good overview, but not much detail.

Jacobs, Thomas A., et al. *What Are My Rights? 95 Questions and Answers about Teens and the Law.* 1997. 208 pp. $14.95. Free Spirit Publishing. 612.338.2068.
A matter-of-fact guide to the laws that affect teens at home, at school, on the job, and in their communities.

Lansky, Vickie. *Feed Me — I'm Yours.* 1994. 141 pp. $9. Meadowbrook, Inc., 18318 Minnetonka Boulevard, Deephaven, MN 55391. 800.338.2232.
An excellent cookbook for new parents. Lots of recipes for making baby food "from scratch." Also includes directions for kitchen crafts.

_____. *Games Babies Play from Birth to Twelve Months.* 1993. 112 pp. $8.95. The Book Peddlers, 15245 Minnetonka Boulevard, Deephaven, MN 55345-1510. 800.255.3379.
Collection of activities — 20-30 ideas for each three months of the first year. Assign several activities each week to students for interacting with their babies as part of your ages and stages curriculum.

Leach, Penelope. *Your Baby and Child from Birth to Age Five.* Revised, 1997. 560 pp. $20. Alfred A. Knopf.
An absolutely beautiful book packed with information, many color photos and lovely drawings. Comprehensive, authoritative, and outstandingly sensitive guide to child care and development.

Lieberman, E. James, M.D., and Karen Lieberman Troccoli, M.P.H. *Like It Is: A Teen Sex Guide.* 1998. 216 pp. $25. McFarland and Co.
Excellent book to offer teen parents (all teens actually). It describes methods of contraception, starting with abstinence, and the risks associated with each one. Gives bias-free information about pregnancy options.

Lindsay, Jeanne Warren. *The Challenge of Toddlers* and *Your Baby's First Year (Teens Parenting Series).* 2004. 224 pp. each. Paper, $12.95 each; hardcover, $18.95 each. Workbooks, $2.50 each.

Morning Glory Press. 888.612.8254.

How-to-parent books especially for teenage parents. Lots of quotes from teenage parents who share their experiences. Board games ($29.95 each), one for each of these titles, provide great learning reinforcement. Also see video series, **Your Baby's First Year,** *described on page 273. For detailed teaching guide, see* **Challenge of Toddlers Comprehensive Curriculum Notebook** *and* **Nurturing Your Newborn/Your Baby's First Year Comprehensive Curriculum Notebook,** pp. 279-280.

_____. *Do I Have a Daddy? A Story About a Single-Parent Child.* 2000. 48 pp. Paper, $7.95; hardcover, $14.95. Free study guide. Morning Glory Press. *A beautiful full-color picture book for the child who has never met his/her father. A special sixteen-page section offers suggestions to single mothers.*

_____. *Pregnant? Adoption Is an Option.* 1996. 224 pp. $11.95. Teacher's Guide, Study Guide, $2.50 each. Morning Glory Press. *Birthparents share stories of responsible, difficult adoption planning. Does not "push" adoption, but suggests* **planning** *and deliberate decision-making. Stresses open adoption and birthparents' role in choosing adoptive parents.*

_____. *Teen Dads: Rights, Responsibilities and Joys (Teens Parenting Series).* 2001. 224 pp. $12.95. Teacher's Guide, Workbook, $2.50 each. Morning Glory Press. *A how-to-parent book especially for teenage fathers. Offers help in parenting from conception to age 3 of the child. Many quotes from and photos of teen fathers. For detailed teaching help, see* **Teen Dads Comprehensive Curriculum Notebook,** pp. 279-280.

_____. *Teenage Couples — Caring, Commitment and Change: How to Build a Relationship that Lasts. Teenage Couples — Coping with Reality: Dealing with Money, In-laws, Babies and Other Details of Daily Life.* 1995. 208, 192 pp. Paper, $9.95 ea.; hardcover, $15.95 ea. Workbooks, $2.50 ea. Curriculum Guide, $19.95. See *Teenage Couples—Expectations and Reality* on p. 280. Morning Glory Press. *Series covers such important topics as communication, handling arguments, keeping romance alive, sex in a relationship, jealousy, alcohol and drug addiction, partner abuse, and divorce, as well as the practical details of living. Lots of quotes from teenage couples.*

_____ and Jean Brunelli. *Nurturing Your Newborn: Young Parent's Guide to Baby's First Month.* (*Teens Parenting Series*) 1999. 64 pp. $6.95. Morning Glory. *Focuses on the postpartum period. Ideal for teen parents home after delivery. For detailed teaching help, see* **Nurturing Your Newborn/Your Baby's First Year Comprehensive Curriculum Notebook,** pp. 279-280.

_____ . *Your Pregnancy and Newborn Journey (Teens Parenting Series).* 2004. 208 pp. Paper, $12.95; hardcover, $18.95; Workbook, $2.50. Morning Glory Press .
*Prenatal health book for pregnant teens. Includes section on care of newborn and chapter for fathers. For detailed teaching help, see **Your Pregnancy and Newborn Journey Comprehensive Curriculum Notebook,** pp. 279-280. Also see **Pregnancy and Newborn Journey board game** and **Pregnancy Two-in-One Bingo game**, p. 270.*

_____ and Sally McCullough. *Discipline from Birth to Three.* 2004. 208 pp. Paper, $12.95; hardcover, $18.95. Morning Glory Press.
*Provides teenage parents with guidelines to help prevent discipline problems with children and for dealing with problems when they occur. For detailed teaching help, see **Discipline from Birth to Three Comprehensive Curriculum Notebook,** pp. 279-280.*

Marecek, Mary. *Breaking Free from Partner Abuse.* 1999. 96 pp. $8.95. Quantity discount. Morning Glory Press.
Lovely edition illustrated by Jami Moffett. Underlying message is that the reader does not deserve to be hit. Simply written. Can help a young woman escape an abusive relationship.

Martin, Margaret, M.P.H. *Pregnancy and Childbirth: The Basic Illustrated Guide.* 1997. 126 pp. $12. Perseus Publishing.
Easy to read basic guide to pregnancy and childbirth.

McCoy, Kathy, Ph.D., and Charles Wibbelsman. *Teenage Body Book Guide.* 1999. 288 pp. $18.95. Perigee Publishing.
Crammed with information for teenagers about everything from their bodies, changing feelings, teenage beauty, and special medical needs of young adults to sexuality, venereal disease, birth control, pregnancy and parenthood. Lots of quotes from young people, sometimes in the form of questions.

MELD Parenting Materials. Nueva Familia: Six books in Spanish and English. *Baby Is Here. Feeding Your Child, 5 months-2 years. Healthy Child, Sick Child. Safe Child and Emergencies. Baby Grows. Baby Plays.* 1992. $12 each. MELD, Suite 507, 123 North Third Street, Minneapolis, MN 55401. 612.332.7563.
Very easy to read books full of information. Designed especially for Mexican and Mexican American families, but excellent for anyone with limited reading skills. Ask MELD for catalog of other materials designed especially for school-age parents.

_____. *The New Middle of the Night Book: Answers to Young Parents' Questions When No One Is Around.* 1999. 163 pp. $12.50.

MELD.
Includes clearly written information about parenting during the first two years of life. An especially good section discusses the benefits and how-tos of shared parenting, whether or not the parents are together as a couple.

Miller, Kathryn Ann. *Did My First Mother Love Me? A Story for an Adopted Child.* 1994. 48 pp. Paper, $5.95; hardcover, $12.95. Morning Glory Press.
A birthmother explains why she made the difficult adoption decision. For every adopted child. The book would be a lovely gift for the birthmother to give her child at time of placement with the adoptive family.

Nykiel, Connie. *After the Loss of Your Baby — For Teen Mothers.* 1994. 19 pp. $4.50 ppd. Spanish edition, *Despues de la Perdida de tu Bebé: Para Madres Adolescentes.* Centering Corp., 7230 Maple St., Omaha, NE 68134. 402.553.1200.
Tremendous resource. Beautifully written to help teens through grief of losing a baby, whether through miscarriage, stillbirth, SIDS, or other death.

Parent Express Series: *Parent Express: For You and Your Infant. Spanish edition: Noticias Para Los Padres. Parent Express: For You and Your Toddler.* Each newsletter, 8 pp. $4 each set. ANR Publications, University of California, 6701 San Pablo Avenue, Oakland, CA 94608-1239. 510.642.2431.
Wonderful series of newsletters for parents. The first set starts two months before delivery and continues monthly through the first year of the child's life. Second set with twelve letters covers second and third years. Good resource for teen parents. Beautiful photos, easy reading.

Pollock, Sudie. *Will the Dollars Stretch? Teen Parents Living on Their Own.* 2001. 112 pp. $7.95. Teacher's Guide, $2.50. Morning Glory.
Five short stories about teen parents moving out on their own. As students read, they will get the feel of poverty as experienced by many teen parents — as they write checks and balance checkbooks of young parents involved.

_____. *Moving On: Finding Information You Need for Living on Your Own.* 2001. 48 pp. $4.95. 25/$75. Morning Glory Press.
Fill-in guide to help young persons find information about their community, information needed for living away from parents.

Porter, Connie. *Imani All Mine.* 1999. 218 pp. $12. Houghton Miflin.
Wonderful novel about a black teen mom in the ghetto where poverty, racism, and danger are constant realities.

Reynolds, Marilyn. **True-to-Life Series from Hamilton High.** *Baby Help. Beyond Dreams. But What About Me? Detour for Emmy.*

Telling. Too Soon for Jeff, Love Rules, If You Loved Me. 1993-2001. 160-256 pp. Paper, $8.95 each (*Love Rules,* $9.95). See *True to Life Series Teaching Guide,* p. 282. Morning Glory Press.
Wonderfully gripping stories about situations faced by teens. Start with Detour for Emmy, award-winning novel about a 15-year-old mother. Students who read one of Reynolds' novels usually ask for more. Topics cover partner abuse, acquaintance rape, reluctant teen father, sexual molestation, racism, fatal accident, abstinence, homophobia, school failure.

Romanchik, Brenda. **The Open Adoption Pocket Guide Book Series: Being a Birthparent: Finding Our Place; What Is Open Adoption? Your Rights and Responsibilities: A Guide for Expectant Parents Considering Adoption;** and **Birthparent Grief.** 1999. 20 pp. ea. $5.95 ea. R-Squared Press.
Concise guides filled with usable information. Excellent for educating family and friends.

Seward, Angela. Illustrated by Donna Ferreiro. **Goodnight, Daddy.** 2001. 48 pp. Paper, $7.95; hardcover, $14.95. Morning Glory Press.
Beautiful full-color picture book shows Phoebe's excitement because of her father's visit today. She is devastated when he calls to say "Something has come up." Book illustrates the importance of father in the life of his child.

Silberg, Jackie. **125 Brain Games for Babies.** 1999. 143 pp. $14.95. Consortium Book Sales. **125 Brain Games for Toddlers and Twos.** 2000. $14.95. Gryphon House.
Packed with everyday games, songs, and other opportunities to encourage the brain development of children from birth through three years. Illus.

Smallwood, Diane, developer. **Board Games: "Challenge of Toddlers," "Baby's First Year," and "Pregnancy and Newborn Journey."** 1999; 1996; 1996. $29.95 each, 3/$80. **Two-in-One Pregnancy Bingo,** 2000. $19.95. Morning Glory Press.
Games based on Teens Parenting series of books. Combine fun and learning as you play.

Wiggins, Pamela K. **Why Should I Nurse My Baby?** 1998. 58 pp. $5.95. Noodle Soup, 4614 Prospect Avenue, #328, Cleveland, OH 44103. 216.881.5151.
Easy-to-read, yet thorough discussion of breastfeeding. Question and answer format. Also ask about the Babies First pamphlets, same source.

Wolff, Virginia E. **Make Lemonade.** 2003. 208 pp. $5.99. Scholastic.
Wonderful novel about a teenager living in a Project who takes a job babysitting for a teenage mom, and who eventually sees the mom back in school, her children in child care, and her life back on focus.

VIDEOS — Sources, Representative Titles
(Contact distributors for complete listings.)

Discipline from Birth to Three. Four videos, **Infants and Discipline — Meeting Baby's Needs, He's Crawling — Help!** (6-12 months), **She's into Everything!** (1-2 years), and **Your Busy Runabout** (2-3 years). 2001. 15 min. each. $195 set, $69.95 each. Morning Glory Press, 6595 San Haroldo Way, Buena Park, CA 90620. 888.612.8254.
Wonderful videos over book of same title. Shows teens talking to teens, sharing techniques for loving care. Teaching guide includes discussion questions, writing and research assignments, and quiz.

Getting Men Involved. Three-video series. 2001. 15-35 min. Prices below. KidSafety of America, 6251 Schaefer Ave., Suite B, Chino, CA 91710, 909.902.1340.
One focuses on the importance of men getting involved in childcare, education, and social work (15 min. $79.95). Another video focuses on young men as fathers, produced for educators and caregivers, and includes suggestions on implementing and maintaining a fatherhood program (35 min. $79.95). The third video is for teens and other young fathers (15 min., $59.95).

Fatherhood USA. Three tapes: **Dedicated Not Deadbeat, Juggling Family and Work,** and **Workshop and Workbook.** 2000. Each tape, $34.95 ppd. for individuals; $114 ppd. for institutions. Three tapes and workbook, $74.95 and $250. Transit Media, P.O. Box 1084, Harriman, NY 10926. 800.343.5540.
PBS series on fatherhood hosted by former Senator Bill Bradley. Shows young fathers, teens and early 20s, in fatherhood groups. Realistic, good.

Fetal Development: A Nine-Month Journey. 15 min. $109.95. Sunburst Communications, 101 Castleton Street, P.O. Box 40, Pleasantville, NY 10570. 800.431.1934.
Traces fetal development from the moment of fertilization of a human egg to the emergence of the baby through the birth canal at nine months.

Healthy Steps for Teen Parents. Three videos, "Prenatal Care," "Labor and Birth," and "Postpartum." 2000. 25 min. each. $195 each; 3/$479.95. Injoy Videos, 1435 Yarmouth, Ste. 102, Boulder, CO 80304. 303.447.2082.
New series for teens features an all-teen cast. Teens will identify with real life footage as they meet a diverse group of peers who are successful teen parents. In "Labor and Birth," viewers follow Marquita, a single 15-year-

old mom, and 19-year-old Samantha and her supportive boyfriend. One
chooses unmedicated childbirth, the other epidural pain relief.

Healthy Touch: Infant Massage for Teenage Parents. 40 min. $95.
Injoy Videos.
Focusing on touch, the simple massage strokes are easy for teen parents to
learn and incorporate into their daily contact times with their babies.
Introduction is for the teacher, but the rest of the film is designed for young
parents, and is excellent.

Looking for Love: Exploring Teen-Adult Relationships. 1998. 22
min. $150. Planned Parenthood, 2314   Auburn Ave., Cincinnati, OH
45219. 513.721.8932.
Focuses on five teens who discuss their real life dating experiences with
adults. Includes 74-page Instructor s Guide with lesson plans.

Project Future: Your Pregnancy, Your Plan. Giving Birth to Your
Baby. Your New Baby, Your New Life. 42 to 56 min. each. One
video, $99; 3 videos, $295. Vida Health Communications, 6
Bigelow Street, Cambridge, MA 02139. 617.864.4334.
Provide comprehensive help for pregnant and parenting teens. Each is
divided into two parts, each of which can be used separately. Excellent
videos, respectful to teen parents, informative, and entertaining. Offer
emotional support as well as teaching basic parenting skills.

Raising Nonviolent Children in Violent Times. 1999. 15 min. $89.
Meridian Education. 888.340.5507.
Stresses the parents role in raising nonviolent children, the importance of
good prenatal care, a nonviolent home, and close family relationships.

Read to Me. Directed by Susan Straub. 2000. $19.95. READ to ME,
Teachers & Writers Collaborative, 5 Union Square   West, 7th Floor ,
NY, NY 10003. 212.691.6590.
Wonderful video which chronicles a series of workshops with teen mothers
reading to their babies in a high school in Brooklyn, NY. Three leaflets
provide valuable tips on reading to babies and toddlers.

Real People: When I Say Stop, I Mean Stop. 1998. 25 min. $109.95.
Sunburst, 101 Castleton St., Pleasantville, NY 10570. 800.431.1934.
Teens discuss how to say No to sex and give practical help to teens
struggling to handle sexual pressure and sexual harassment.

Still Shiny. 1998. 35 min. plus 20 min. segment on breastfeeding.
$119.95. Injoy Videos.
Whimsical look at the first 28 days after birth told in the guise of two babies

talking. Includes excellent information about caring for the baby. Ideal for
new parents to help them understand what their newborn needs from them.

Teen Breastfeeding: The Natural Choice. 20 min. **Teen Breastfeeding: Starting Out Right.** 30 min. Both for $139.95. Injoy Videos.
Wonderful videos. Part 1 provides reasons to breastfeed, and Part 2 tells
how. Several teen moms star. A lactation specialist shows a young mom still
in the hospital how to get her baby latched on to her breast. It s a fast
moving and colorful series. I wish I had had it when I was breastfeeding our
five kids.

Teen Parents: Three Birth Stories. 1999. 18 min. $295. Injoy .
Created to educate and inspire pregnant teens, this program presents the
real-life experiences of three birthing teenagers in a positive, encouraging
light.

Teens and Sex in Europe: A Story of Rights, Respect & Responsibility. 2000. 16 min. $79.95. Advocates for Youth, Suite 200, 1025 Vermont Ave., NW, Washington, DC 20005. 202.347.5700.
Provides a fascinating glimpse into the sexual health attitudes of Dutch,
German, and French teens and their parents as well as the attitudes of
government officials, educators, and health care providers. Excellent for
anyone interested in preventing teen pregnancy in the U.S.

Too Soon for Jeff. 1996. 40 min. $89.95. Films for the Humanities and Sciences, P.O. Box 2053, Princeton, NJ 08543. 800.257.5126.
ABC After-School TV Special was based on the award-winning novel by
Marilyn Reynolds. Starring Freddie Prinze, Jr., it s an excellent adaptation
of novel about reluctant teen father.

Working with Teens   Pr egnant or Parenting. Vol. 1, For Parents of Teens; Vol. 2, For Teens; Vol. 3. For Educators and Caregivers. Vol. 1 & 2 (1 video) in Spanish. 2003. $69.95 each, 4/ $249.95. KidSafety of America. 909.902.1340.
Can help parents of pregnant and parenting teens, as well as educators and
teens themselves, understand the world of teen parenting.

Your Baby s First Year. 2001. Four videos. **Nurturing Your Newborn, She s Much More Active** (4-8 months), **Leaving Baby Stage Behind, Keeping Baby Healthy.** $195 set; $69.95 each. Morning Glory Press.
Teens talking to teens, sharing techniques for loving care. Based on book
with same title. Includes teacher s guide with questions, projects, quiz.

Resources for Professionals

Adolescent Parent Resource Guide. Revised 1997. 800 pp. $125 +
   10% shpg. Center on Education and Training for Employment, The
   Ohio State University, 1900 Kenny Road, Columbus, OH 43210.
   800.848.4815. Web site for catalog: www.cete.org/publications.asp>
   *An amazingly huge and good curriculum prepared by and for teachers in
   teen parent programs. Group and individual learning activities are written
   for each competency in the **GRADS Ohio Competency Analysis Profile.**
   Each unit also contains teacher background information, family involvement and leadership activities, processing questions, and action projects.*

*Alternative Assessment: A Family and Consumer Sciences Teacher's
   Tool Kit.* 1996. 118 pp. $25. Center on Education and Training for
   Employment, The Ohio State University.
   *The guide assists you in understanding issues related to and purposes of
   assessment, developing an overall assessment plan, and selecting or
   creating specific product, performance, and process assessment tools.*

Barr, Linda, M.N., and Catherine Monserrat, Ph.D. *Working with
   Pregnant and Parenting Teens.* 1996. 175 pp. $27.95. New Futures,
   Inc., 4919 Prospect NE, Albuquerque, NM 87110. 505.872.0164.
   *Can help professionals who work with teen parents. Includes teacher's
   guide for **Teenage Pregnancy: A New Beginning.***

Batten, Susan T., and Bonita Stowell. *School-Based Programs for
   Adolescent Parents and Their Young Children: Guidelines for
   Quality and Best Practice.* 1996. 64 pp. $5.00. Center for
   Assessment and Policy Development (CAPD), 111 Presidential
   Boulevard, Ste. 234, Bala Cynwyd, PA 19004. 610.664.4540.
   *A wonderful description of components needed for child care, prenatal care
   and reproductive health services, preventive health care for children,
   parenting and life skills education, and case management/family support.*

Bavolek, S. *Research and Validation Report, Adult-Adolescent
   Parenting Inventory.* 2002. $122/kit. Family Dev. Resources, Inc.
   P.O. Box 982350, Park City, UT 84098. 435.649.5822.
   *To be used by professionals to assess the parenting and child-rearing
   attitudes of adults and adolescents.*

Berne, Linda, and Barbara Huberman. *European Approaches to
   Adolescent Sexual Behavior and Responsibility.* 1999. 74 pp. $15.
   Advocates for Youth, Suite 200, 1025 Vermont Ave. NW,
   Washington, DC 20005. 202.347.5700.

Teen pregnancy prevention study tour leaders (covering the Netherlands, France and Germany) share their experiences, research, and amazing findings which can provide invaluable help in fostering teen pregnancy prevention in the U.S.

Brick, Peggy, et al. *The New Teaching Safer Sex.* 1998. $25. Center for Family Life Education, Planned Parenthood of Greater New Jersey. 973.539.9580. www.ppgnnj.org>
Advocates "safer sex" and provides lessons that actively involve students in learning how they can protect themselves.

Cahill, Michele, J. Lynne White, David Lowe, and Lerner E. Jacobs. *In School Together: School-Based Child Care Serving Student Mothers: A Handbook.* 1991. 135 pp. $16. Academy for Educational Development. Contact Elayne Archer, AED, 100 Fifth Avenue, New York, NY 10022.
Provides practical research-based guidance in setting up school-based child care. Covers all phases of the program development process including support strategies, staffing, program and policies, funding, and evaluation. Request current catalog from AED — good materials!

Card, Josefina J., Ed. *Handbook of Adolescent Sexuality and Pregnancy Research and Evaluation Instruments.* 2003. 294 pp. $134. Sage Publications, 2455 Teller Road, Thousand Oaks, CA 91320. 805.499.0721.
Provides tools to create research instruments. Descriptions of more than sixty field-tested instruments with information on obtaining them. Includes two questionnaires to be used by adolescent care and prevention programs.

Centerfocus. "Using Data for Program Improvement: How Do We Encourage Schools to Do It?" May, 1996. Download from Web site: ncrve.berkeley.edu/CenterFocus>
Brief information on using data for program improvement.

Choices: Charting a Positive Future for Teen Parents. 1993-1995. 200-300 pp. each. $35 per volume. IFAS Extension Bookstore, P.O. Box 110011, University of Florida, Gainesville, FL 32611-0011. 352.392.1764.
Curriculum designed to help pregnant teens chart a more positive future. Components include "Focus on Teens," "Nutrition," "Resource Management," and "Parenting." Multiple learning activities for each concept. Three volumes, with each of the four components included in each volume.

Coles, Robert. *The Youngest Parents: Teenage Pregnancy as It Shapes Lives.* 2000. 224 pp. $19.99. W. W. Norton and Company, 800.233.4830.

An absorbing book which offers the compelling voices of young women and men, either pregnant or already parents, to provide yet another dimension to the realities of teen parents' lives. Includes nearly 100 pages of wonderful black and white photos.

Complete Teens Parenting Curriculum. 2002. Includes two books, five *Comprehensive Curriculum Notebooks,* and quarterly newsletter for teacher; and, for students, six books and workbooks, eight videos, four games. $1085. Morning Glory Press. 888.612.8254.
Everything you need to teach parenting to teen parents. See descriptions of Teens Parenting books on pp. 266-268, videos, pp. 271, 273; games, p. 270.

Dash, Leon. ***When Children Want Children: An Inside Look at the Crisis of Teenage Parenthood.*** 2003. 270 pp. $18.95. U of Ill. Press.
Based on living 18 months within one of Washington, DC's poorest ghettos. Dash provides the reader with a valuable first-person account of a small group of teen parents and their families.

Dryfoos, Joy G. ***Adolescents at Risk: Prevalence and Prevention.*** 1991. 280 pp. $29.95. Oxford University Press. 800.451.7556.
Unique overview of 10-17-year-olds in the United States today. Dryfoos examines four problem areas — delinquency, substance abuse, teen pregnancy, and school failure. She describes techniques and programs that work, and some that haven't.

Earle, Janice. ***Counselor/Advocates: Keeping Pregnant and Parenting Teens in School.*** 1990. 47 pp. $5. National Association of State Boards of Education, 277 South Washington St., Ste. 100, Alexandria, VA 22314. 703.684.4000.
Report of a demonstration project testing the effects of using counselor/ advocates to help pregnant and parenting teens stay in school. Good resource to offer administrators when you're trying to develop special services for teenage parents within the regular school.

Francis, Judith, and Fern Marx. ***Learning Together, Volume 1: A National Directory of Teen Parenting and Child Care Programs***, $10; ***Volume 2: Proceedings of a National Conference of Teen Parenting and Child Care Programs***, $10; ***Volume 3: A Supplement to the National Directory of Teen Parenting and Child Care Programs,*** $10. All 3 volumes, $25. 1989-1991. 196, 97, 189 pp. Publications Department, Center for Research on Women, Wellesley College, Wellesley, MA 02481. 781.283.2510.
The 430+ programs profiled in these directories illustrate the range of services needed to help teen parents become competent and self-sufficient adults. Designed for use by policy makers and program planners.

Frederickson, Helen L. M.D., and Louise Wilkins-Haug, M.D., Ph.D.
Ob/Gyn Secrets: Questions You Will Be Asked . . . on Rounds, in the Clinic, on Oral Exams. 1997. 368 pp. $39.95. Hanley & Belfus.
Presents an overview of obstetrics and gynecology in question-and-answer format, emphasizing common problems encountered in practice. Good reference for your program's nurse.

Gelperin, Nora, M.Ed. *Teaching with SEX, ETC: Articles and Activities.* 2002. 161 pp. $29.95. Network for Family Life, Center for Applied Psychology, Rutgers University, 41 Gordon Road, Suite A, Piscataway, NJ 08854.
Forty activities, each accompanied by articles from past issues of Sex, Etc., a wonderful newsletter written by and for teens. Topics include abstinence and sexual decision-making, love and relationships, contraception, STIs, pregnancy issues, sexual orientation, sexual violence and abuse, substance use and abuse, and sexual health and wellness. All reproducible.

Goldberg, Linda, Ginny Brinkley, and Janice Kukar. *Pregnancy to Parenthood.* 2001. 342 pp. $12.95. Avery Penguin Putnam. 800.548.5757.
Provides month-by-month breakdown of physical changes to expect during pregnancy, describes the emotional aspects of pregnancy, and much more.

Gonzalez-Mena, Janet. *Multicultural Issues in Child Care.* 1993. 91 pp. $19.68. Mayfield Publishing Company.
Focuses on cultural differences relevant to all caregiving settings. Daily caregiving routines are stressed, emphasizing practical concerns.

GRADS Ohio Competency Analysis Profile. 1996. 20 pp. $10. The Ohio State University, Voc. Instruc. Materials Laboratory (p. 274).
Competency listing developed for Ohio and other GRADS programs. Broad areas covered include adolescent development, pregnancy, parenting, health and safety, relationships, and economic independence. See sample on p. 80.

Great Beginnings Nutrition Curriculum for Pregnant and Parenting Teens. 1999/2001. $495. Available in Spanish. AGC/United Learning, 1560 Sherman Avenue, Ste. 100, Evanston, IL 60201.
Ten lesson nutrition curriculum, each containing instructor's materials and reproducible activities. Includes two 13-minute videos, "Pregnant and Growing" and "Baby, It's You." Evaluation by University of New Hampshire showed pregnant teens receiving this curriculum had healthier babies.

Hardy, Janet B., and Laurie Schwab Zabin. *Adolescent Pregnancy in an Urban Environment: Issues, Programs and Evaluation.* 1991 400 pp. $51.50. Urban Institute. 800.462.6420.
Authors describe five clinical adolescent pregnancy and parenting service programs conducted during the last 20 years at Johns Hopkins University. Helpful for clinicians and researchers who are designing or evaluating effective interventions aimed at high-risk, disadvantaged urban youth.

Hatcher, Robert A., et al. *A Personal Guide to Managing Contraception.* 2000. 179 pp. $14.95. Bridging the Gap Communications. 706.265.3912.
Remarkably complete and medically accurate coverage of the various contraceptive methods. Good resource for teens.

Heart to Heart Program. For information, Heart to Heart, Ounce of Prevention Fund, 122 South Michigan Avenue, Ste. 2050, Chicago, IL 60603. 312.922.3863.
An innovative approach to preventing child sexual abuse by teaching teen parents to protect their children from abuse. Program can be implemented in a school or community-based setting. Practitioners participate in a two-day training and purchase the curriculum and facilitator's guide.

Horn, Wade F., Ph.D. *Father Facts.* Fourth Edition. 2002. 106 pp. $15. The National Fatherhood Initiative, One Bank Street, Suite 160, Gaithersburg, MD 20878. 301.948.0599.
This book is filled with important facts, information, and research concerning the plight of fatherlessness.

It Takes Two: For Teen Parents. 1997. 124 pp. Teachers Manual, $50; 26-page Student Manual, $6. Legacy Resource Group, P.O. Box 700, Carlisle, IA 50047. 515.989.3360.
It's a five-hour pregnancy prevention curriculum for teen parents. Encourages participants to look at their own values and their dreams, and to discuss how parenting has impacted those dreams. Emphasizes shared responsibility between men and women.

Johnson, Jeffery, and Pamela Wilson. *Fatherhood Development: A Curriculum for Young Fathers.* 1994. 400 pp. $600 for curriculum and training. National Center for Strategic Nonprofit Planning and Community Leadership (NPCL), 2000 L Street NW, #815, Washington, DC 20036. 202.822.6725.
Excellent curriculum for teen father programs. Available only with training.

Kanfer, Frederick H., Susan Englund, Claudia Lennhoff, and Jean Rhodes. *A Mentor Manual for Adults Who Work with Pregnant and Parenting Teens.* 1995. 136 pp. $16.95. Child Welfare League of America, 440 First Street NW, Third Floor, Washington, DC 20001-2085. 202.638.2952.
Based on a school mentor program for pregnant and parenting teens, the book offers guidelines for adults working with a teenage partner. Good tips for teachers and others working with young people.

Kotulak, Ronald. *Inside the Brain. Revolutionary Discoveries of How the Mind Works.* 1997. 224 pp. $19.95. Andrews McMeel Pub.
An in-depth look at the latest scientific findings about the brain — about how nature builds the brain then develops it during early life. Wonderful resource for teacher and for motivated students.

Lerman, Evelyn. *Safer Sex: The New Morality.* 2000. 240 pp. Paper, $14.95; hardcover, $21.95. Adult Leader's Guide, $5. Participant's Guide, $2.50. Morning Glory Press.
Safer Sex provides an honest appraisal of the impact of unprotected sex on the lives of teens, along with proven strategies for positive change. Wonderful guide for parents, teachers, clergy, counselors, all who love, care and worry about teens in our world of free sex in the media and our passion for keeping teens away from sex in the real world.

_____. *Teen Moms: The Pain and the Promise.* 1997. 192 pp. Paper, $14.95; hardcover, $21.95. Workbook, T.G., $2.50 each. Adult Leader's Guide, $5. Participant's Guide, $2.50. Morning Glory.
Stories from teen moms together with illuminating research. Especially good for board members and others who don't know much about the realities of teen parents' lives. Offers good background material for people working on teen pregnancy prevention.

Levin-Epstein, Jodie. *Teen Parent Provisions in the Personal Responsibility and Work Opportunity Reconciliation Act of 1996.* 1996. 80 pp. $7.50. Center for Law and Social Policy, CLASP Publications, 1015 15th St. NW, Ste. 400, Washington, DC 20005. 202/906.8000.
Reviews Act and highlights restrictions on assistance to teens, incentives to states to invest in pregnancy prevention, and other provisions of the new law that may affect teen parents and teens at risk of early parenting.

_____. *Tapping TANF for Reproductive Health and Teen Parent Programs.* 1999. Center for Law and Social Policy, 202.906.8000. Available free on CLASP website, www.clasp.org.
Provides answers to often-asked questions about how to use TANF funds for prevention and teen parent services. See other and more recent publications available on the same web site.

Leving, Jeffery M., Kenneth A. Dachman, and Jeffrey Leving. *Fathers' Rights: Hard-hitting and Fair Advice for Every Father Involved in a Custody Dispute.* 1998. 240 pp. $15. Basic Books.
This powerful book provides accurate and authoritative information regarding child support and custody issues. Good for program providers.

Lindsay, Jeanne Warren. **Five *Comprehensive Curriculum Notebooks* for *Teens Parenting Series: Your Pregnancy and Newborn***

Journey; Nurturing Your Newborn/Your Baby's First Year; The Challenge of Toddlers; Discipline from Birth to Three; Teen Dads. 2002. 175-190 pp. loose-leaf notebooks. $125 each; 5/$500. Morning Glory Press.

Each notebook contains, for each chapter of that book, objectives, supplementary resources, teacher tips, group and independent study activities list, reproducible activities, handout listing high points of chapter, quiz, answer key, and suggested responses for all workbook assignments.

_____, Ed. *PPT Express.* Published quarterly. 12 pp. Annual subscription, $15; two years, $25. Morning Glory Press.

Newsletter especially for teachers and others who work with pregnant and parenting teens. Contains lots of curriculum ideas including input from readers. Conference listings, Washington, DC, news, resource reviews. Free sample copy on request.

_____. *Teenage Couples — Expectations and Reality: Teen Views on Living Together, Roles, Work, Jealousy and Partner Abuse.* 1996. 192 pp. $14.95. Morning Glory Press.

For teachers — insight into the world of teenage couples. Based on a survey of 3700 teens, the book provides valuable background information for relationship classes. Documents surprising changes during past decade.

Luker, Kristin. *Dubious Conceptions: The Politics of Teenage Pregnancy.* 1996. 283 pp. $8.50. Harvard University Press.

Shows the complex reality and troubling truths of teenage mothers in America today. Helps explain the public's increasingly hostile attitude toward this social, economic, and political problem.

Males, Mike A. *The Scapegoat Generation: America's War on Adolescents.* 1996. 330 pp. $17.95. Common Courage Press. 207.525.0900.

Males takes on politicians, private interests, and the media and accuses them of being unfair in their condemnation of teens. Refutes myth after myth. Book can help you raise awareness of the needs of teen parents.

Maynard, Rebecca A., Ed. *Kids Having Kids: A Robin Hood Foundation Special Report on the Costs of Adolescent Childbearing.* 1996. 20 pp. Free download: www.nnfr.org/curriculum/topics>. The Robin Hood Foundation. 212.227.6601.

Excellent summary of recent research book on costs of teenage pregnancy and parenting.

The MediaWise™ Teen Parent Program. 2002. $159.95. National Institute on Media and the Family: 111.mediafamily.org or 888.672.5437.

Four-week program includes three videos, Leader's Guide, reproducible activities, handouts, homework assignments, overheads. Can help teens become "media-wise parents."

Montfort, Sue, and Peggy Brick. ***Unequal Partners: Teaching About Power and Consent in Adult-Teen Relationships.*** 1999. 156 pp. $29. Planned Parenthood, Greater Northern New Jersey, Inc. 973.539.9580, x 149.
Series of lessons with activities designed to help teens think about older person/teen and power/non-power relationships. Excellent curriculum.

Morris, Jon. ***The For Males Only Curriculum.*** 1997. 103 pp. $15. The Fatherhood and Families Program. 141 Campbell Avenue SW, Roanoke, VA 24011. <www.roadprogram.org>
Curriculum used by For Males Only staff for teen pregnancy prevention programs.

_____. ***ROAD to Fatherhood: How to Help Young Dads Become Loving and Responsible Parents.*** 2002. 208 pp. $14.95. Morning Glory Press.
Book shows the many needs of young fathers through their real stories together with strategies for helping them meet their individual and unique challenges. Also excellent planning guide for starting or expanding a program for young fathers.

Musick, Judith S. ***Young, Poor, and Pregnant: The Psychology of Teenage Motherhood.*** 1995. 271 pp. $16. Yale University Press. 203.432.0940.
Musick, an expert on adolescent pregnancy, discusses how psychological pressures of adolescence interact with the problems of being poor to create a situation in which early sexuality, pregnancy, and childbearing — often repeated childbearing — seem almost inevitable.

Nurturing Program for Teenage Parents and Their Families.
Complete program (manuals, handbooks, videos, instructional aids, assessment tools), $1577.15. Family Development Resources, Inc., P.O. Box 982350, Park City, UT 84098. 435.649.5822.
Instructional program designed to help treat and prevent child abuse and neglect. Focuses on the needs of the parent as well as those of the child. Designed for weekly sessions with teenage parents.

Organizing TAPP: Useful Forms for Teenage Parent Programs.
1997. $4.95. Morning Glory Press.
Booklet of reproducible forms to be used in the classroom and for program evaluation. Includes sample child care center handbook. Also available on disk so forms can be personalized. $9.95.

Parenting Education for School-Age Parents. 1991. 107 pp. $10.
Curriculum Center for Family and Consumer Science, Box 41161,
Texas Tech University, Lubbock, TX 79409-1161. 806.742.3029.
*A guidebook for use in establishing and implementing school-age parenting
programs. Includes information on needs assessment, funding, sample
curriculum, facility ideas, program options, evaluation techniques, and
other areas.*

Parents as Teachers National Center, Inc. 10176 Corporate Square
Drive, Ste. 230, St. Louis, MO 63132. 314.432.4330.
*PAT is an early childhood parent education and family support program
designed to empower all parents to give their child the best possible start in
life. "Issues in Working with Teen Parents" is a specially designed training
for professionals working with teen parents and their young children.*

Ransom, Scott B., and S. Gene McNeeley, Jr. *Gynecology for the
Primary Care Provider.* 1997. 294 pp. $73.50. W. B. Saunders Co.
*Advice on dealing with the day to day issues that primary care providers see in
woman's health care. It is concise and the topics are very useful for day to day
primary care disorders.*

Reading Is Fundamental®. **Shared Beginnings®.** 1993. Leader's Guide,
125 pp. $25. *Idea Book* (for students). 30 pp. $5, 10/$40. Contact
Program Division — Shared Beginnings, Reading Is Fundamental,
Inc., 600 Maryland Avenue SW, Ste. 600, Washington, DC 20024.
202.287.3220.
*RIF program for teen parents and their children. The Idea Book for teen
parents is excellent.*

Renfrew, May, Chloe Fisher, and Suzanne Arms. *Bestfeeding: Getting
Breastfeeding Right for You.* 2000. 272 pp. $14.95. Celestial Arts
Publishing, P.O. Box 7123, Berkeley, CA 94707. 800.841.2665.
*Marvelous description, with lots of photographs and drawings (150+) of the
importance of breastfeeding, and of how to make the process work.
Wonderful resource for teacher. While many students may not want to read
the whole book, simply looking at the photos and drawings could be helpful.*

Reynolds, Marilyn, and David Doty. *True-to-Life Series from Hamil-
ton High Teaching Guide.* 1996. 144 pp. $21.95. Morning Glory.
*Comprehensive teaching guide for four novels by Marilyn Reynolds: Detour
for Emmy, Too Soon for Jeff, Telling, and Beyond Dreams. Reproducible.
Individual guides for But What About Me? Baby Help, Love Rules, and If
You Loved Me also available, $2.50 each.*

Sipe, Cynthia L., and Susan T. Batten et al. *School-Based Programs
for Adolescent Parents and Their Young Children: Overcoming*

Barriers and Challenges to Implementing Comprehensive School-Based Services. 1995. 115 pp. $5.00. Center for Assessment and Policy Development (CAPD). 610.664.4540.
Guidelines for developing services critical to helping adolescent parents and their children achieve positive outcomes. Excellent resource.

Sonenstein, Freya L., Kellie Stewart, Laura Duberstein Lindberg, Marta Pernas, and Sean Williams. ***Involving Males in Preventing Teen Pregnancy.*** 1997. 176 pp. $10. The Urban Institute. 2100 M Street NW, Washington, D.C. 20037. <www.urban.org>
Guide for program planners wanting to start or enhance their teen pregnancy prevention program. Highlights several successful male focused programs.

Stephens, Susan A. ***School-Based Programs for Adolescent Parents and Their Young Children: Community Assessment Workbook.*** 1996. 100 pp. 1 copy, n/c. $3/additional copy. CAPD.
Wonderful document to help you figure out how to do a needs assessment for pregnant and parenting teens in your community.

Successful Parenting for School-Age Parents. Teacher's Resource Guide. 544 pp. $30. ***Student Reference Book.*** 1993. 303 pp. $24. Curriculum Center for Family and Consumer Science, Box 41161, Texas Tech University, Lubbock, TX 79409-1161. 806.742.3029.
Teacher's Resource *contains teaching strategies, paper-and-pencil activities, teaching aids, tests, and answer keys for use in teaching school-age parenting programs. Use with* ***Student Reference Book.***

Taking It to the Streets: Raising Public Awareness of Teen Pregnancy Policies and Programs, Advocacy Leadership Training Facilitator's Guide. 2002. $35. Limited supply. CACSAP (California Alliance Concerned with SchoolAge Parents), 1127 11th St., #548, Sacramento, CA 95814. 916.454.1450.
Purpose is to train advocates to educate policymakers and the public about the issue of teen pregnancy and the need for effective policies to reduce teen pregnancy rates. California statistics, but could easily be changed to facts from your state.

Way, W., & Rossman, M. ***Lessons from Life's First Teacher: The Role of the Family in Adolescent and Adult Readiness for School to Work Transition.*** 1996. 85 pp. Download from web: www.ncrve.Berkeley.edu>
Research report stressing the family's strong influence on work readiness for both children and adults. Concludes that it makes sense to include parents as partners in instruction to improve the transition from school to work.

ABOUT THE AUTHORS

Sharon Githens Enright currently is assistant director of Ohio's Career-Technical and Adult Education in family and consumer sciences and former director of Ohio's GRADS (Graduation, Reality, And Dual-Role Skills) program, an in-school program for pregnant and parenting teens. In addition to working with Ohio's 280 GRADS teachers, she directed the GRADS national dissemination project, and has worked with teachers and other professionals in more  than 35 states. Schools in 16 other states have adopted and adapted the GRADS program model.

Enright began an 11-year tenure in 1974 as a teacher in an alternative school for teen parents. She earned her B.S. and M.S. degrees in Home Economics Education from Indiana State University, and her Ph.D. in Family Science from The Ohio State University.

Enright lives in Columbus, Ohio, with her husband Steve. She has two sons who live in Michigan and a young step-daughter in Oregon. Family time is a challenge as well as a priority.

Jeanne Warren Lindsay founded and, for sixteen years, coordinated and taught a teen parent program in a Los Angeles County school district. She is the author of seventeen other books for and about pregnant and parenting teens including the *Teens Parenting* five-book series and *Teen Dads: Rights, Responsibilities and Joys.*

She edits the *PPT Express,* quarterly newsletter for teachers and  others working with pregnant and parenting teens. She speaks frequently at conferences across the country, but says she is happiest while interviewing young people for her books or writing in her backyard.

Lindsay, a transplanted Californian for 43 years, grew up on a farm in Kansas. She has MA degrees in anthropology and consumer and family science. She and Bob have five children and seven gorgeous and brilliant grandchildren.

INDEX

Morning Glory Press
6595 San Haroldo Way, Buena Park, CA 90620
714.828.1998; 888.612.8254   Fax 714.828.2049
Contact us for complete catalog including quantity and other discounts.

		Price	Total

Resources for Teen Parent Teachers/Counselors:

__ *Books, Babies and School-Age Parents*

	1-885356-22-6	14.95	_____
__ *ROAD to Fatherhood*	1-885356-92-7	14.95	_____
__ *Safer Sex: The New Morality*	1-885356-66-8	14.95	_____
Teen Moms: The Pain and the Promise			
	1-885356-25-0	14.95	_____

Resources for Teen Parents:

__ *Pregnant? Adoption Is an Option*	1-885356-08-0	11.95	_____
__ *Surviving Teen Pregnancy*	1-885356-06-4	11.95	_____
Your Pregnancy and Newborn Journey			
__ Paper	1-885356-30-7	12.95	_____
__ Hardcover	1-885356-29-3	18.95	_____
__ Workbook	1-885356-31-5	2.50	_____
__ *PNJ Curriculum Notebook*	1-885356-96-x	125.00	_____
__ **PNJ Board Game**	1-885356-19-6	29.95	_____
__ **Pregnancy Two-in-One Bingo**	1-885356-64-1	19.95	_____
__ *Nurturing Your Newborn*	1-885356-58-7	6.95	_____
__ Workbook	1-885356-61-7	2.00	_____
Your Baby s First Year			
__ Paper	1-885356-33-1	12.95	_____
__ Hardcover	1-885356-32-3	18.95	_____
__ Workbook	1-885356-34-x	2.50	_____
__ *BFY/NN Curriculum Notebook*	1-885356-97-8	125.00	_____

Four-video series   **Your Baby's First Year**

__ **Nurturing Your Newborn**	1-885356-86-2	69.95	_____
__ **She s Much More Active**	1-885356-87-0	69.95	_____
__ **Leaving Baby Stage Behind**	1-885356-88-9	69.95	_____
__ **Keeping Your Baby Healthy**	1-885356-89-7	69.95	_____
__ **All Four Videos Baby s First Year Series**		195.00	_____
__ **Baby's First Year Board Game**		29.95	_____
Discipline from Birth to Three			
__ Paper	1-885356-36-6	12.95	_____
__ Hardcover	1-885356-35-8	18.95	_____
__ Workbook	1-885356-37-4	2.50	_____
__ *Discipline Curriculum Notebook*	1-995357-99-4	125.00	_____

Four-video series   **Discipline from Birth to Three**

__ **Infants and Discipline**	1-885356-82-x	69.95	_____
__ **He s Crawling Help!**	1-885356-83-8	69.95	_____
__ **She s into Everything!**	1-885356-84-6	69.95	_____
__ **Your Busy Runabout**	1-885356-85-4	69.95	_____
__ **Four-Video Discipline from Birth to Three Series**		195.00	_____

SUB-TOTAL (Carry over to top of next page) _____

SUB-TOTAL FROM PREVIOUS PAGE _____

More Resources for Teen Parents:

The Challenge of Toddlers

__	Paper	1-885356-39-0	12.95	_____
__	Hardcover	1-885356-38-2	18.95	_____
__	Workbook	1-885356-40-4	2.50	_____
__ *CT Curriculum Notebook*		1-885356-98-6	125.00	_____
__ **Challenge of Toddlers Bd. Game**		1-885356-56-0	29.95	_____

Teen Dads: Rights, Responsibilities and Joys

__	Paper	1-885356-68-4	12.95	_____
__	Workbook	1-885356-69-2	2.50	_____
__ *Teen Dads Curriculum Notebook*		1-995357-95-1	125.00	_____

__ *Teenage Couples: Expectations and Reality*			
__		0-930934-98-9	14.95	_____
Caring, Commitment and Change			
__		0-930934-93-8	9.95	_____
Coping with Reality		0-930934-86-5	9.95	_____
__ *Breaking Free from Partner Abuse*	1-885356-53-6	8.95	_____
__ *Will the Dollars Stretch?*	1-885356-78-1	7.95	_____
__ *Moving On*	1-885356-81-1	4.95	_____

Novels by Marilyn Reynolds:

__ *Love Rules*	1-885356-76-5	9.95	_____
__ *If You Loved Me*	1-885356-55-2	8.95	_____
__ *Baby Help*	1-885356-27-7	8.95	_____
__ *But What About Me?*	1-885356-10-2	8.95	_____
__ *Too Soon for Jeff*	0-930934-91-1	8.95	_____
__ *Detour for Emmy*	0-930934-76-8	8.95	_____
__ *Telling*	1-885356-03-x	8.95	_____
__ *Beyond Dreams*	1-885356-00-5	8.95	_____

TOTAL _____

Add postage: 10% of total Min., $3.50; 15%, Canada _____
California residents add 7.75% sales tax _____

TOTAL _____

Ask about quantity discounts, teacher, student guides.
Prepayment requested. School/library purchase orders accepted.
If not satisfied, return in 15 days for refund.

NAME _____

PHONE _____ Purchase Order # _____

ADDRESS _____